A Theory of Conceptual Intelligence

A Theory of Conceptual Intelligence

Thinking, Learning, Creativity, and Giftedness

Rex Li

Westport, Connecticut
London

Library of Congress Cataloging-in-Publication Data

Li, Rex.
  A theory of conceptual intelligence : thinking, learning,
creativity, and giftedness / Rex Li.
     p.   cm.
  Includes bibliographical references and index.
  ISBN 0–275–95326–2 (alk. paper)
  1. Intellect.   2. Thought and thinking.   3. Learning, Psychology
of.   4. Creative ability.   5. Gifted persons.   I. Title.
  BF431.L467   1996
  153.9—dc20   95–37642

British Library Cataloguing in Publication Data is available.

Library of Congress Catalog Card Number: 95–37642
ISBN: 0–275–95326–2

First published in 1996

Praeger Publishers, 88 Post Road West, Westport, CT 06881
An imprint of Greenwood Publishing Group, Inc.

Printed in the United States of America

The paper used in this book complies with the
Permanent Paper Standard issued by the National
Information Standards Organization (Z39.48–1984).

10 9 8 7 6 5 4 3 2 1

To the memory of

Pauline

who teaches me how to fly

Contents

Contents   ix

x Contents

Tables and Figures

Preface

The scientific study of intelligence is barely a hundred years old. The founding fathers (Paul Broca, Francis Galton, Alfred Binet) began by measuring human heads. Their utter failure to discover any significant relationship between skull characteristics and intelligent behavior did not deter later searchers. They began searching from another direction: to detect and measure an invisible entity called "intelligence quotient" (IQ). The contemporary fad is to measure electroencephalogram (EEG) and reaction time (RT). This book begins by a brief outline of the three generations of intelligence research and their modern reinterpretation.

The 1980s witnessed the competition between two theories, Robert Sternberg's (1984, 1985) triarchic theory of intelligence and Howard Gardner's (1983) theory of multiple intelligences. By the 1990s we saw some integration effort (Anderson, 1992) as well as some revival of interest in IQ (Herrnstein & Murray, 1994). This was counterbalanced by David Perkins (1995) who tried to outsmart IQ by learning it, thus learnable intelligence. Few researchers today would equate intelligence to IQ; most would probably subscribe to Perkins's view that "intelligence quotient is not intelligence but one aspect of the complex phenomenon of intelligence" (Perkins, 1995, p. 57). So, what is that complex phenomenon?

Unfortunately, contemporary experts cannot agree on what intelligence is. Twenty-five experts gave 24 different definitions and opinions of intelligence (one paper was co-authored) in a 1986 survey by Robert Sternberg and Douglas Detterman. One researcher characterizes intelligence as *"describing the elephant"* (Humphreys, 1986). Amidst such confusion, I was able to trace an evolving consensus for over seven decades that intelligence is composed of *thinking and learning*. Regrettably, however, major contemporary theories of intelligence fail to treat the two subjects adequately despite the strong need for a comprehensive theory of intelligence based on learning and thinking.

My theory is that the precursors of human intelligence lie in the human language capacity and human mental ability. Evolutionary pressure favors the interaction between the symbolic world of language and the mental world, leading to the creation of concepts. In this book I propose the notion of *conceptual intelligence*, that is, *intelligence as a result of thinking and learning through concepts*. Conceptual intelligence is the essence of human intelligence: it enables us to represent reality in concepts, to think and understand in concepts, to learn more efficiently and deeply in concepts, and subsequently create the human knowledge enterprise. Here I trace the development of concepts, the growth of conceptual thought, and how conceptual thinking and conceptual learning make the human species intelligent and creative. There is a complex co-evolution between language and thought, and between thinking and learning, which I explore in chapters 4 and 5.

But do theories of intelligence matter? After all it is just a theory, skeptics may say. Evidences abound that theories of intelligence have significant impact on society and public policy. For example, Mark Snyderman and Stanley Rothman (1988) traced how the IQ controversy has divided the American society in its dilemma between equalitarianism and individual attainment. Richard Herrnstein and Charles Murray's controversial book, *The Bell Curve* (1994), argue fervently that blacks as a group are less "intelligent" than whites, as evidenced by measured IQ, which they presume to be the "cause" behind the dismal result of affirmative action. The authors go as far as to take IQ as a major determinant of social ills such as poverty, unwed mothers, the chronically unemployed, or even criminals. However, Herrnstein and Murray's arguments stand and fall with IQ, but where lies the theoretical foundation of IQ? This I will try to answer in chapter 2. Meanwhile, my point is that theory does play an important role in human action.

One unifying theme across this book is that while lower animals can think and learn in rudimentary ways, what distinguishes us from them is our capacity for conceptual thinking and conceptual learning. With the advent of langauge and the subsequent growth of concepts, the human species slowly evolves to a new plateau unparalleled in intelligence with other species on this planet. By extending conceptual learning and conceptual thought to new frontiers, we see the development of creativity and giftedness. My conclusion is simple: *Better thinking and more learning will make us intelligent.* How to think better and what to learn to make us intelligent are important questions that require the effort of a whole generation of researchers. Fortunately we are already on our way to thinking skills (de Bono, 1986, 1992; Marzano, 1989), learning strategies (Pressley, 1990; Dryden & Vos, 1995) metacognition (Flavell, 1977), metacurriculum (Perkins, 1992) and metalearning (Novak & Gowin, 1984; Li, 1995b).

This book is for general readers as well as for researchers in the field. The busy general reader will find the chapter summary at the end of each chapter convenient and informative. But if you are a graduate student, remember that statements in the chapter summary cannot replace details of argument within the chapter. In addition, each chapter comes with an "Intelligent food for thought" on the anecdotes of intelligence research. Unlike brain-teasers that may confuse you, they are thought-openers that hopefully bring delights to your thinking and reflection on the subject.

It is my hope that this work could bring intelligence research to a new light and serve as a common ground for future research. I believe that knowledge has no national boundary and cross-cultural fertilization will only enhance it. Intelligence research was an international effort a century ago (Galton in England, Binet in France, Terman in America, Piaget in Switzerland), and it should be more so as we enter the next millennium.

Rex Li
1996
Hong Kong

Acknowledgments

It gives me indescribable pleasure to thank all my friends who have given me invaluable encouragement and support to my work. They wrote to me from all over the world, notably: In America, Professor James Borland and Professor Dennis Mithaug (Teachers College, Columbia University), Professor Dean Simonton (University of California, Davis), Professor Howard Gardner (Harvard University), Professor Richard Ripple (Cornell University), and Professor Phillip Ackerman (University of Minnesota); in the United Kingdom, Professor Hans Eysenck (University of London) and Dr. David George (National Association for Curriculum Enrichment); in China, Professor Zha Zixiu and Professor Zhang Meiling (Chinese Academy of Sciences), Professor Zhu Ying (Peking University), and Dr. Meng Hong Wei (China National Institute for Educational Research); in Hong Kong, Dr. Jimmy Chan (University of Hong Kong), Professor Chung-Kwong Wong (Chinese University of Hong Kong), and Professor Elizabeth Rudowicz (City University of Hong Kong); in Taiwan, Professor Wu-Tien Wu (National Taiwan Normal University), and Professor Lung-An Chen (Taipei Municipal Teachers' College); in Germany, Professor Kurt Heller (University of Munich); in South Korea, Dr. Jeong-hwa Moon (Korea Creativity Development Institute); in South Africa, Professor Cedric Taylor (University of Port Elizabeth); in Canada, Professor Kieran Egan (Simon Fraser University), and Professor Carolyn Yewchuk (Universtiy of Alberta).

Finally, I wish to thank my colleagues at Gifted Education Council of Hong Kong for their comments on my manuscript, notably C. K. Chan, Eugene Ho and David Chan, my secretaries Michelle Hui and Carmen Wong for their professional typing, and Alex Yam for his wonderful artwork. At Greenwood Publishing Group Inc., my thanks are due to copyeditor Wanda Giles, production editor Lori Blackwell, and editorial assistant Marcia Goldstein for their wonderful editorial work in bringing this book to its completion.

1

How It All Started and Where Are We?

A SHORT HISTORY OF INTELLIGENCE RESEARCH

We Began by Measuring Heads

It may sound awkward today, but the modern study of intelligence began about one and a half centuries ago with the measurement of human heads. At that time, researchers were measuring skulls with as much precision and seriousness as a scientific enterprise. Craniometry, the study and measurement of human skulls, is actually the forerunner of modern brain science. Our story of intelligence began with Paul Broca (1824-1880), a pioneering brain surgeon to whose name we owe for his discovery of the speech area in the human brain. As a professor of clinical surgery and founder of Anthropological Society of Paris, Broca amassed enormous data about brain size of different races: these data included weight, circumference, cranial capacity; he also refined the technique of measurement by pouring lead shot into the skull; then he compared the quality of frontal lobes with occipital lobes between races and did many then-empirical studies. Eventually Broca (1861) declared the superiority of white men over black women for their having larger heads (presumably larger skulls and brains as well) and subsequently their higher intelligence. Craniometry gained much popularity for many decades and was treated as a scientific enterprise until researchers slowly lost their naivete and discovered that they have erred.

In the decade when Broca was measuring heads in France, Sir Francis Galton (1822-1911) wrote his *Hereditary Genius* (1869) in Britain. A cousin of Charles Darwin, Galton studied the family trees of eminent people, applied statistics to quantify his data, and concluded, not too surprisingly, that eminent people had offsprings who later became eminent. Giving a Darwinian account of the transmission of characteristic traits through heredity, Galton believed that intelligence, one of the most important traits of human species with high survival value, is no exception. Darwin hypothesized that there exist some tiny "gemmules" in body cells which migrated through the bloodstream, accumulated at reproductive cells, and transmitted through fertilization between the sperm and ovum. This biological hypothesis was taken without question as the hereditary interpretation of intelligence.

Galton had high hopes that genetics would reveal the secrets of intelligence. In 1884, he set up a laboratory in London to measure intelligence. In addition to measuring skulls, Galton also measured physical strength, sensory perception, sight sensitivity, and reaction time and computed the first mental test scores of his subjects. His laboratory became some sort of a fun fair for the British aristocracy: many dignitaries, including the then-British prime minister, had their heads and intelligence measured there.

The French Won the Contest

While Broca was busy measuring skulls and Galton measuring reaction time, Wilhelm Wundt (1832-1920), the father of modern experimental psychology, ventured into other measurements in Germany, In 1879, Wundt set up his psychometric laboratory in Leipzig to study mental events by introspection. Caught in this measuring euphoria, an American student, James McKeen Cattell (1860-1944), learned his trade from both Wundt and Galton and imported it to the United States. Before the turn of the twentieth century, every psychometric pioneer was racing toward measuring something out of human heads to get something called "intelligence."

The French won the contest. Alfred Binet (1857-1911) and Theodore Simon (1873-1961) were the first to develop an intelligence test for French children. Binet started his psychometric laboratory at the Sorbonne in 1890 and followed Broca's footsteps in measuring heads of schoolchildren. The results had been disappointing. When the minister of public instruction in Paris asked Binet to develop a test to identify the "mentally defective" for separate school placement in 1904, Binet changed his course. He abandoned craniometry altogether and designed numerous short tasks of real-life problems, sequenced them in order of difficulty, and administered them to these children. Unknowingly Simon and Binet were devising a reasoning test which later became the blueprint of an IQ test (Sattler, 1988, chapter 3).

If Broca, Galton, and Wundt were considered the first generation in intelligence research, Binet belongs to the second. Binet's contemporaries include Cattell in the United States, who measured some invisible entities of intelligence, and Charles Spearman (1863-1945) in Great Britain, who perfected statistical techniques to measure intelligence. A psychometrics professor at the University of London, Spearman invented factor analysis in 1904 to treat mental test scores and came up with a two-factor theory, a single general factor, "g," to denote general intelligence, and several independent specific factors, "s," to represent interrelations among tests. In both generations, researchers were working under the empirical paradigm of scientific research with the assumption that intelligence is innate, mostly heritable, like something inside the head and manifest in certain physiological characteristics such as skull shape and size. Intelligence is assumed to be a single entity amenable to measurement. With improved statistical techniques and apparent success in mental testing, intelligence researchers were hopeful that they could isolate, detect, and measure intelligence.

The American "Great Leap Forward"

Like thousands of Europeans finding their homes in the United States during the First World War, intelligence research also landed in that land of opportunity. The third generation of intelligence researchers began with Americans refining IQ tests. Lewis Terman (1877-1956), a Stanford professor in psychology, revised Binet's scales to become the Stanford-Binet Scales for American children in 1916. Terman also inherited Spearman's factor g position in revising the Binet Scales, taking intelligence as a general, global factor. While Spearman takes intelligence as the "eduction of correlates" and grounds g in mental energy of cortical activity in light of the then-fashionable atomic energy theory, Terman was more pragmatic: he simply defined "superior intellectuality (intelligence)" as high IQ scores in Stanford-Binet and started measuring giftedness (Vol. l, 1925, p. 631). Using his newly developed measuring instrument, he crusaded in a talent search in California and began a longitudinal study of more than 1,000 gifted children in 1920. His mass marketing of IQ tests has helped popularize intelligence as a single innate entity and a single score. Stanford-Binet remains one of the most popular IQ tests in the United States today. Monism by the third generation is firmly established.

The First World War was a great leap forward for intelligence tests in the United States. Robert Yerkes, a Harvard professor of psychology sold his idea to the United States Army and had 1.75 million recruits take IQ tests as a screening mechanism for posting and officer training, with the rationale that only recruits with higher intelligence are suited for more demanding tasks requiring special skills. IQ tests, no more the toys of academicians, now gained their American flavor of business and marketing. On the other side of the Atlantic, Sir Godfrey Thomson quarrelled with his colleague Spearman in England on the interpretation of g. Thomson accepted Spearman's data and factor analysis but interpreted it the opposite way. He argued that there is no single factor; the overlapping bonds of multiple factors give its unitary appearance (1919). So born into this troublesome factor-analytic family a quarrelling sibling: pluralism.

The Swiss Turn from Studying Snails to Children

A suprising turn of intelligence research took place in Europe in 1926. In that year, Jean Piaget (1896-1980), a Swiss biologist turned psychologist, published his first book on children, *Language and Thought in the Child*. As a schoolboy Piaget studied snails (mollusks) and received his Ph.D. for doing so (He was then twenty-one.) In 1920, he went to Paris and worked in the Binet Laboratory with Simon. His job was to standardize an IQ test. Instead of scoring children's incorrect responses in a standardized procedure, Piaget toyed with their wrong answers and came to the realization that young children are not less intelligent, but that they think differently. Without joining the IQ test gang, Piaget returned to Geneva in 1921, became director of the Rousseau Institute and studied children's thought by watching his own offsprings (an observant father!). From 1923 to 1932 he published many papers and five books on children, recasting intelligence in cognitive-developmental terms.

Back in America, Columbia professor Edward Thorndike (1874-1949) was busy studying intelligence in another direction. Instead of studying people, he experimented with hungry cats and found animal intelligence in an experimental study of the associative process in animals (1898). For Thorndike, the most rudimentary intelligence (problem solving by cats) is trial-and-error behavior and the stimulus-response association. He further refined his position into a number of laws in learning: the law of repetition, the law of readiness, and the law of effect (1913), which soon became the behaviorist view of intelligence.

By the third generation (see Figure 1.1), the major paradigms of intelligence were in shape. From Thomson's pluralism we saw its expansion to L. L. Thurstone's vectors of mind (1935) and seven primary mental abilities (1938): verbal comprehension, word fluency, number, spatial visualization, associative memory, perceptual speed, and reasoning. As that is not enough, J. P. Guilford proposes a structure of intellect (1967) with 4 contents, 5 processes and 6 operations, making up a total of 120 abilities! From Terman's monism there emerged the Cattell-Horn (Horn, 1965; Horn & Cattell, 1966; Cattell, 1971) version of fluid ability and crystallized ability. Cognitive developmentalism progressed in Europe under Piaget while behaviorism dominated the American scene for many decades. The modern information-processing paradigm did not come into being until the 1960s, with the advent of the computer metaphor.

Figure 1.1
Three Generations of Intelligence Research

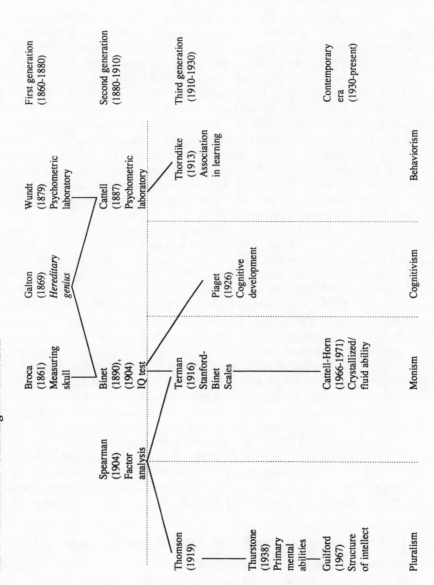

SO, WHAT IS INTELLIGENCE? EXPERTS CANNOT AGREE

Describing the Elephant

Once we enter the contemporary scene, intelligence research becomes very confusing. There is no consensus in sight with respect to the meanings, conotations, or assumptions of intelligence. Piaget (1952), for example, used the term to mean the growth of the intellect of the normal child, but Terman's usage (1925) denotes the study of genius and the exceptionally gifted. The strangest thing is that *creativity* has been consistently excluded from the concept of intelligence, which is equated to a number commonly thought to be what an intelligence test is supposed to measure and confer (Boring, 1923). When in recent years Robert Sternberg (1985) proposed a triarchic theory of intelligence, the conception was so broad that intelligence could mean any conceivably related entity, for example, adaptation, automatic processing, novelty, knowledge, behavior, and so on. So, what is intelligence?

Robert Sternberg and Douglas Detterman (1986) surveyed 25 experts on this question. The experts were asked (a) what intelligence is and how they measure it and (b) what the most crucial "next" steps in research were? As might be expected, 25 experts gave 24 different definitions and opinions on the subject (one paper was co-authored). It would be difficult and unnecessary to summarize all their conceptions here. Morever, this list of experts is not exhaustive since many experts were, for one reason or another, not included in this survey. For example, Piaget was not included, obviously because of his death in 1981; yet his theory is still very influential. Phillip Ackerman's radex model of structure of abilities (1989) was not included, nor was Mike Anderson's minimal cognitive architecture (1992): both were developed a few years later. Richard Skemp, a British educator cum philosopher who has written a whole book on learning and intelligence, was not included (Skemp, 1979). The fact is that we have more than 24 different theories of intelligence. The diversity of opinions regarding intelligence has led to Lloyd Humphreys's characterization of intelligence as "describing the elephant," where "no one aspect (of description) is sufficient to encompass the elephant of intelligence" (1986, p. 95).

Convergence Among Social Scientists and Educators

On the other hand, there is a convergence of conception among social scientists and educators on the important elements of intelligence. Mark Snyderman and Stanley Rothman (1988) surveyed 1,020 social scientists and educators on many topics dealing with the nature of intelligence and the adequacy of intelligence testing. It is so far the most recent and comprehensive survey of expert opinions in this area.

Snyderman and Rothman found that opinions of those respondents not only converged on the basic elements of intelligence but also converged on the view that intelligence was a less stable characteristic trait than height: 73 percent of them agreed on this point. In the same survey, over 85 percent of respondents believed that intelligence tests could adequately measure general knowledge, linguistic and mathematical competence and memory. On the whole, however, only 53 percent agreed somewhat or strongly that there was a consensus among psychologists and educators as to the kinds of behaviors that were labeled intelligent, as compared with 39.5 percent who disagreed in some manner (Snyderman & Rothman, 1988, p. 55).

Table 1.1 is adapted from Snyderman and Rothman's survey on the important elements of intelligence. While experts have no consensus as to whether intelligence should include creativity (59.6 percent thought it should) or goal directedness (only 24 percent thought so), they do have a common understanding that intelligence should include elements such as abstract thinking or reasoning (99.3 percent), problem-solving ability (97.7 percent), and capacity to acquire knowledge (96 percent). These top three elements far excel other elements lower in the list: following them are memory (80.5 percent), adaptation (77.2 percent), mental speed (71.7 percent), and so on.

Such convergence can be viewed as a strong consensus among scholars about the elements of intelligence. As Snyderman and Rothman put it,

Accompanying the disagreement about the scope of the definition of intelligence is very strong agreement at its core. It can reasonably by concluded that when different psychologists and educators use the term "intelligence" they are *basically* referring to the same concept, having to do with the capacity to learn and with more complex cognitive tasks like abstract reasoning and problem solving, and that they would generally exclude purely motivational and sensory abilities from this definition. (1988, pp. 56-57)

Intelligence as Thinking and Learning

How are we going to characterize these top three elements of intelligence? First of all, they all belong to higher-order conceptual activities. In other words, the consensus is that intelligence includes conceptual activities such as abstract thinking, reasoning, problem-solving ability, and the capacity to acquire knowledge. Next, since "abstract thinking" and "reasoning" are used interchangeably, we can delete the latter and keep the former intact. A question thus arises: Are the three elements distinct, or can one be reducible to the other?

Notice that in most basic texts on cognitive psychology, such as John Anderson (1990), reasoning and problem solving are treated as two different topics, with the former covering subtopics such as inductive and deductive reasoning, conditional reasoning, hypothes is formation, and so on, while the latter is concerned with problem space, insight, means-ends analysis, and the like. Upon closer analysis, however, we discover that to search through the problem space is an abstract

Table 1.1
Important Elements of Intelligence

Descriptor	% of Respondents Checking as Important
Abstract thinking or reasoning	99.3
Problem-solving ability	97.7
Capacity to acquire knowledge	96.0
Memory	80.5
Adaptation to one's environment	77.2
Mental speed	71.7
Linguistic competence	71.0
Mathematical competence	67.9
General knowledge	62.4
Creativity	59.6
Sensory acuity	24.4
Goal directedness	24.0
Achievement motivation	18.9

Source :   M. Snyderman and S. S. Rothman, *The IQ Controversy* (New Brunswick, New Jersey: Transaction Publishers, 1988), p. 56. Copyright 1988 by Transaction Publishers. Adapted by permission.

thinking activity; to devise heuristics to solve a problem also involves abstract thinking. There are many methods to solve a problem, such as difference-reduction method, means-ends analysis, working-backward method, analogy, and so on (see Anderson, 1990, chapter 8); all of them invariably involve deep and abstract thinking. It is therefore conceptually sound to consider problem-solving ability as a subset of abstract thinking.

Now "to acquire knowledge" is a term almost synonymous with "learning." In fact the writers of one textbook have defined learning as "acquiring facts and skills that can be retained and used when necessary" (Biggs & Telfer, 1987, p. 147). So "the capacity to acquire knowledge" is very synonymous with "the capacity to learn." Going back to the important elements of intelligence, we can safely point to the consensus that it includes abstract thinking and the capacity to learn. More specifically, the general consensus is that intelligence has two major components, namely, thinking and learning.

The Evolving Consensus

That social scientists and educators take thinking and learning as the two major components of intelligence is hardly surprising. In fact, we can trace the historical development of this consensus. In 1921, the editors of the *Journal of Educational Psychology* invited prominent psychologists to define intelligence. Naturally, the conceptions of intelligence among them varied widely. Nevertheless, the highest consensus was reached among 8 out of 14 respondents, or 57 percent that intelligence is about "higher-level components" (abstract reasoning, representation, problem solving, decision making). This was remarkably similar to what we conceptualize today. At that time, the ability to learn ranked second, that is, the second highest consensus was reached among four respondents, or 29 percent, who thought that intelligence included "the ability to learn."

The idea of a symposium on intelligence is not new. In 1974, a conference was held at the Learning Research and Development Center at the University of Pittsburgh. The contributors addressed the question of the nature of intelligence. Surprisingly, no participant ever mentioned the connection between learning and intelligence. Learning theory seems to be the domain of behaviorists, who dismiss intelligence as unobservable behavior. At that time, cognitive psychologists were casting doubt on the scientific validity of the psychometric paradigm of intelligence. They were busy formulating their information-processing concept of intelligence by reinterpreting factorially the findings of intelligence tests in an information-processing framework of long-term memory, problem solving, specific cognitive tasks, and so on. They were also responding to the Piagetian challenge of development and intelligence.

A decade later, another symposium on intelligence was organized (Sternberg & Detterman, 1986). As pointed out by one of its editors, "Although extraordinary diversity can be found within these definitions, there are striking commonalities as well" (Sternberg, 1986a, p. 3). More specifically, a consensus was reached among 12 out of 24 scholars, or 50 percent, that intelligence can be viewed with "higher-level components, (abstract reasoning, representation, problem solving, decision making)." This was by far the highest frequency of defining attributes of intelligence reached, followed by intelligence as "that which is valued by culture" (seven scholars, or 29 percent), and intelligence as "ability to learn" (six scholars, or 25 percent).

Thus, despite the diversity of opinions on the subject, it is fairly safe to conclude that there is a strong consensus about the core of intelligence, which is thinking and learning. More strikingly, this consensus seems to have changed very little over time. In fact, the consensus is especially strong and unanimous in the 1988 survey. These has led Snyderman and Rothman to conclude, "These same threads run through both the 1921 and 1986 symposia. In many ways, Terman's 1921 definition of intelligence as abstract thinking remains at the heart of current thought about intelligence," (Synderman & Rothman, 1988, p. 57).

More recently, Harvard psychologist David Perkins proposed the interesting notion of learnable intelligence (1995). In Perkins's view, intelligence has three aspects, the neural dimension (intelligence as determined by genetic and physical maturation), the experiential dimension (intelligence as contribution of context-specific knowledge), and the reflective dimension (intelligence as a result of reflective thinking, metacogntion, and mental self-management). The first dimension is determined by human genetic predisposition and cognitive structure while the other two are learnable, thus learnable intelligence. In fact Perkins has worked for years on the teaching of thinking to raise IQ and proposed the idea of "metacurriculum" and "smart schools" for "better thinking and learning" (Perkins & Simmons, 1988; Perkins, 1992). Perkins's view of intelligence can be seen as the latest exposition of this consensus.

THE INADEQUACY OF MAJOR CONTEMPORARY THEORIES OF INTELLIGENCE

Given the consensus that intelligence has two major components, namely, thinking and learning, how are these two components treated in major contemporary theories of intelligence? Upon deeper study of the subject, I come to the conclusion that these two components have not been treated adequately. The following are a brief sketch of what contemporary theories of intelligence are and how they maltreat thinking and learning. More details of critique can be found in chapter 2. There are numerous theories of intelligence in the field, but most of them fall into the following four paradigms: the information-processing paradigm, the learning paradigm, the factor-analytic paradigm, and the cognitive-developmental paradigm.

The Information-Processing Paradigm

The information-processing paradigm is best represented by Sternberg's triarchic theory of intelligence (Sternberg, 1984, 1985). Basically it is a cognitive reinterpretation of intelligence in an information-processing framework. Sternberg formulates his theory in terms of three subtheories: the contextual subtheory, the experiential subtheory and the componential subtheory, each further divided into sub domains of conern. The triarchic theory's treatment of thinking is not comprehensive enough: while the contextual and experiential subtheories have little to do with thinking, while the componential subtheory deals with only one aspect of thinking, that is, thinking as a process. Here Sternberg mentions two important forms of thinking: inductive reasoning and deductive reasoning. Regrettably a more comprehensive taxonomy of thinking is missing, such as concept formation, reflective thinking, conceptual thinking, problem solving and so on. Moreover, Sternberg focuses only on the information-processing aspect of thinking, breaking it up into metacomponents and performance components, but has nothing to theorize about the nature and mechanism of thinking, rules of thought, thought and language, levels of thinking, and so on. Sternberg's domain of inquiry is limited to the processing aspect of only a few types of reasoning.

On the other hand, Sternberg is very explicit about learning and develops his knowledge-acquisition component within the componential subtheory. However, the whole notion of learning is broken down into parts to fit into different subtheories, where learning and vocabulary belong to the componential subtheory, concept acquisition, and insight belong to the experiential subtheory, and tacit knowledge belongs to the contextual subtheory. Thus, Earl Butterfield criticized Sternberg's knowledge-acquisition component as an ad hoc construct that "does not specify mechanisms of acquisition nor their relations to other mechanisms of the cognitive system" (1986, p. 45).

Morever, Sternberg's treatment of knowledge-acquisition component is a very preliminary and sketchy one: Sternberg merely shows the complex process of knowledge acquisition, pointing out that there is vast individual difference in how one learns from one's experience and that the knowledge acquisition process can be amenable to measurement through ingenious design. He never spells out the underlying mechanism of knowlege acquisition, knowledge characteristics and representation, the principles underlying learning, and so on. In conclusion, Sternberg has not treated thinking and learning adequately in his triarchic theory of intelligence.

The Learning Paradigm

Many contemporary theorists, notably Ann Brown, Joseph Campione, Earl Butterfield, Richard Snow and Roger Schank, take learning as crucial to intelligence. However, their treatment of learning in relation to intelligence has been less comprehensive than a theory would require. Moreover, they focus exclusively on learning to the extent that they neglect the thinking dimension of intelligence. For example, Butterfield sees learning exclusively from the cognitive perspective. He defines intelligent action as the creation of a novel executive routine after searching through knowledge base, meta-cognition, and cognitive strategies (Butterfield, 1986). He provides a cognitive framework of learning, but not a comprehensive theory of intelligence based on learning. Brown and Campione equate intelligence with learning potential and try to measure it through dynamic assessment of domain-specific indices of learning potential (Brown & Campione, 1985, 1986; Campione, 1989). They are more concerned with school learning of academic subjects, that is, learning in a formal sense, than learning in a more informal and general sense. While they should be credited for bringing learning back to the center of focus on intelligence, they have yet to spell out the concept and ramifications of "learning potential" and its relation to intelligence. Snow defines intelligence as a "family resemblance" concept with six aspects. He is concerned with the cognitive aptitude for learning and proposes a typography of ability and learning (Snow & Lohman, 1984; Snow, 1986), but he offers no comprehensive theory of intelligence based on learning. Schank is able to propose a theory of intelligence by piecing together a few very basic concepts such as understanding, explanation, and learning (Schank, 1982, 1986); yet he is more concerned with cognitive understanding than learning and defines the latter in terms of the former. In fact, I would take Schank's theory as a special case of learning in my typology. (See elaboration in chapter 5.)

The Factor-Analytic Paradigm

The factor-analytic approach to intelligence has caught the imagination of many scholars ever since Spearman invented factor analysis and put it to use in the study of intelligence (Spearman, 1904, 1927). Their concern is mainly with the manifestation and quantification of intelligent behavior, that is, intelligence test scores and how to measure intelligence. The euphoria of measurement has ranged from Spearman's "g" to reaction time to evoked potentials in EEG (Jensen,

1982, 1986). The latest representatives are John Horn's mixture theory (Horn, 1989) and Phillip Ackerman's radex model of structure of abilities (Ackerman, 1989) for pluralism and Hans Eysenck's EEG for monism (1982, 1986a, 1986b). In general, this tradition is more concerned with whether there exist single or mutliple abilities (intelligence) and how one might measure them. They have eschewed more general and foundational issues such as how intelligence comes into being, what the relations are among intelligence, thinking and learning, and so on. On the whole, the factor-analytic paradigm has little foundational theory to offer, least about thinking and learning.

The Cognitive-Developmental Paradigm

The cognitive-developmental paradigm has a lot in common with my concern here, especially in how it relates to thinking and learning. Piaget, the founding father of this paradigm, proposes a developmental theory of intelligence and a theory of learning of his own. He offers a theory of the developmental process of how intelligence grows in a child (1952). There is no doubt that Piaget is concerned with thinking, and indeed he defines intelligence in terms of thinking or the growth of intellect (Piaget, 1950, 1952). On the other hand, Piaget is also concerned with learning. He takes learning in a general sense, that is, development. Piaget's theory of learning (development) is aimed at showing the process and mechanisms (such as equilibration) that make the human species intelligent. What Piaget has neglected is formal learning and the issue of individual differences. This I will elaborate in chapter 2.

It now becomes clear that my concern in intelligence, that is, thinking and learning, is in fact a domain shared and studied extensively by Piaget. His focus and mine, however, are different. Piaget's focus is on giving a developmental account of the growth of intelligence (or thinking), plus an explanatory account of learning (development). My focus is, on the other hand, on the possibility of thinking, the nature and scope of thinking, how learning takes place and what principles underlie learning. Piaget's theory is a very comprehensive and sophisticated one, but there is a missing link in his theory of intelligence; for while he is able to give a descriptive account of the development of intelligence with the emergence of many phenomena, he does not explain why this is possible. It is my hope to connect this link, build on it and go beyond Piaget. This I will elaborate in chapters 2, 4 and 5. Although I am no Piagetian, I have the deepest admiration for Piaget, to whom I always have to come back whenever I address a new topic and domain as a result of his breadth, relevance, and insight.

WHAT THIS BOOK IS ABOUT

Why Theorize at All?

A common question raised would be why theorize at all. What is the significance of theories in general and theories of intelligence in particular? To the general question, I would give a simple answer. Theory guides action. A theory is like a lens through which we see the world. A good theory will lead us to penetrate deeper into reality and will enhance our understanding of the world. We build bridges, we send space shuttles to outer space; they all depend on theories in physics and engineering. Without adequate and proper theories we just cannot make advances in science and technology.

A critic may not object to the need for theories in the physical sciences but have reservations in the significance of theories in the social sciences. The critic may argue that physical theories have pragmatic uses and implications, but social scientific theories are just about human affairs. It is just a theory, not the real thing. Even if the theory is proved correct, it may not have any practical use apart from enchancing our understanding of ourselves. To this I would respond that theory guides action, in both the science and the social realm. Take the example of Marxism. It is just a theory, but it has had an enormous impact on the history of humankind. Marxist theory guides human action in both the political and the economic realms; this ideology has dictated Eastern European and Russian practices for years. It is still the state ideology of China today.

How Theories of Intelligence Affect Human Action

When we look at theories of intelligence, there is no doubt that they have significant impact on society and human action. Take the example of IQ. The belief in the existence of an innate intelligence, quantifiable as IQ, led Terman to the mass marketing of intelligence tests and the identification of over 1,000 "gifted children" and the subsequent publication of four volumes of work (Terman, 1925; Burks, Jensen & Terman, 1930; Terman & Oden, 1947, 1959). The belief that IQ is a heritable trait led H. H. Goddard, an American educator, to advocate that "feebled-minded" people should not be allowed to mate and give birth to "feebled-minded" children (Goddard, 1914). The belief that brain size has something to do with intelligence led to the development of craniometry and to Broca's conclusion that white, eminent men have bigger brains than ordinary women of other races (Broca, 1861). All these are examples of how our misconceived ideas or theory may have enormous impact on society and human action. To this I would add the latest belief of Herrnstein and Murray (1994) that blacks as a group are intellectually inferior to whites, as evidenced in measured IQ, which could not be explained by environmental factors alone. If blacks are genetically less intelligent than whites, it surely has enormous implications for society and social policies. Note that their belief, rightly or wrongly, is based on IQ, but where lies the theoretical foundation of IQ? This I would discuss in some detail in chapter 2.

Of course, it could be argued that in the above examples, theory did not direct or guide action. Rather, theory may serve as a post hoc justification for what was already believed. As a consequence, theory justifies belief and belief justifies action. Whichever the case, it is undeniable that theory does affect to a very great extent human action directly or indirectly. The quests for better theories, or theories that are more encompassing and closer to truth, are genuine pursuits. Better theories may lead to better beliefs, so to speak, and these may result in better-reasoned human action and better lives.

The Purpose of This Book

The purpose of this book is to offer a foundational theory of intelligence based on thinking and learning. The theory will take these two major components as its starting point. I will try to offer a theory to explain how these two major components of intelligence develop and also show how they relate to each other. It is a foundational theory because it attempts to give a micro explanation of intelligence; it will ground the human intelligence phenomenon on thinking and learning; it will outline the basic mechanisms of intelligent operation, and it will address the fundamental issues on intelligence: what intelligence is, how it develops, and how it relates to basic human abilities. With this basic conception of intelligence, I hope we would be able to delineate what is relevant from what is irrelevant in the study of intelligence, distinguish what we should measure from what we should not measure in intelligence, and finally specify the broad shape of how one might improve intelligence.

On the conceptual thinking dimension of intelligence, I will try to answer some very basic questions, such as: How is conceptual thought possible? How does the human species grow into thinking? What is the nature, scope, and characteristics of thinking? How does the advent of language transform thinking? What are the relations between language and thought? On the conceptual learning dimension of intelligence, I will try to answer the following questions: What is conceptual learning? How is conceptual learning possible? How does conceptual learning take place? What are the nature, scope, content and principles of conceptual learning, and how does it contribute to intelligence?

My theory starts from the human species' unique capacity for language. This unique capacity interacts with the human mental ability in the creation of concepts, and subsequently the development of conceptual thought and conceptual learning. By extending conceptual thought and conceptual learning to new frontiers, we see the development of creativity and giftedness. In other words, I am trying to integrate four domains in one theory: thinking, learning, creativity, and giftedness.   Like Gardner's theory of multiple intelligences and Sternberg's triarchic theory, my attempt is to give a comprehensive account of the human intelligence phenomenon.   But my theory goes beyond information-processing and human cognition.   I have brought forth the issue of the human conceptual system in our study of intelligence.   I hope this is a new way of looking at old issues and has made some progress in the field. As stated earlier, intelligence research is an international effort and I hope researchers of different nations can work together to uncover this universal human phenomenon.

CHAPTER SUMMARY

The modern study of intelligence began with craniometry, the study and measurement of human skulls.   Paul Broca (1824-1880) believed that the shape and size of human heads were related to intelligence.   He measured human heads with great precision and concluded that white men have larger heads than black women and are subsequently more intelligent. Sir Francis Galton (1822-1911) wrote his *Hereditary Genius* in 1869 in Britain.   He studied the family tree of eminent people and concluded that intelligence is a characteristic trait transmittable through heredity, thus setting the stage for hereditarian intelligence research.   At the turn of the century, Alfred Binet (1857-1911) and Theodore Simon (1873-1961) succeeded in devising the first intelligence test with intelligence quotient (IQ) for the French government for school placement purposes. The Americans "leap" forward by Stanford professor Lewis Terman (1877-1956) importing Binet Scales. Terman revised and popularized it in the United States for the talent search of over 1,000 American gifted children with a large-scale longitudinal study.

The debate between Professor Charles Spearman and Sir Godfrey Thomson has divided intelligence research into two camps: monism and pluralism. The former hypothesized that intelligence is a unitary entity while the latter argued that intelligence is composed of multiple abilities.   In 1926, Jean Piaget (1896-1980), a Swiss biologist began studying children's thought and published his first book, *Language and Thought in the Child*. An apprentice-turned rebel of the IQ test gang, he questioned the validity of IQ test and studied intelligence in cognitive and developmental terms.   The behaviorist view of intelligence as learning was established in America by Columbia professor Edward Thorndike (1874-1949) who studied cats instead of men and came up with laws of learning. The modern information-processing view arrived in the 1960s with the advent of the computer metaphor.

In the contemporary era, experts cannot agree on what intelligence is and how to do intelligence research. Nevertheless there is an evolving consensus since 1920s that intelligence is composed of thinking and learning. This latest manifestation appears in Mark Snyderman and Stanley Rothman's 1988 survey of 1,020 social scientists and educators.

There are four major paradigms in intelligence research, namely the information-processing, factor-analytic, cognitive-developmental and learning paradigm. Except for the cognitive-developmental paradigm under Piaget, all other paradigms treat thinking and learning inadequately. This book tries to offer a theory of conceptual intelligence based on conceptual thinking and conceptual learning. My theory starts from the human species' unique capacity for language, which interacts with the human mental ability in the creation of concepts, and subsequently the development of conceptual thought and conceptual learning. By extending thinking and learning to new frontiers, we see the development of creativity and giftedness. This work hopes to offer a common ground for future research on intelligence.

Intelligent Food for Thought I

Ever since Alfred Binet devised the first IQ test, researchers have been keen on devising other human measurements. David Perkins jokingly mentioned athletic quotient (AQ), and Daniel Goleman seriously professed emotional quotient (EQ) in his new book *Emotional Intelligence* (Bantam, 1995). Guess what SQ would stand for for Freudian psychologists.

Exercise: List in alphabetical order all Qs and outline how to measure them. Example: QQ=quotient of all quotients. Calculation: add all Q scores and divide the sum by 26 (or 25?).

2

A Critique of Contemporary Theories of Intelligence

In chapter 1, I gave a short historical review of intelligence research and have touched upon many important theorists, notably Francis Galton, Alfred Binet, Charles Spearman, L. L. Thurstone and J. P. Guilford. Their ideas have been frequently reviewed in books and articles on intelligence, for example, Robert Grinder (1967, 1985), Robert Siegler and D. Dean Richards (1982), Robert Sternberg and Janet Powell (1983), and Robert Sternberg and Janet Davidson (1985). Since many of their ideas have been incorporated into contemporary thinking, this chapter will focus on contemporary theories and ideas only; theories of these old masters will not be reviewed here.

THE COGNITIVE-DEVELOPMENTAL PARADIGM

Piaget's Cognitive-Stage Theory

Jean Piaget (1896-1980) tries to account for human knowledge through the study of the growth of the human intellect. Instead of studying knowledge and logic in their own terms as philosophers and logicians do, Piaget turned to the empirical study of a child's intellectual development in stages: the psychological structures, the growth process and the underlying mechanisms. This, Piaget believed, could lead to the creation of a new discipline—genetic epistemology—"to explain knowledge . . . on the basis of its history, its sociogenesis, and especially the psychological origins" (1971, p. 1).

Piaget's Research Program

It is not an overstatement to state that Piaget devoted almost all his lifetime to the study of intelligence. His whole research program focused on the psychology of intelligence, attempting to bridge the gap between biology and epistemology or, more specifically, to explain epistemology through biology, the mechanism being intelligence. In Piaget's words: "If the sciences of nature explain the human species, humans in turn explain the sciences of nature, and it is up to psychology to show us how" (1978, p. 651).

Piaget defines intelligence in terms of biology, calling it a "particular instance of biological adaptation" (1952, p. 3). An infant is born with a set of biological/physical structures, such as the mouth and the ear, which manifest themselves in automatic behavioral reactions, such as the sucking reflex. The infant also comes with innate general tendencies such as primary circular reaction, secondary circular reaction, primitive anticipation, and so on. Through interaction with the environment, the automatic behavioral reactions are transformed into psychological structures, such as the sucking scheme, which the infant uses to adapt, assimilate, and accommodate to the world. This is an instance of psychological adaptation, or intelligence. In other words, intelligence is the growth of psychological structures.

Intelligence or psychological structures can be as basic and narrow as the sucking scheme. But Piaget spent much time detailing the more complex psychological structures that the human species uses to adapt to the environment. For Piaget, psychological structure is a very broad term covering constructs such as action schemes, higher-order schemes, classification, language, egocentric speech, preoperational thought, and so on. These constructs are employed to describe organized behavior and thought which help a child to adapt to his or her environment.

Another definition offered by Piaget is that intelligence is "the form of equilibrium towards which the successive adaptation—and exchanges between the organism and his environment are directed" (1950, p. 6). According to Piaget, the child is in constant interaction with the environment and has to construct knowledge and action schemes to deal with it. New and more powerful action schemes naturally grow out of old ones, and this moves the child to a higher level of equilibrium in its successive stage of intellectual development. So intelligence can be seen as (a) the product of innate endowment and interaction with environment and (b) a constructivist outcome with active involvement and creation by the child.

Axiomatizing Piaget's Theory of Intelligence

Piaget's theory of intelligence is basically a structural functionalist approach. A brief account of structural functionalism is as follows: for an organism to survive, it must perform certain functions, such as breathing, eating, reproduction, and so on. These functions are invariants because every species has to perform them in order to survive. But the physical structures of performing these functions may vary: Primates breathe with noses, but fish use gills. Thus, the functions will be the same but the structures may vary.

Piaget's version of structural functionalism in his theory of intelligence can be axiomatized into three premises and one conclusion.

Premise 1: Functionalism
             The existence of functional invariants: organization and adaptation
Premise 2: Structuralism
             The development of psychological structures
Premise 3: Interacting principles
Conclusion: Premise 1 interacts with premise 2 through principles in premise 3, propelling growth of intelligence in stages.

In premise 1, it is postulated that the human species, like other species, has a tendency to organize its processes in coherent systems. In Piaget's structural functionalism, subsystems will interact within an organized whole to achieve coherence and coordination, where the whole system is bigger than the sum of its parts. Premise 1 also postulates the tendency of the organism to adapt to the environment. Here Piaget introduces two notions: assimilation and accommodation. Assimilation refers to the process whereby an external event or object is actively processed and incorporated into existing psychological structures. Accommodation is the adjustment and modification of the psychological structures in question in the process of assimilation due to its inadequacy to incorporate the event.

Premise 2 postulates the existence of various psychological structures, defined earlier, to deal with the environment.

Premise 3 is the interacting principles between structure and function. There are two principles:

1. Active Constructivism
    The nature of interaction is an active one. The child does not passively receive information; rather he or she actively seeks out what interests him or her for his or her interaction through which psychological structures are constantly exercised, improved, and reconstructed. The child is also constantly tending towards a better understanding, or a higher-order equilibrium.

2. Emergent Property
    When the child handles a new object by using an old scheme, the old scheme is constantly undergoing internal reorganization, refinement, and improvement. New and more complex schemes naturally emerge out of the old ones to deal better with the environment.

The three premises should necessarily lead to the conclusion that the growth of intelligence is propelled from a lower stage to a higher one in an inherently dynamic system. Such are the underlying assumptions of Piaget's cognitive-stage theory with insightful descriptions of the sensorimotor period, pre-operational period, concrete operations period, and formal operations period. Piaget also studies the growth of adolescent thought (See my chapter 4 for review.)

Piaget's Theory of Learning

Does Piaget have a theory of learning? Gallagher and Reid said yes, and they wrote a whole book on the subject (Gallagher & Reid, 1981). I tend to be more cautious and argue that Piaget has a theory of development instead of learning.

To begin with, Piaget distinguished learning in a narrow sense and learning in a general sense. The former refers to learning of the particular, and memory in a specific sense, while the latter is what Piaget is concerned about: development, deeper understanding, growth of the intellect, memory and knowledge in a wider sense. In fact, the more general form of learning, or development, is the precondition for specific learning. Without development in the sense of maturation and gradual growth of the child's mind, specific learning simply cannot take place. For example, a child at four can be asked to memorize by rote the law of transitivity (A>B, B>C, then A>C), but he or she simply cannot understand, master, or apply the rule until he or she gets older, say around seven, at the stage of concrete operations.

Piaget pointed out that four factors affect development: maturation, experience, social transmission, and equilibration. Maturation is the physical boundary that sets the limits and provides opportunities for learning. It is the specific heredity of the human species, the physiological aspects that give the baby ways of knowing, such as sight and hearing, processing and thinking.

Physical versus Logico-Mathematical Experience

Experience is what a child gets when he or she comes in contact with the environment. Here Piaget distinguishes two types of experience: physical experience and logico-mathematical experience. In the former the child acquires physical knowledge and works with empirical abstraction; in the latter the child acquires logico-mathematical knowledge and works with reflective abstraction. Take the example of an apple. A child learns what apples are like by acting on them: edible, heavy, red, round, and so on. The subject (i.e., the child) comes in contact with the object (apple) and extracts the empirical properties from it, thus empirical abstraction. Now suppose there are two apples, one bigger than the other. All the physical experience a child can get is two instances of apples. The relationship between the two apples (one bigger than the other) is not extracted from the objects themselves, but from the child's own mental activity of comparison. This abstract understanding of relationship is a reflection on one's physical experience and is thus called reflective abstraction. According to Piaget, this is a higher-order abstraction which is much removed from physical experience. The logico-mathematical experience does not come from the object itself. It is the child's mental activity of gradual discovery of abstract relations such as correspondence, functions, identities, equivalence, differences, class, and so on.

Apart from the sharp distinction between empirical knowledge and logico-mathematical knowledge, Piaget also introduces the notion of pseudo-empirical knowledge and pseudo-empirical abstraction that serves as a stepping stone from the empirical to the logico-mathematical knowledge. As for social transmission, Piaget focuses on the relationship between thought and language, the socializing function of language, and how language socializes thought. Piaget's position can be briefly outlined as follows:

1. Thought is broader and more encompassing than language.
2. The operation aspect of thought need not involve language.
3. Representations (mental image, drawing, etc.) are examples of thought that do not involve language.
4. When thought is not mature, language training cannot speed up thought.

Finally, Piaget proposed the notion of equilibration, in which there may be equilibrium as well as disequilibrium. Here Piaget comes with a whole package of new terminologies. Equilibrium itself is not static; it has the tendency of always moving toward better equilibriums through reflective abstraction and concept development. Reflective abstraction can progress through projection and reorganization, while concept development may progress through differentiation and integration, relativization of concepts and quantification of relations. On the other hand, disequilibrium is the motor of intellectual development. It may create distortion, disturbance, and contradiction. The degree of distortion is a function of a child's cognitive development. Disturbance may manifest itself in three reactions: alpha, beta, and gamma, while contradiction can be analyzed through affirmation and negation. An alpha reaction is one in which a child distorts an event to fit his or her schemes. A beta reaction is one in which a child partially reorganizes his or her scheme to accommodate the disturbing event. A gamma reaction is one in which a child has matured enough to construct a whole new system to anticipate all variations of disturbances by means of inferences.

Spiral of Knowing

Piaget also proposes a "spiral of knowing" to explain development. Figuratively, it is like an inverted cone shape with a spiral growing bigger and bigger from bottom to top. The spiral is the internal construction of knowledge of the child through empirical and reflective abstraction and successive reorganization (see Figure 2.1). There are three vectors acting as the impetus to this spiral: (a) the succession of cognitive structures and stages; (b) disequilibrium and the modification of structures; (c) exploration of the environment. I also summarize Piaget's theory of learning in graphic form in Figure 2.2.

Evaluating Piaget's Theory of Intelligence

Piaget's Scope. Piaget's theory of intelligence is interwoven with and in support of his theory of learning. Piaget defines intelligence as a particular instance of biological adaptation, but what he really means is the study of how the human intellect grows to adapt to the world. In other words, Piaget's theory of intelligence is a theory of cognitive development. As for his theory of learning, it is a theory of

Figure 2.1
Piaget's Spiral of Knowing

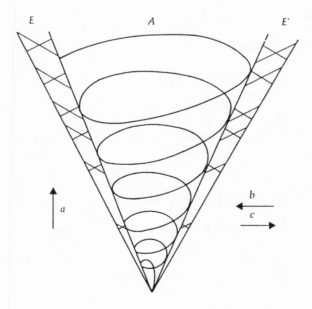

Source: From *Adaptation Vitale et Psychologie de l'Intelligence: Selection Organique et Phenocopie,* by J. Piaget. 1974, Paris: Hermann. Copyright 1974 by Hermann Editeurs Des Sciences Et Des Arts. Reprinted by permission.

Figure 2.2
Piaget's Theory of Learning in Summary

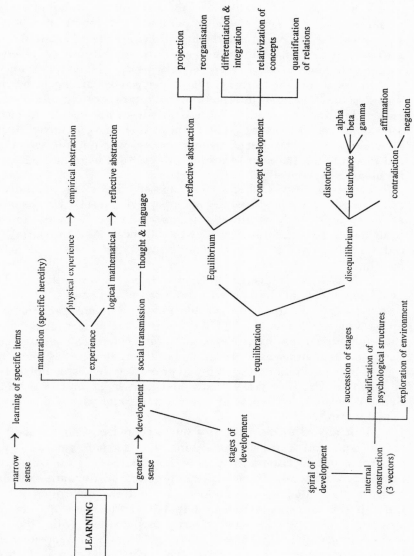

learning in a general sense, a theory of development. Again, Piaget is talking about cognitive development. In fact, Piaget's theory of learning (development) is to show the process and mechanisms (such as equilibration) that make the human species intelligent; on the other hand, his theory of intelligence focuses on the different stages of cognitive development, which operate in different psychological structures but the same interacting principles: here again we come across equilibration, equilibrium and disequilibrium. It is entirely legitmate to look at the two theories as two sides of the same coin.

In his theory of learning, Piaget neglected learning in a narrow sense: school learning, information absorption, growth of substantive knowledge domains, and so on have not been discussed. In fact, the central notion of learning, that is, how a child consciously acquires knowledge in the teaching/learning process was not addressed. Nor did Piaget touch the micro-learning process of a learning item despite his breadth in scope.

Piaget is also said to have missed the issue of individual differences in learning (Ginsburg & Opper, 1988, p. 14). He has ignored extreme cases, such as gifted learners and slow learners, and their contribution to a general theory of intelligence. And of course Piaget did not address the issue of emotion and the affective domain in learning.

This is to be expected. Piaget's theory is an outline of broad development of intelligence with milestones and stages. It is not a comprehensive theory covering every aspect, domain, and content area in learning. If Piaget did not discuss transfer of learning, it merely shows that this is not his research question. When we evaluate Piaget's theory on its own terms, it would be fair to say that he has made many significant contributions, especially in proposing the distinction between empirical and reflective experience and knowledge and in detailing a dynamic growth system of the intellect through disequilibrium and equilibration.

With regard to the nature of human intellect, Piaget rejects both empiricism and rationalism, calling the former genesis without structures and the latter structures without genesis. His middle-ground position is that intelligence is the product of dynamic interaction between the initial genetic endowment and the environment. It is through this dynamic interaction that a child creates psychological structures (also called cognitive structures) to deal with the world around him or her. In Piaget's words, "Nor do any apriori/innate cognitive structures exist in man. The structure is created through action on objects. Knowledge proceeds from action" (1980, p. 23).

Piaget made explicit his position that there is no a priori cognitive structure with which the human species is born. Piaget did accept that humans have certain innate genetic endowments, such as general heredity (organizational tendencies within an organism to integrate external stimuli, adaptation, assimilation, and accommodation), and specific heredity (e.g., the physical structures, reflexes, automatic behavioral reactions, and so on). While Piaget accepted the existence of innate reflex such as sucking that a child possesses at birth, he denied that humans are born with cognitive structures. For Piaget, these cognitive structures are the result of the human's interaction with the environment, a construction by humans to cope with the outside world.

Fodor's Challenge.   The constructivist position has led to serious challenges from innativists, such as Jerry Fodor and Noam Chomsky. Fodor's (1980) argument runs as follows: The Piagetian stage is a development from simple to complex, from lower stages to higher stages, with the latter incorporating the former. All along, the child is doing hypothesis testing in the environment to confirm his or her views and to seek better understanding in the process of equilibration. But it is entirely inconceivable that a child can construct a richer logic on the basis of a weaker logic. In Fodor's words, "it is never possible to learn a richer logic on the basis of a weaker logic, if what you mean by learning is hypothesis formation and confirmation" (1980, p. 148). For example, how can a child "build the concept of reversible operations out of a conceptual system that contains only the concepts of 'fat' and 'thin,' 'tall' and 'short?' It just does not have the requisite expressive power. Therefore, Piaget's story does not really explain how new and richer hypotheses are constructed" (Flanagan, 1991, p. 139). Let us call this the "constructivist fallacy."

I think the "constructivist fallacy" is a very serious assault on Piaget's theory, because the whole of Piagetian theory rests on the notion of the active knowing subject and his or her constructivism. If constructivism is untenable, Piaget's theory will have to be extensively revised. In fact, what Fodor and Flanagan are asking is a more general question: How can constructivism in any form be possible, Piaget's included?   How far can constructivism carry a child in his or her growth of knowledge?

I would argue that the constructivist fallacy is not a real fallacy. The argument of constructivist fallacy is valid: a richer logic cannot be constructed out of a weaker logic.   Here Fodor is referring to a deductive system, a weaker premise cannot deduce a stronger, all-embracing premise.   But in a child's activity of constructing knowledge, it is not only hypothesis testing and deduction. In dealing with a new world, children not only hypothesize, deduce, and test; they may assume, induce, explore, create, reconceptualize, reclassify. In short, they do reflective thinking through a lot of cognitive tools. Especially through induction, a lot of new inputs can be integrated with old structures which are reorganized into a new framework. It is entirely conceivable that new knowledge can grow out of the old through reconstruction and admission of new data, and this is the case with children.

Reinventing the Foundations of Mathematics? On the substantive side, however, Piaget's constructivism is not without problems. If we accept it without reservation, we would come to the logical conclusion that every child invents for himself or herself the foundations of logic and mathematics. In Piaget's words,

This brings us back to the child, since within the space of a few years he spontaneously reconstructs operations and basic structures of a logico-mathematical nature, without which he would understand nothing of what he will be taught in school. Thus after a lengthy preoperative period during which he still lacks these cognitive instruments, he reinvents for himself, around his seventh year, the concepts of reversibility, transitivity, recursion, reciprocity of relations, class inclusion, conservation of numerical sets, measurements, organization of spatial references (coordinates), morphisms, some connectives, and so on—in other words, all the foundations of logic and mathematics. (1980, p. 26)

It is really like magic that every child reinvents the foundations of mathematics and logic at about seven, but this is Piaget's conclusion.

My disbelief is based on the following: Given different environments, different cultures, different experiences, different initial starting points, nurturing practices, interacting patterns, how can every child in every part of the world end up at the same place? How can it be plausible that they all construct the same thing? If this is a verifiable fact, how can we account for this learning end-point, or learning sameness given such vast diversity and difference in experience?

I think the case is that we do not always end up in the same place at the same time. Just think of exceptional children. Some gifted children at age seven may be capable of understanding and manipulating algebraic symbols while most children are still struggling with numbers. On the other hand, if the majority of children do construct the foundation of mathematics, as Piaget claims, exactly what does a child do to reinvent the whole foundation of mathematics? Also, in that case Piaget will have to face another serious challenge: innativists would argue that logico-mathematical thought, or the foundation of mathematics, are all "prewired" in each child's mind, only waiting for the signal of "maturation," at which specified time it would "pop up."

I think Piaget could have avoided this innativist nightmare by adding some supporting hypotheses to his framework. For example, he could stress the importance of species-specific heredity and species-specific conditions that are instrumental to the growth of learning structures. What I mean is something like this: We as human species share the same physical structures and capacities, similar oral-aural apparatus, similar hearing frequencies, similar language capacities, similar brain structures and organization, similar time-tables for brain maturity, and so on. Also, we share the same life world—we live in social groups, we communicate through language, we share the same meta-reality of time, space, causality of relations, and so on. In fact, our human mind, our learning apparatus, reflect the reality we are able to capture. With the same biological roots and species-specific conditions, it is entirely conceivable that we construct and grow into similar learning structures, which Piaget held so strongly. In fact, I would argue that most children invent their foundations of mathematics, not miraculously, but through their cognitive residues. I will elaborate my position in chapter 5.

Is Piaget's Theory Descriptive or Explanatory? Another criticism of Piaget's theory is that it is a descriptive theory without explanatory power (Flanagan, 1991, p. 130). In Piagetian terminology, for example, most eight-year-olds get the conservation task right because they are in the concrete operations stage. Since concrete operations stage is defined as one in which a child can handle reversibility, conservation included, Piaget's explanation is self-defining. The explicandum merely asserts the explican. It is true that Piaget has given a detailed account of the growth of cognitive structures, but describing what happened is not the same as explaining why it happened. Worse still, Piaget was charged with offering truism, as "logical truths dressed up in psychological guise, such as that learning must proceed from the simple to the complex, or that concrete operations with objects must preceed abstract thoughts about them" (Peters, 1966, p. 229).

The real problem is that Piaget's theory seems to have failed to explain the emergence of new phenomena. It is true that Piaget's basic premises assert the emergent property of a child's interaction with his or her environment and explain the growth into higher stages through equilibrium. But Piaget has not explained why and how this emergent property should happen. Take the example of object permanence. How does an infant grow from no object concept at four months old to object permanence at around ten months old? (According to Piaget, object permanance did not emerge until 18 to 24 months old, but recent research dates it much earlier.)   Piaget merely describes the two end-points of the situation, invoking very general concepts such as growing from simple to complex, without explaining why. Another example is the transition from action schemes to conceptual schemes. In Piaget's words,

A good example is the passage of action to representation due to the formation of the semiotic function. Sensorimotor assimilation consists only of assimilating objects to schemes of action, whereas representative assimilation assimilates objects to each other, hence the construction of conceptual schemes. Now, this new form of assimilation already was virtual in sensorimotor form since it bore on multiple but successive objects; it was then sufficient to complete these successive assimilations by a simultaneous act of setting into transversal correspondence before passing to the next level. But such an action implies the evocation of objects not presently perceived, and this evocation requires the formation of a specific instrument, which is the semiotic function (deferred imitations, symbolic play, mental image which is an interiorized imitation, sign language, and so on, in addition to vocal and learned language). (1980, p. 28)

What Piaget meant is that nearing the end of sensorimotor stage, there are already preconditions for transition from action schemes to conceptual schemes: the multiple but successive objects, the evocation of hidden objects (object permanence), and so on. However, these preconditions are only necessary but not sufficient conditions for the transition from action schemes to conceptual schemes. A sufficient condition would be to explain why the infant gives up action on objects and focuses on objects themselves. Why does not the infant keep his or her highly successful action schemes instead of giving them up in favor of conceptual ones? In other words, why does an infant abandon action at all? Why does a child jump the gap from action to concept? Why is there a qualitative change? This is an intruiging question Piaget failed to address.

Following the same line of argument, we can ask how a child grows from passive looking to active looking, from primitive anticipation to passive expectation, from babbling to early language, from preoperational thought to concrete operations, from no transitivity to transitivity, and so on. Of course, Piaget might claim that he has answered all these by his concept of equilibration, or autoregulation, that is, the tendency to move toward better equilibrium. But equilibration has its problems too. First it is a theoretical construct. It is highly abstract and can be applicable to almost any type of phenomenon for explanation by virtue of its level of generality. Second, it seems to command immense explanatory power, but in reality this explanatory power is too general to be of any real value, unless it is capable of being related to a more specific schemes or levels of discourse. In this case, the transition from nothingness (such as no reversibility, no transitivity, no reciprocity) into somethingness is a puzzle too difficult for equilibration to solve.

In summary, Piaget outlines many new phenomena and asserts the emergence of many new phenomena. He also gives a detailed account of the growth of these phenomena, but when it comes to explaining the transition from the old phenomenon to the new phenomenon, Piaget is unable to give a satisfactory explanation because his notion of equilibration is too general to be of any use.

Furthermore Piaget seems to have committed the fallacy of circularity of argument. Here our explicandum, the issue to be explained, is the development of intelligence, or acquisition of learning structures. Piaget explained it by equilibration, which is the explican, or the statements explaining the explicandum. In other words, Piaget explains intelligence by equilibration. But when we look deeper into equilibration, Piaget cited reflective abstraction as the actual rule and procedure of equilibration. However, reflective abstraction is in fact what intelligence is all about: The development and acquisition of learning structures are all due to reflective abstraction. In other words, Piaget is explaining intelligence by itself.

Glaser's Cognitive Efficiency Theory

Robert Glaser (1986) sees intelligence as cognitive proficiency, that is, proficiency (or competence) in intellectual cognitive performance. More specifically, Mitchell Rabinowitz and Robert Glaser (1985) proposed a cognitive efficiency theory to explain intelligence and giftedness. According to them, knowledge is an associative network with automatic spread of activation. Highly competent performance is seen as a result of better knowledge representation and retrievability and the development of automaticity and controlled processing, where automatic processing equates to learned behavior while controlled processing equates to a learning process. The cognitive efficiency theory deals with the most basic unit of cognitive processing and can serve as a micro-foundation for Sternberg's triarchic theory.

Intelligence is also related to knowledge. Here Glaser distinguishes two domains of knowledge: artifactual knowledge and natural knowledge. Artifactual knowledge is the knowledge "invented" by a society and which is valued by its culture. This includes the conventional knowledge domains such as physics, chemistry, economics, and so on as well as professional, vocational, or social skills. Natural knowledge consists of those competencies that occur early in human development, such as existential concepts, first-language proficiency, general spatial knowledge, perceptual abilities, concepts of time, number, causality, and so on. While the two domains overlap, the former is generally learned formally whereas the latter is acquired informally and unconsciously.

According to Glaser, intelligence is attained competence, which is more than the ability to learn. In other words, intelligence is the outcome of learning, the end-point of learning (attained competence), not just the ability to learn. To learn, in fact, is to gain competence. Glaser stresses that existing knowledge structures of a domain-specific area will enable acquisition of further proficiency (or competence). In other words, learning is to utilize existing competence (proficiency) to attain further or more competence (proficiency), which is regulated by cognitive mechanisms such as organized memory, chunking, forms of representation, self-regulatory skills, and so on.

What psychometric analyses and cognitive studies reveal as attention span, perception, memory span, Glaser calls "generalized cognitive processes." Glaser postulates that they are acquired as "an individual operates in a wide variety of domains" (1986, p. 81), and that they are applicable to all knowledge domains and novelty situations. In other words, Glaser accepts the existence of general intelligence despite his stress on domain-specific intelligence.

As to the nature of competence, Glaser points out that it is domain specific; that is, competence in one domain is no guarantee of competence in others. Also, competence (or intelligence) is characterized by dynamic proceduralized knowledge bound by concepts and declarative knowledge. It is also manifested in better knowledge representation, seeing a larger, meaningful picture, and the extent (and speed) of multiple representation/perspectives in face of new information, accompanied by skilled self-regulatory (meta-cognitive) process, such as performance monitoring, allocation of attention, sensitivity to feedback, and so on. By elucidating intelligence in modern cognitive terms, Glaser looks forward to the possibility of enhancing intelligence through reorganization of schooling (1976).

Zigler's Social Competence and Other Neo-Piagetians

Edward Zigler is basically a developmentalist/Piagetian who stresses the importance of motivational aspects in learning that lead to increases in IQ (Zigler & Butterfield, 1968). His definition of intelligence is most similar to a polygenic model which stresses that "experience interacts with a variety of autochthonous factors in development of the intellect" (Zigler, 1986, p. 150). According to Zigler, formal cognitive processes and their structural features, as defined in Piagetian and neo-Piagtian terms, are the appropriate referents for the construct of intelligence. Yet at the same time, Zigler stresses individual differences which Piaget neglected and proposes the notion of "social competence" (Zigler, 1984) as an addition and alternative to pure IQ or Piagetian task measurements.

"Neo-Piagetian" is a very general term covering scholars and researchers who acknowledge Piaget's stage theory of intellectual development and work in line with that paradigm. P. Arlin (1975), for example, suggested the existence of a "post-formal operational period" characterized by the issue of problem-finding ability, as contrasted to the problem-solving ability in formal operations. On the other hand, John Flavell (1977) showed that many adults do not even reach the fully formal-operations stage. Robbie Case (1978) characterized the formal-operational stage as one of seeing second-order relations and suggested the searching for third-order relations and operations. Based on Case's notion, R. J. Sternberg and C. Downing (1982) developed tests of third-order operations, the ability to recognize relations between analogy and analogy. Following this line of research, M. L. Commons, F. A. Richards, and D. Kuhn (1982) proposed the existence of fifth and sixth period in cognitive development later in life, corresponding to the recognition of third-order relations requiring "systematic operations" and fourth-order relations requiring "meta-systematic operations" respectively. So far, data seem to support that these two periods require cognitive abilities beyond those of formal operations (Sternberg & Davidson, 1985).

Gardner's Theory of Multiple Intelligences

Howard Gardner, (1983), a Harvard psychologist who works in a hospital in Boston, tries to go beyond Piaget in another direction. He proposes a theory of multiple intelligences and is more than a cognitive-developmentalist. Gardner is concerned with the neuropsychological mechanisms underlying cognition and intelligence and should be most appropriately called a neural-developmentalist.

The idea of multiple intelligences is not new. L. L. Thurstone (1938) proposed seven primary mental abilities, and J. P. Guiford's structure of intellect (1967) includes 4 contents, 5 operations, and 6 processes, making up to 120 combination of abilities. MIT philosopher Jerry Fodor also suggests the idea of *The Modularity of Mind* (1983). What is new in Gardner is that he tried to ground intelligence in its biological basis and is able to isolate 7 "distinct" human abilities, thus 7 intelligences. In addition, Gardner's theory includes many different types of abilities while Thurstone and Guilford talk about the different facets of only one type of ability—intellectual ability.

Gardner's "Symbol Systems" Approach

Gardner began by criticizing different contemporary approaches to intelligence:

The I.Q., the Piagetian, and the information-processing approaches all focus on a certain kind of logical or linguistic problem solving; all ignore biology; all fail to come to grips with the higher levels of creativity; and all are insensitive to the range of roles highlighted in human society. Consequently, these facts have engendered an alternative point of view that focuses precisely upon these neglected areas. (1983, p. 24)

Gardner tries to remedy this by electing to take the human symbol systems as a primary focus of attention. These include linguistic, logical, numerical, as well as musical, bodily, spatial or even personal symbol systems. Gardner's goal is "to arrive at the 'natural kinds' of symbol systems: the families of symbol system which hang together (or fall apart), and the ways they might be represented in the human nervous system" (1983, p. 29). Thus, his research questions are: Do common processes cut across diverse symbol systems, or does each symbolic system have its unique developmental course? How and when do they break down, under what conditions of brain damage? How do they develop, organize and fall apart? By posing questions this way, he is trying to relate cognitive processing to underlying neuropsychological mechanisms. He has expanded our conception of intelligence both in breadth and depth. In breadth, he has introduced more symbol systems into intelligence, such as musical, bodily, and personal symbols traditionally neglected by cognitive psychologists. In depth, he has drawn on neuropsychology to deepen our understanding on the underlying neurophysiological mechanisms of intelligence. Following this research direction, Gardner discovers seven relatively independent and lowly correlated intelligences, each with its own symbol system, end-state performance, special pathology and brain localization, summarized in Table 2.1.

The Structure of Gardner's Theory

Gardner's theory can be axiomatized in the following two premises and one conclusion:

Premise   1:   If it can be found that certain brain parts can distinctively map with certain cognitive functioning (A), then that cognitive functioning can be isolated as one candidate of multiple intelligences (B). (If A, then B).

Premise   2:   Now it has been found that certain brain parts do distinctively map with certain cognitive functioning, as evidenced by certain brain damage leading to loss of certain cognitive function. (Evidence of A).

Conclusion: Therefore, multiple intelligences. (Therefore B).

Evidence of Gardner's Theory

The above is a valid argument, provided that both premise 1 and premise 2 are true. The problem lies in premise 2, evidence from neuroscience. It is clear that Gardner has taken great pains to gather evidence from neuroscience, neuroanatomy, and clinical cases to support his claim of brain modularity and thus multiple intelligences. However, it must be pointed out that neuroscience is a young and growing field, and all evidence should be taken as tentative rather than definite. In neuroscience, research is still going on, speculating about the existence of 100 distinct areas in the cerebral cortex, still trying to stain them, to identify them, and to see how they relate to one another. The tentative and flimsy nature of neural evidence has been described aptly by Francis Crick, a foremost practitioner in the field, "If each area could be clearly stained postmortem, so that we could see exactly how

Table 2.1
Gardner's Multiple Intelligences

Types of intelligence	Symbol system	End-state performance	Pathology	Brain localization
Linguistic	• Verbal language • Written language	• Poets • Novelists • Writers	• Aphasia • Dyslexia • Dysphasia • Hyperlexia	• Left hemisphere • Broca's area
Musical	• Pitch • Rhythm	• Musicians • Conductors • Composers	• Amusia	• Right hemisphere • Frontal lobe • Temporal lobe
Spatial	• Pictures • Visual symbols	• Artists • Painters	• Turner's syndrome • Visual impairment	• Right hemisphere
Bodily	• Gesture • Movement	• Dancers • Gynastists	• Apraxia	• Left hemisphere • Motor cortex
Interpersonal	• Feelings • Personality	• Social leaders • Religious leaders	• Inability to give appropriate feelings	• Dorsal (parietal) region
Intrapersonal		• Sagehood • Wise persons	• Indifference to others' feelings	• Ventral (temporal) region
Logico-mathematical	• Number system • Abstract system	• Mathematicians • Scientists	• Gerstmann syndrome	• Left parietal lobe • Left temporal lobe • Left occipital lobe • Angular gyrus

Sensory cortex —
Parietal lobe —
Occipital lobe —
— Motor cortex
— Frontal lobe
— Temporal lobe

many there are, how big each one is, and exactly how it is connected to other areas, we would have made a big step forward" (Gardner, 1983, p. 50).

Furthermore, if we find brain localization (modularity), that is, that certain brain parts do correspond with certain cognitive functioning, it may merely reflect the paradigm of neuroscience research than the real state of affairs.   In this young science, researchers have constantly follow a brain-mapping-cognition approach. They tend to divide the brain into small distinct parts and try to map each part with specific cognitive functioning. Their working assumption is that each distinct brain part must be functional, and the brain is organized along functional lines. This approach has generally paid off: for example, they do discover certain neurons in our visual system responsible for forming dots and lines but not higher processing functions. But this approach may have difficulty explaining higher conceptual activities such as thinking, planning, self-awareness, and so on, for such activities require the coordination of the whole brain.

Non-Modularity in Logical-Mathematical Intelligence

While I am impressed and sympathetic with Gardner's over-whelming evidence for brain localization and multiple intelligences, there is one area that is not susceptible to modularity. Most of us could tentatively accept that linguistic ability is generally related to the left hemisphere of most right-handed individuals, while musical and spatial abilities are more related to the right hemisphere. However, there seems no hemispherical dominance for logical-mathematical ability. According to Gardner, "In fact, two recent electrophysiological studies document considerable involvement of both hemispheres during the solution of mathematical problems. As one author puts it, 'Each task produces a complex, rapidly changing pattern of electrical activity in many areas in front and back of both sides of the brain' " (1983, p. 158). Such findings have led Gardner to confess:

In sum, there is a rationale to the neural organization of logical-mathematical abilities, but it is a far more general kind of representation than we have hitherto encountered.   Wielding Ockham's razor, one could conclude that logical-mathematical ability is not as "pure" or "autonomous" a system as others reviewed here, and perhaps should count not as a single intelligence but as some kind of supra- or more general intelligence. (1983, p. 158)

Why is it that there are distinct neural areas for linguistic, spatial, and musical abilities but that the "whole brain" seems to be involved in logical-mathematical ability? This puzzle can be better understood if we look at the nature of logical-mathematical intelligence as defined by Gardner. At first glance, there seems to be no problem: Gardner is using the term much in line with Piaget's concept of logico-mathematical reasoning. Gardner alludes to the intelligence of handling number system, logic, and abstract systems. Using this definition, Gardner is in fact talking about the conceptual activity of abstract thinking.

In my view, abstract thinking is the most important among all intelligences. It is the essence of intelligence. As I pointed out earlier, intelligence includes higher-order conceptual activities such as thinking, problem solving, and acquisition of knowledge. For me, it is not at all surprising that thinking would involve the whole brain because thinking would make use of as many modalities as the situation may require. We may have to think through the medium of language (left hemisphere), we may have to think through visual images (right hemisphere), we may have to comprehend the problem and solve it step-by-step (frontal lobe), we may have to draw on our memory (temporal lobe), and we may even have to use our bodily movement (motor cortex). Thus it is entirely conceivable that thinking in a general sense can be viewed as general intelligence involving the whole brain.

Thus we have come to a very fruitful lesson from Gardner. He has shown us that humans possess multiple abilities (intelligences) modulated in relatively distinct parts of the brain. His evidence further shows that those abilities (intelligences) are relatively independent of one another and are related to different symbol systems. He has also broadened the scope and deepened the study of intelligence. While Gardner indicates the plausibility of multiple intelligences, he has, unknowingly and paradoxically, revived the notion of general intelligence as evidenced in his logical-mathematical intelligence.

After proposing a pioneering theory of multiple intelligences based on neuropsychology, Gardner turned to write a short history of cognitive science (1985), did a few case studies on creative individuals (1993a), and put his theory of multiple intelligences to work in school (1991, 1993b). Gardner also visited China and reviewed its educational system (1989). To be sure, Gardner possesses 'multiple' talents and is a scholar with "multiple" interests.

THE INFORMATION-PROCESSING PARADIGM

Sternberg's Triarchic Theory of Intelligence

The most widely cited theory of intelligence in recent years is Sternberg's triarchic theory of intelligence (1984, 1985). It is a comprehensive theory, more encompassing than Guilford's structure of intellect model (Guilford, 1967) because it takes into account social and contextual factors apart from human abilities. It is also broader than the psychometric tradition represented by the factor g (Spearman, 1927).

Basically, it is a cognitive reinterpretation of intelligence in an information-processing paradigm.

Theory Outline

In Sternberg's general theory, there are three subtheories: the componential subtheory, the experiential subtheory and the contextual subtheory, each divided into subdomains of concern. The contextual subtheory deals with the context of intelligence, that is, intelligence in the real world requiring adaptation, selection, and/or shaping the environment. Measurement of contextual intelligence would relate to the issue of social perception, culture fairness, and cultural relativeness. The experiential subtheory deals with the issue of novelty and automatizing of processing. It is related to the notion of learning and the dynamic interplay between controlled and automated processing in the competition for cognitive resources.

Finally, there is the componential subtheory, which is subdivided into (a) metacomponents, (b) performance components, and (c) knowledge acquisition components, which are directly related to learning. Here, Sternberg sees knowledge acquisition as having three variables: contextual cues, mediating variables, and processes, through which knowledge is learned or acquired into the repertoire of crystallized abilities. Sternberg does not make clear whether we can learn or acquire "fluid abilities," nor does he specify how learning is related to other subtheories, namely the experiential and contextual aspects. For Sternberg, each subtheory has its own task models that can be operationalized into tests. Whether these tasks overlap is another area of concern. On the whole, Sternberg acknowledges the crucial role of learning in intelligence, but his focus is mainly on the processing side, not the content side (knowledge) or the nature of it. I summarize Sternberg's triarchic theory in graphic form in Figure 2.3.

Sternberg does not talk much about knowledge representation or knowledge networks. Nor does he specify what makes knowledge acquisition succeed or fail. The whole notion of learning is broken down into parts to fit into different subtheories, where learning and vocabulary belong to the componential subtheory, concept acquisition and insight belong to the experiential subtheory, and tacit knowledge belongs to the contextual subtheory. Such a treatment does not do justice to learning as an independent concept (1985, pp. 320-321).

Evaluating the Contextual Subtheory

When we examine a theory, we may be interested to extract statements that are its axioms, assumptions and premises from which we can derive deductions, implications, and conclusions. We are also interested in the explanatory power and predictive validity of the theory. We may wish to isolate the explicandum from the explican to

Figure 2.3
Sternberg's Triarchic Theory of Intelligence in Summary

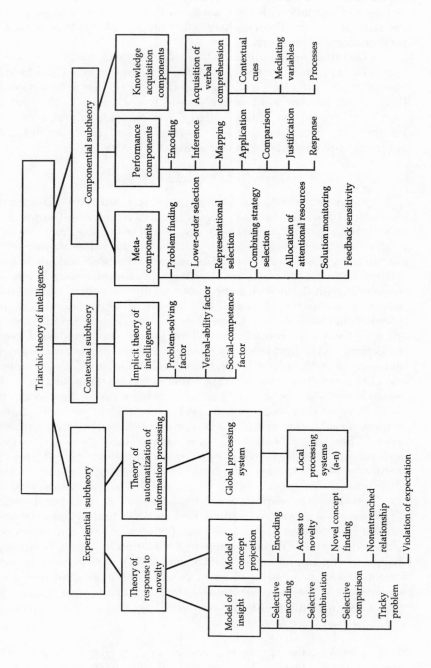

avoid circular argument. We may wish to identify statements for testing and refutation. If we want to go deeper, we may as well analyze the structure of the theory, that is, its ontological, epistemological, and methodological questions.

I find it extremely difficult to evaluate Sternberg's theory on those grounds. Let me start with his contextual subtheory. Here Sternberg identifies six different characteristics of context. Then he proceeds to the issue of measurement and responses to challenges to the contextual view. It would be better called "a conception about," or "some preliminary consideration of," contextualism than a full-fledged subtheory because it lacks the structure of a theory.

Evaluating the Experiential Subtheory

In the experiential subtheory, we are led into an intriguing question of how the human species handles novelty and automaticity. In fact, novelty and automaticity are two sides of the coin: input and processing are novel to start with and are slowly turned into automaticity. Sternberg gives a taxonomy of the issue and spells out the relation between the two, also alluding to measurement and comparing the expert with the novice in processing. Here Sternberg claims to have proposed a theory of response to novelty and automatization of information (1985, p. 78). Upon closer examination, I find no theory at all, only two task models: model of insight and model of concept projection. In the first model he brought in three processes proposed by him and Janet Davidson (1982, 1983) to account for insight: selective encoding, selective combination, and selective comparison. Their research is like reclassifying "insight problems" according to the three problem types they so proposed . When an "insight problem" does not fit their classification system, it is termed unclassified "tricky problem" type! Then they calculated the correlation between subjects' performance with IQ (1985, p. 81). As for model of concept projection, Sternberg studied how an individual mentally moves from a conventional conceptual system to a novel one in five critical processes: (1) encoding the expectation of a change in conceptual system; (2) accessing a novel conceptual system; (3) finding an appropriate concept in a new conceptual system; (4) allowing for a nonentrenched relationship; and (5) responding to a violation of an expectation of a change in conceptual system (1985, pp. 83-84). Sternberg studied the formation and processing of novel concepts by exploiting our discrete steady-state words of color, (blue-green), maturity forms (child-adult), chemicals (freezing-melting) and changing them into variable-state words such as the following:

bleen — an object that appears blue now but appears green in the year 2000
grue — an object that appears green now but appears blue in the year 2000
balt — a child that grows to be an adult

pros — an adult that grows to be a child

Subjects answered multiple choice questions on these problems in verbal and graphic form and their solution strategies were examined in terms of task analysis of novel processing in 17 steps represented in a flowchart (1985, p. 88) and so on.

In my view, Sternberg's experiential subtheory is narrowly grounded on a few task models and lacks a broad perspective. How does previous experience (prior knowledge) affect novelty processing? How does one describe them in knowledge network and solution strategies? How does different experience bring to bear on intelligence? What are the rules and conditions underlying selective encoding, combination, and comparison? These questions have scarcely been answered. It does not seem that Sternberg has solved the problem of insight by reclassification. It is true that his study of novelty by artificial problems may provide a basic skeleton for, and is an important step to, our understanding of real-life novelty. But we need to move forward by more research on real-life novelty problems.

Evaluating the Componential Subtheory

A "Component" or a Process? Let us finally look at the component-ial subtheory. This is by far the most substantial part of Sternberg's theory. Here Sternberg defines his unit of analysis as a component. He identifies seven metacomponents, and spells out the characteristics of performance components and knowledge-acquisition components. Upon closer examination I find the term "component" used by Sternberg very misleading. Readers usually expect a "component" to refer to some entity, abstract or concrete, with certain formal characteristics. But that is not the case here. For Sternberg, a component is "an elementary information process that operates on internal representations of objects or symbols" (Sternberg, 1984, p. 281). In other words, a component is a process whereby intelligent behavior is represented and realized. That is, the whole componential subtheory is about the process of intelligence.

As stated above, Sternberg further divides the intelligent process into three subprocesses (subcomponents): the metacomponent, the performance component, and the knowledge-acquisition component. It is quite reasonable to suggest that in the process of an intelligent behavior, there is a metacomponent that governs, controls, and monitors the performance components. For example, in approaching a word-analogy task, there is a role for metacomponents to define the problem as word analogy, select an information representation of verbal cues, decide on the attentional resources allocated to the task, monitor the solution, and so on. It is entirely legitimate, or even necessary, to divide an intelligent process into meta and performance parts. My question is, while metacomponents are closely related to performance components, they are both only remotely related to knowledge-acquisition components.   The former two components are directly related to a task performance, but the latter is not related to a task, but rather to one's learning. Sternberg never justifies how the latter is related to the former, nor does he explain why the knowledge-acquisition component should be a part of the componential subtheory.

The Inadequacy of Knowledge-Acquisition Components.   I do not deny the significance of knowledge-acquisition components. I think knowledge acquisition is imperative in intelligence. What I find difficult is that it cannot be readily integrated into the immediate performance components of intelligence.   Rather, it may itself form a separate subtheory with underlying connections with the experiential and contextual subtheories. Moreover, Sternberg's treatment of knowledge-acquisition components is a very preliminary and sketchy one: Sternberg merely shows the complex process of knowledge acquisition, pointing out that there are vast individual differences in how one learns from experience and that the knowledge-acquisition process can be amenable to measurement through ingenious design (1985, p. 232-235). But his exposition is a restricted one; he merely examined one type of knowledge acquisition: the acquisition of verbal comprehension (p. 214). Even within that type he focused mostly on vocabulary acquisition through context (p. 232-235, p. 237-239). Here Sternberg distinguishes external from internal context each with eight and four contextual cues respectively (p. 221, 236). He put artificial words (e.g., blumen) in a sensible paragraph to test children's ability to infer meaning.

While I agree with Sternberg that "there is reason to believe that vocabulary is such a good measure of intelligence" (p. 307), vocabulary acquisition is only one important subset of verbal comprehension, which is again a subset of knowledge acquisition. To equate vocabulary with knowledge acquisition is a gross misrepresentation.   In fact, Sternberg has no knowledge-acquisition theory to offer here: he never spells out the underlying mechanism of different types of knowledge acquisition, knowledge characteristics and representation, the stages and principles underlying acquisition, and so on.   His knowledge-acquisition components propose nothing new: he merely borrows his and Davidson's insight model of selective encoding, combination, and comparison from his contextual subtheory with two subtheories sharing the same idea and leading to the awkward conclusion that "learning always requires at least minor insights" (p. 107)!   As for his representation of information, it is much similar to David Rumelhart and Donald Norman's node model (1975). His model focuses only on vocabulary learning in context.

Super-Rationality and Mechanistic Response.   If the componential subtheory is the core of Sternberg's triarchic theory of intelligence, an intelligent action is an ideal type characterized by super-rationality and mechanistic response. For example, in the metacomponent, intelligent action has the image of a professional manager: it defines a problem, makes a decision on strategy and solution, monitors progress and feedback, allocates resources, and so on. In the performance component, intelligent action is merely an improved version of stimulus-response with a mediational and representational variable. Of course, in reality we always perform subrationally and our responses are not easily predictable by a stimulus-response model. What Sternberg depicts is an ideal case of intelligence and in no way has he related intelligence to affective, motivational, or personality domains.

Sternberg's Research Methodology and Subsequent Theory Development

Sternberg's research methodology, reflecting the whole approach underlying the information-processing paradigm, is briefly summarized as follows: To conduct research in intelligence, first define a mental task. Break it up by task analysis into subtasks or subprocesses. Administer the task to a number of subjects of a heterogeneous or homogeneous sample. Score the task in terms of speed, level of difficulty, probability of correct responses, and so on. Obtain subscores relative to subtasks. Analyze the scores and correlate them with IQ scores of the subjects. Depending on the amount of correlation found, the task is said to have certain predictive value for intelligence. Sternberg's triarchic theory can be seen as an abstraction and generalization resulting from the above research practice of an information-processing approach. Readers may see my criticism on this research methodology later in the chapter.

Sternberg advanced his componential theory of intelligence as early as 1981. It was transformed into triarchic theory of intelligence in 1984. Two years later he reconceptualized intelligence again as mental self-government (1986b). Here Sternberg retains his triarchic framework but exploits the metaphor of government and tries to see the parallel between political entities and mental entities. In a government there are different functions (judicial, executive, legislative, etc.), levels (hierarchy, ministries, federal, state), forms, scope, and political spectrum. So is intelligent behavior, which Sternberg represents as mental self-government. It is not clear how powerful or useful this metaphor is or how serious Sternberg is, for by 1988 intelligence for Sternberg is no more self-government, but self-management (1988b) "[T]he self-management of one's life in a constructive, purposeful way ... adapting to environments, selecting new environments and shaping environments." (1988b, p. 11). Two years later, intelligence changes again to become the *Metaphors of Mind* (Sternberg, 1990b). Whether he borrows terms from political science (government), business studies (management), computing (information), or coins a new word (triarchic), he has so far retained his componential framework, and successful or not, his integrating effort has been "intelligent," "triarchic," and "metaphoric."

Support of the Information-Processing Approach

Within the mainstream of the information-processing paradigm, there are many supporters who elaborate upon and supplement Sternberg's theory. Since the information processing paradigm takes learning as automatic processing, Norman et al. (1985) pointed out there are certain natural constraints in learning. They showed that mentally retarded children have an automatic processing deficiency that affects their performance on a task designed to preclude the use of cognitive strategies. In other words, certain children learn differently because of the problem in the mechanism of automatic processing.

In the same light, R. D. Tennyson (1989) suggested the use of instructional technology to improve higher-order thinking strategies. Tennyson specifically focused on the importance of cognitive complexity, leading to improvement in problem solving and intelligence. In other words, what is implicit in Tennyson as well as Sternberg's framework is that intelligence can be improved through learning. Similarly, B. M. Shore and H. C. Dover (1987) made use of the triarchic theory to explain giftedness as a result of availability and flexibility of cognitive style among gifted children.

THE LEARNING PARADIGM

When we talk about theories of learning, it is important to note that there are three historical traditions and two modern approaches. They are mental discipline, natural unfoldment, apperception (historical traditions), and behaviorism and cognitivism (modern approaches). The historical traditions have their roots in Plato and later Enlightenment philosophers such as Jean-Jacques Rousseau (see chapter 5 for review). However, the three historical traditions are theories of education that seldom relate themselves explicitly to intelligence, while behaviorism is a doctrine that focuses on observable behavior and its relationships to observable stimuli in the environment rather than unobservable mental activities such as intelligence. This leaves us with the cognitive approach, the only paradigm of learning that is related to intelligence. The following five scholars are theorists of intelligence who emphasize the importance of learning, and they all approach the issues from a cognitive point of view.

Butterfield's Components of Intelligent Action

Earl Butterfield's view of intelligence and learning may be seen as growing out of and beyond Sternberg's triarchic theory of intelligence (Sternberg, 1985). It is one of the latest attempts at integrating learning with the information-processing paradigm at intelligence. When Sternberg postulated a knowledge-acquisition component, Butterfield criticized it as an ad hoc construct in which learning is treated as an incidental consequence of particular cognitive process. He identified four cognitive differences among people of different intelligence:

Younger and less intelligent people have been said to have smaller and less elaborately organized knowledge bases (Butterfield, Nielsen, Tangen, & Richardson, 1985; Chi, 1981; Holzman, Pelligrono, & Glaser, 1983); to use fewer, simpler, and more passive processing strategies (Belmont and Butterfield, 1969; Brown, Campione, Bray, & Wilcox, 1973; Flavell, 1970); to have less metacognitive understanding of their own cognitive systems and of how the functioning of these systems depends upon the environment (Brown, 1978; Flavell & Wellman, 1977); and to use less complete and flexible processes for controlling their thinking (Butterfield & Belmont, 1977; Campione et al., 1982). (Butterfield, 1986, p. 46)

Figure 2.4 can best illustrate what Butterfield meant. When a problem situation exists, a person will utilize his or her knowledge base, metacognition, and cognitive strategies to solve a problem. He or she will search an appropriate executive routine to execute the problem-solving (intelligent) activity. But when the problem is novel and there is no executive routine available, or all the existing executive routines fail to work, there is a demand for the creation of a novel step; learning is said to occur.

Figure 2.4
Butterfield's Four Components of Intelligent Action

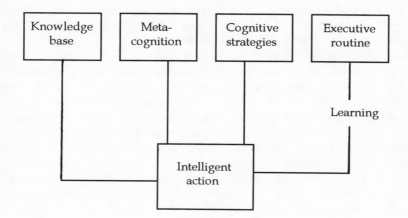

Since we are facing hundreds of problem situations every day, learning will take place quite frequently, although not at every moment. According to Butterfield, then, learning is a function of the exposure to a novel situation and the utilization of internal cognitive mechanisms such as knowledge base, metacognition, and cognitive strategies. The generation of a new executive routine is defined as learning including: (a) setting a goal, (b) selecting known alternatives or creating new combinations of responses, (c) mapping strategies, and (d) assessing progress. Thus, Butterfield claims that "intelligent action, learning and cognitive development might all be explained by the same theory" (Butterfield, 1986, p. 45). In Butterfield's view, intelligence is a very broad theoretical construct which has correlates with different problem-solving strategies among gifted, average, and mentally retarded children (Butterfield & Ferretti, 1989).

Brown and Campione's Learning Potentials

Ann Brown and Joseph Campione, researchers on learning disabilities at University of Illinois, are very explicit about the role of learning in intelligence. They point out, as many learning theorists do, that an IQ test is "a measure of past learning" (Brown & Campione, 1986, p. 42). They subscribe to the view that intelligence is "the capacity to acquire capacity" (Woodrow, 1938), or the capacity to learn. Their research indicates that learning is correlated with IQ and that transfer of learning is also correlated with IQ. They also found that aids in learning can affect improvement in performance, with different effects in far transfer items, near transfer indices, and learning efficiency (Brown & Campione, 1984a, 1984b). For them, learning potential is synonymous with intelligence. With their background in learning disabilities and special education, they further propose dynamic assessment (Brown & Campione, 1985) and assisted assessment (Campione, 1989) as alternatives to IQ testing.

Brown and Campione's work focuses on current learning rather than past learning. They are less interested in increasing speed in learning than in the amount of help needed in acquisition and application of knowledge in domain-specific areas.

While Brown and Campione are uncertain about the existence of a general learning facility, they suggest the possibility of measuring domain-specific indices of learning potential. They also suggest developing procedures for the assessment and diagnosis of readiness to acquire information in various academic domains. Such assessment should go beyond the traditional static assessment of past learning. Learning capacity should be viewed not as a stable characteristic but as a fluctuating characteristic that will vary across domains and over time. To further their research in this direction, Brown and Campione suggest developing adaptive testing procedures that would specify learning paths and developmental milestones of individual learners with normal or subnormal intelligence.

Snow's Six Aspects of Intelligence

Richard Snow, an educator from Stanford, defines intelligence in terms of six aspects: adaptive purposeful striving (Snow, 1978), mental playfulness (Snow, 1980), idiosyncratic learning (Snow, 1981), knowledge-based thinking, fluid-analytic reasoning, and feeling and knowing (apprehension;) (Snow, 1986). Basically, Snow stresses that

Persons differ *within* themselves in how they solve parts of a problem, or different problems in a series (Bethell-Fox, Lohman, & Snow, 1984; Kyllonen, Lohman & Woltz, 1984; Snow, 1981). It appears that adaptive learning, reassembly, and strategy shifting occur within persons and within tests (or tasks). (1986, p. 135)

Also, Snow proposes a topography of ability and learning and a theory of cognitive aptitude for learning (Snow, Kyllonen, & Marshalek, 1984) in which he stresses the vast individual differences in aptitude, attitude, ability, and so forth for learning. For Snow, then, people learn differently, and this is the central issue of intelligence. Snow further suggests that intelligence is the part of the internal environment of a person handling cognitive tasks. Each person possesses a very large bank of cognitive processing components and chunks of organized knowledge, and individual differences consist of the different methods and purposes between individuals with respect to how these components and knowledge are organized, assembled, and decomposed. Individual differences may also be manifested in aptitude, achievement motivation, anxiety, and so on.

As for the measurement of the six aspects of intelligence, Snow argues that fluid-analytic reasoning and knowledge-based thinking can be measured in terms of fluid (Gf) and crystallized (Gc) intelligence factors, respectively, in which Gf represents short-term adaptive performance on novel tasks while Gc represents long-term performance on familiar tasks. Apprehension and adaptation processes are also implicitly measured in this manner. The measurement of mental playfulness and idiosyncratic learning has hardly begun and requires further research.

Schank's AI Metaphor

Understanding, Explanation, and Learning

Roger Schank, a theorist of artificial intelligence from Yale, proposes a theory of intelligence by piecing together in an ingenious way a few very basic concepts: understanding, explanation, and learning (Schank, 1982, 1986).   Like other theorists of artificial intelligence, Schank gives a rational account of human understanding and intelligence without taking into account the affective domain or those sub-rational understandings that are essential characteristics of human beings.   Nevertheless, Schank's theory (1982) is an interesting starting point for further theory development.

Schank's starting question is: how do we understand an event? His answer is that we understand by processing incoming information, bringing in our memory to bear on it, and then relating it to our goals, beliefs, and expectations.   The two steps are when processing current information bringing in our closest previous experience and then creating a new knowledge structure adjacent to our previous ones. Whenever there is any difference between previous and current experience, we take note and index it.   In Schank's words,

In this view, then, understanding is finding the closest higher-level structure available to explain an input and creating a new memory structure for that input that is IN TERMS OF the old closely related higher-level structure. Understanding, then, is a process that has its basis in memory, particularly memory for closely related experiences accessible through reminding and expressible through analogy. (Schank, 1986, p. 123)

Spectrum of Understanding

Then Schank postulates a spectrum of understanding: making sense, cognitive understanding, and empathy. Making sense is the most elementary level of understanding; when we are told of an event, we do not process the information per se but try to match it into our knowledge structure (schema, scripts, and knowledge recipes are more or less all the same thing). We will fill in the missing links by inference. In case some missing links cannot be inferred, we may ask for that piece of missing information. When this is done, we would tie together all the inputs (plus inference) into a coherent picture and say the event "makes sense." If it is still unintelligible, we simply say it does not make sense.

At the second level, cognitive understanding, we compare the input with our past experience. We go beyond the making-sense level. We note the similarities and differences between the present experience and our past experience. We pinpoint and take note of the differences and point out where the present experience does not match our expectation. We explain to ourselves satisfactorily, we hope, why it is so. Then we index it to this particular input or experience. By doing so we can be said to have achieved cognitive understanding.

At the third level, we are seeking an understanding of the reason behind someone's action, that is, to understand one's motivation, fears, needs, and so on. When two persons share the same goals, beliefs, expectations—in short, ideology—and receive the same input, they may achieve complete empathy. It is the second level, cognitive understanding, that interests us most.   Notice that we do not mechanically compare the most relevant previous experience with current experience and then note and index the difference.   We explain why the current experience does not meet the expectations of past experience.   We explain why the expectation fails.   By comparing current experience that differs from former expectations, we create "a new set of expectations that capture the generalization created by similar failures with similar explanations" (Schank, 1986, p. 128).   This process of explaining failure and creating new expectation and knowledge structures serves as the basis of learning.

How do we know we have achieved understanding?   Schank proposes a very interesting criterion: the explanation test.   He postulates coherency explanations, failure explanations, and contributory explanations, respectively, to correspond with the three levels of understanding.   Piecing together all these conceptions, understanding, explanation, and learning, Schank defines intelligence as follows:

It is this explanation at the cognitive understanding level that really is the hallmark of our intellectual capacities.   Having a powerful memory, rich with experiences and cleverly indexed, is at the base of intelligence.   Being able to recover from failed expectations by recalling prior similar experiences, and being able to learn from the comparison of the current failure to a prior experience, is what intelligence, in its richest form, is all about. (Schank, 1986, pp. 128-129)

Perkins's Learnable Intelligence

"Intelligence can be learned" (Perkins, 1995, p. 117).   This is the major theme of David Perkins's *Outsmarting IQ: The Emerging Science of Learnable Intelligence* (The Free Press, 1995).   A colleague of Howard Gardner at Harvard Graduate School of Education, Perkins not only argues that intelligent behavior can be improved by instruction, but also points out that IQ is not a good measure of intelligence.

In response to Herrnstein and Murray's (1994) claim that the low intelligence of the blacks cannot be raised by intervention programs, Perkins pointed out that "IQ is the wrong focus for efforts to raise intelligence and the wrong measure of success.   IQ is not intelligence but one aspect of the complex phenomenon of intelligence.   We need a much broader conception of what intelligence is" (1995, p. 57).

Basically Perkins reconceptualizes intelligence into three distinct kinds: neurological intelligence, experiential intelligence, and reflective intelligence.   Neurological intelligence is relatively fixed by genetic and physical maturation.   Experiential intelligence is the specialized or context-specific knowledge and experience one acquires over time.   Reflective intelligence is one's mindware underlying one's thinking: mental habits, metacognition, memory strategies, imagination, mental attitudes and so forth.   Perkins argues fervently that both experiential intelligence and reflective intelligence are and can be learned, thus learnable intelligence.

So, how can we learn to be more intelligent? Perkins's research on thinking, learning, and education shows that we should avoid many "intelligence traps," such as hasty thinking, narrow thinking, fuzzy thinking and sprawling thinking (p. 153). He further points out that the future of intelligence lies in:

Distributed Intelligence. Good thinking relies on cultural artifacts, symbol systems, and collaboration patterns among people.

Embracing Complexity. To overcome mental overload in demanding situations.

Dialectical Thinking. A phase in the development of reflective intelligence that involves cutting across and integrating multiple frames of reference.

Metacurriculum. The teaching of thinking in the classroom with focus on dispositional realms, challenge realms, tool realms, technical realms, field realms and situational realms (p. 336).

Obviously, Perkins belongs to the learning paradigm of intelligence which starts from the assumption of equating intelligence with the capacity to learn. His innovation is to take up the "two-thirds position," that is, only two out of the three kinds of intelligence are learned. Perkins does not deny certain genetic endowment underlying intelligence.

THE FACTOR-ANALYTIC PARADIGM

Jensen's Resurrection of Spearman's *g*

Arthur Jensen can be said to represent the latest version of factor analysis in the tradition of Charles Spearman's *g*. His approach to the study of intelligence is to design and collect a large set of mental tests and apply factor analysis to it. His "working definition" of intelligence is to discover "the *g* factor in a large collection of diverse mental tests" (Jensen, 1986, p. 110). Such tests may vary considerably, differing with respect to modalities, media, task requirements, complexity, and so on. Jensen points out that there are always low positive correlations among cognitive test items, indicating a common source of variance in all cognitive tests.

Jensen's Research Program and Methodology

Jensen's enterprise can be outlined as follows: first, get mental tests, of any imaginable kind, that are not affected by physical capacity such as sensory or muscular strength. Then create a large bank of test items and administer them to a "representative sample." Make use of item analysis to get "internal consistency reliability" and reject those inconsistent items. Afterward, collect test scores and apply factor analysis to estimate the common source of variance among tests. The first principal component represents the g factor. Finally, it may be necessary to get rid of the non-g variance by regressing out other group factors (such as verbal, spatial, numerical, and so forth) and extracting g factor scores.

Jensen further points out three important findings related to g. First, "g is the single largest source of individual differences in all cognitive activities that involve some degree of mental complexity" (Jensen, 1986, p. 111). Second, g has predictive validity for individual performance in school, education, and employment. Third, g is highly correlated with some very elementary measurements of human capacities, such as choice reaction time and average evoked potential (Jensen, 1982).

Jensen has devoted a whole book (1980) to the existence of the g factor. He reports that g defined in his enterprise is correlated with Wechsler's full-scale IQ at 0.9 and with Stanford-Binet at 0.8. In other words, Jensen's g measure is only slightly different from our conventional intelligence measurements. By studying intelligence through factor analysis, Jensen has by implication aimed at discovering a unitary trait called "intelligence," or g, which is presumably relatively stable among individuals. This g is assumed to be identifiable and demonstrable through mental tests. This has to be so because if "intelligence" is not a single, unitary, stable trait, then it follows that it cannot be discovered and isolated by factor analysis. The very fact that we find positive correlations among cognitive test items, Jensen's argument goes, is proof of the existence of g (Jensen, 1984).

The logical development of this line of argument is the hereditarian theory of IQ. Since intelligence is seen as a single, unitary, stable trait that does not change over time, it follows that intelligence must be inherited and remain unchanged. In the nature-nurture debate, Jensen takes an extreme hereditarian position. He argues that the failure of large-scale compensatory educational programs to raise IQs significantly is best explained by the limitations placed on intellectual plasticity by an individual genetic endowment. Based on the currently available evidence, Jensen placed the heritability of intelligence at about 0.8, that is, 80 percent of the individual difference in IQ in the American population could be traced to genetic differences (Jensen, 1969).

Jensen Challenged

Jensen's position has been challenged by nurturists such as Leon Kamin (1974) and Stephen Gould (1981). Specifically Kamin takes the opposite side and argues that there is no reasonable evidence for any heritable component in learning disabilities or IQ. Later, Kamin softened his positions slightly by saying that "the data on heredity and IQ are, at best, ambiguous" (Kamin & Eysenck, 1981, p. 154). The nurturist stresses the importance of experience, social factors, and education in the development of intelligence and by implication places learning in a central role in intelligence. Nevertheless, discussion about the mechanism or process of learning is conspicuously absent in Kamin's and Gould's treatment of the subject. In fact, the effects of the IQ controversy are more noticeable in the media and public policy than in the theories of intelligence (Snyderman & Rothman, 1988).

But the more serious assault on Jensen is from John Horn (1989), who applied factor analysis more cautiously and came up with a completely opposite conclusion. Horn rejects the notion of single, unitary intelligence and advocates the existence of overlapping cognitive abilities. (Horn's theory will be discussed later in the chapter). Horn argues that Jensen's method did not follow the spirit of Spearman. Specifically, Spearman theorized the functional unity of cognitive processes, that is, eduction of relations and correlates, and demanded a careful selection of abilities to represent one common factor. But what Jensen did was just to put together any collection of mental tests, observe that they were positively correlated, calculate the first principal factor, again observe that it was large and conclude the existence of g. This way of doing factor analysis is incorrect because the size of first principal factor is just a function of redundancy. "If many tests measuring the same thing are included in a battery, the first principal component will be large" (Horn, 1989, p. 31). Also it is incorrect to assume, as Jensen did, that any sizable collection of mental tests can represent the universe of all mental tests. The fact is that we cannot even define the universe of mental tests, let alone sample it. Furthermore, both Gould (1981) and Horn (1989) pointed out the inherent arbitrary nature of factor analysis. In Horn's words:

Just as one can always calculate a first-principal component for the inter-correlations among any set of abilities, so one can always continue factoring at higher orders until only one factor is indicated, whence the results can be transformed via the Schmid-Leiman algebra to define a general factor operationally. But one can calculate this general factor for any mixture of abilities, and there is no assurance that the factor thus calculated in one arbitrarily formed battery is at all equivalent to a factor calculated in the same way in another such battery. (Horn, 1989, p. 38)

Thus, it is not unreasonable to conclude that Jensen's research program is less scientific than it appears. The application of factor analysis to discover factor g hinges on the validity of unitary intelligence. Jensen's research program will rise and fall with this conception.

Eysenck's EEG Manifestation

Hans Eysenck, professor of psychology at University of London Institute of Psychiatry, studies the biological basis of intelligence and points out that Spearman's g has its biological source. Eysenck gathered evidence to show that average evoked potentials (AEP) in EEG is highly correlated with psychometric g. He measured the complexity of the AEP waveform (the contour parameter) and the variance of stimulus across waveform epochs and discovered that the contour parameter, variance, and composite AEP correlate with WAIS IQ at .72, -.72, and -.83 respectively (1982, p. 205). Interpretation: the more intelligent an individual, the longer his/her AEP contour and the lower its variance.

Recently Eysenck proposes an interesting taxonomy of intelligence ranging from genetic to social intelligence (Figure 2.5). Earlier he tried to distinguish intelligence (A) from intelligence (B). Intelligence (A) stands for basic abilities, such as learning capacity, memory, reasoning, problem-solving abilities, and so on. It is a set of "pure abilities" inherent in humans. Intelligence (B) stands for the level of cognitive performance actually observed. Intelligence (B) is the layperson's notion of intelligence; it is not only a reflection of intelligence (A) but is also influenced by factors such as education, personality, socioeconomic status and so on (Eysenck, 1979). This distinction was first proposed by Hebb (1949), to which Vernon (1971) later added intelligence (C)—score on an IQ test. Eysenck's research is to ground intelligence (B), layperson's version of intelligence, in intelligence (C), IQ measures, which is further grounded in EEG measures.

Figure 2.5
Eysenck's Taxonomy of Intelligence

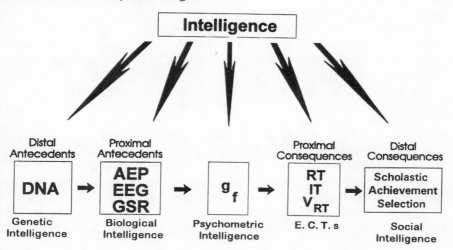

Source: Personal communication with Professor Hans Eysenck. Adapted by permission.

Does faster processing speed indicate higher intelligence? Eysenck's (1982) complex reaction time (CRT) investigation reveals so. CRT is a measure of choice or decision making when a subject must respond to several stimuli. Cognitve processing begins with perception, which is measured by inspection time (IT). It then goes on to processing, measured by decision time (DT), to be followed by an action, which is measured in movement time (MT). Eysenck found that they all correlate negatively with g. Interpretation: a person scoring high in an IQ test tends to perceive, decide and act faster (i.e., lower latency score) in an CRT experiment of pushing buttons. Eysenck also discovered that as the natural log number of stimuli increases, intelligence measures will increase linearly.

Eysenck took IQ as an unitary variable decomposable into mental speed, error checking and persistence (Eysenck, 1982). According to Eysenck, intelligence is "error-free transmission of information through the cortex" (1986a, p. 71). By combining an integrity of circuitry hypothesis and a theory of speed of processing, Eysenck concludes that the speed of processing is a function of neural circuit integrity, which depends on errorless information transmission and processing (1993, p. 26). However, other researchers pointed out that CRT, LAEP, and VAEP account for only a small proportion of human cognitive functioning (Horn, 1989). CRT does not accurately represent, predict, or account for the repertoire of intellectual abilities; CRT correlates only from 0.2 to 0.5, with many cognitive abilities such as short-term memory, long-term memory, attentional capacity, reasoning, and so on. Furthermore, Schucard and Horn (1972) pointed out that LAEP indicates a volitional activation, not the essence of intelligence. If we take IQ to be a higher-level cognitive measure, and social intelligence as an even higher-level performance outcome, it is doubtful they can be reduced to more basic measures such as CRT or LAEP.

Eysenck embraces less genetic determinism than his research program implies. In fact he accepts that while psychometric intelligence "is strongly determined by biological intelligence, . . . environmental factors are also important" (1993, p. 2). EEG, after all, is only a biological measure with distal consequences to social intelligence (Figure 2.5).

Eysenck should be credited for his contribution in grounding intelligence on a neuro-biological basis. How fruitful this research direction will be in terms of its findings, application, and linkage to real-life intelligence remains to be seen. One corollary of Eysenck's biological theory of intelligence is to prescribe vitamin and mineral supplementation instead of education programs for the improvement of intelligence (1993, p. 28)! Educators may hate it but policy-makers may find it cost-effective, if it works.

Horn's Mixture Abilities Theory

Three Kinds of Theories of Intelligence

John Horn also belongs to the psychometric tradition which applies factor analysis to the study of intelligence. Horn (1989) suggests classifying theories of intelligence into three kinds:

1. **Compound theories.** Compound theories take intelligence as a functional unity in which different intellectual capacities stem from a common core of genetic determinants. Horn refers to Spearman's g—eduction of relations and correlates—as an example of functional unity.

2. **Mixture theories.** Intelligence is a collection of many different abilities, possibly representing many different capacities (Horn, 1989, p. 32). Horn quotes his teacher Lloyd Humphreys's definition of intelligence as "the entire repertoire of acquired skills, knowledge, learning sets, and generalization tendencies considered intellectual in nature that are available at any one period of time" (Humphreys, 1979, p. 106).

3. **Essence theories.** Essence theories try to uncover the underlying mechanisms of various manifestations of intelligence. They aim to discover one basic process, one element, as the essence of intelligence. Along this research direction, Jensen (1980, 1982) proposes reaction time (RT) as an indirect measure of psychometric g, while Eysenck's EEG research hopes to show that the essence of intelligence lies in shortness of latency of average cortical evoked potentials (LAEP) or smallness of variance of average evoked potentials (VAEP).

Horn reviewed our present state of knowledge and observed that research evidence does not support essence theories or compound theories. For example, Schucard and Horn (1972) pointed out that LAEP is a volitional concept and not the essence of intelligence. Also, CRT, LAEP and VAEP overlap with each other and are very weakly correlated with other intelligence measures. As for compound theories, Horn's stipulation of functional unity is too stringent a criterion to fulfill. In Horn's words, "No compound model has been found to represent a broad spectrum of intellectual abilities" (1989, p. 35).

Basic Features of Horn's Mixture Theory

The remaining plausible theories, then, are mixture theories. But the problem with mixture theory is that they have no definite specifications. Each theorist can specify his or her abilities set according to his or her conception of intelligence. This lapse into relativism and lack of consensus results in no single mixture theory of intelligence. The two basic features of Horn's version of mixture theory are that (a) there is an infinity of abilities and thus an undefined universe of intelligence, and (b) there is an inevitable overlap among abilities when we try to measure them. In other words, one ability test will measure many abilities, not just the ability in question. From these two basic features, the mixture theorist is forced into a very difficult position: he or she dare not make claim for a complete set of abilities or intelligences. He or she further has to accept the arbitrary demarcation between abilities and hope for scientific validation through convergence of evidence from different sources.

Seven Human Abilities Among Infinite Intelligences

However, Horn is hopeful that he has discovered, in his long-term research and through the use of factor analysis, seven important human abilities. His position, an extension and refinement of Cattell's (1971) fluid intelligence and crystallized intelligence, was termed Well-replicated common-factor abilities (WERCOF), where

>   Gc = Crystallized intelligence
>   Gf = Fluid intelligence
>   TSR = Long-term storage and retrieval
>   SAR = Short-term apprehension and retrieval
>   Gs = Inspection speed
>   Gv = Visual and spatial abilities
>   Ga = Auditory abilities.

Brought up in the tradition of factor analysis, Horn is not uncritical of it. He agrees with Humphreys's (1979) characterization of factor analysis as little more than efforts to slice smoke. There are infinite ways to factorize, mostly arbitrarily, to the extent that "First-order and second-order factors reflect mainly procedures of test construction and selection" (Horn, 1989, p. 38). Nevertheless, he also points out the merits of factor analysis: empirically founded, analytic, hierarchically organized, multi-dimensional, psychometrically distinct, and so on. His own findings through factor analysis in discovering the above abilities have been consistent under different conditions at different ages and with objectively rotated solutions. Most importantly, the factor coefficients have consistently remained low. In a summary of his position, Horn says,

No compound theory of Gf has been constructed. Gc, also, is a mixture. Yet Gf and Gc represent broadly different sets of intellectual capacities (and each of these sets might, with justification, be called intelligence). Gf and Gc have different courses of development over the life span. Each is developmentally different from Gv, visual intelligence; Ga, auditory intelligence; SAR, short-period apprehension and retrieval; TSR, long-term storage and retrieval; and Gs (inspection speed) and CDS (speed of discrimination). (1989, p. 59)

Thus, if we follow Horn, we would enter into an incomplete universe of infinite human abilities. When we select any one ability and measure it, we discover that it would necessarily overlap with other abilities. This is a puzzle we have yet to solve. We cannot find one single test that would measure only one ability. Table 2.2 outlines what we measure behind psychometric tests.

In fact any test can measure Gf provided that we raise the requirement of memory. Similarly, any test can measure Gc if we raise the knowledge component, and we can measure Gs by any test if we increase the speed requirement. In other words, Horn has painstakingly arrived at the following conclusion: abilities overlap with one another and their demarcation is arbitrary.

What Horn and his colleagues have done so far is to show that the idea of a single or unitary intelligence is untenable. Instead they show the existence of an infinite array of abilities, each of which can be called intelligence, hence multiple intelligences or infinite intelligences. In fact, the idea of multiple intelligence is not new. Its roots can date back to Thomson (1919), and more recent examples include Thurstone's seven primary mental abilities (1938), Guilford's structure of intellect with 120 abilities (1967), and Gardner's multiple intelligences, with a more moderate claim of seven distinct intelligences (1983).

Horn's No-Win Position

Horn and his colleagues are in a no-win position because on the one hand they reject the notion of unitary intelligence, and yet on the other hand they cannot establish a strong claim of multiple intelligences because of its arbitrariness. Of the 30 primary abilities Horn and his colleagues assemble for tests, they came up with 7 abilities by factor analysis. Yet Horn made no claims that they are distinct and exhaustive. Moreover, since their intercorrelations are consistently low but not zero, they must overlap one another. This is inevitable when we use factor analysis to discover arbitrarily underlying structures. Horn confessed that "these results represent no more than fanning smoke,"

Table 2.2
Abilities Measured in Psychometric Test Items

Test Items	Abilities Measured
Verbal analogy	Gc, Gf, TSR, SAR
Synonyms	Gc, TSR, SAR
Antonyms	Gf, TSR, SAR
Arithmetic	Gc, Gf

(Horn, 1989, p. 43), and we have to live with the imperfection of having no distinct abilities being discovered.

But the most serious problem is with the 30 primary ability tests that Horn started with. My question is: are they really what intelligence is about? They are abilities, all right, but are they primary? Upon closer examination of these primary ability tests, I discover they are more like cognitive abilities than intellectual (or intelligence) abilities. Alternatively put, Horn's 30 primary abilities are a confusion of the two kinds without a distinction.

Let me make a conceptual distinction between cognitive abilities and intellectual/conceptual abilities. The former are concerned with the structure of the human mind and how it operates. Thus, cognitive psychologists would be interested in different aspects of cognition. For example, they may be interested in how large our memory set is. Consequently, they design tasks like digit span for subjects to retrieve and recall. Or they may be interested in divided attention and design artificial and yet appropriate tasks to uncover this ability. One seemingly innocent visual task of cognitive processing is to ask subjects to cross out the letter b in a sheet of random b's and h's. But taking cognitive abilities as intellectual abilities is a category mistake. The latter are concerned with the application of the human mind and human cognition to thinking, problem solving, learning, and so on. They are based on the lower level of cognitive abilities, such as attention, perception, memory, and so on but are concerned with problems of a higher level. Most notably they are concerned with reasoning and inference, evaluation and synthesis, abstraction and seeing relationship and the like. They take as their domain semantic representation and problem solutions toward a meaningful end. The task of crossing out b's among h's is categorically a cognitive task, *not* an intellectual one.

By taking intelligence as intellectual or conceptual abilities, I am in no way putting cognitive abilities in a derogated position. In fact, cognitive abilities are so fundamental that we cannot carry out intellectual or conceptual tasks without the implicit assumption that we possess those basic cognitive abilities. For example, how can a subject solve a paper-and-pencil mathematical problem if he or she cannot do visual processing, such as crossing out b's among h's? In other words, cognitive abilities serve as the foundation without which higher-level conceptual abilities would not be possible. Seen in this light, intelligence is an activity of utilizing many of these subprocesses or cognitive abilities in the attainment of higher-level objectives related to thinking, problem solving, learning, and human purposes.

Solving the Puzzle of Overlapping Abilities

Horn's research on WERCOF, applying factor analysis, has come up with seven somewhat distinct abilities. The list looks impressive, but the factors Horn uncovers are mostly cognitive abilities: TSR and SAR are related to memory, Gv and Ga are related to basic processing, Gs is related to processing speed. They are all elementary cognitive processes, *not* intellectual (intelligence) process. What is left on the list is Gc and Gf. Also, the relationship between speed and accuracy in basic cognitive abilities and intellectual performance still remains unclear. Alternatively put, there is still no evidence that a person crossing out b's swiftly would think faster and better.

So Horn comes full circle. He starts with the notion of crystallized and fluid intelligence and hopes to advance to a fuller description of human abilities, or intelligence. However, what he discovers amounts to cognitive processes that underlie intelligence, these cognitive processes are not themselves intelligence. Furthermore, Horn is guilty of subjecting intelligence research to the whims and development of cognitive psychology. When cognitive psychologists are studying auditory capacity, auditory span becomes a primary ability; when spatial organization is in vogue in cognitive psychology, visual memory becomes another primary ability, and so on. It seems the list of human abilities is not a constant reality but is subject to the fad and research interests of cognitive psychology.

With this distinction between cognitive and intellectual abilities, the puzzle of overlap of abilities becomes transparent. Gv and Ga are very elementary cognitive processes; they will necessarily become subprocesses in higher-level processing in Gc or Gf tasks. How can we possibly have a Gf task without doing visual or auditory processing? Similarly, memory is so pervasive in all human intellectual abilities that TSR and SAR necessarily overlap with Gc and Gf. Horn's problem of ability overlap is necessarily true because cognitive abilities always serve as the foundation for intellectual processing.

Ackerman's Radex Model of Structure of Abilities

The Issue of Individual Differences

Phillip Ackerman, a psychologist at University of Minnesota, studied individual differences and proposed a radex model of the structure of abilities to explain skill acquisition. Ackerman reviewed the literature on individual differences and posed a perplexing question: Does between-subject variability increase or decrease over practice? In other words, how does practice of, say, number of trials to a task, affect individual performance? Will performance converge or diverge (i.e., increase variability) over practice? The question is more complex than it seems; there are many factors affecting individual differences in performance, such as task complexity, transfer of learning, and task consistency. Generally speaking, during the normal course of skill acquisition of a moderate and consistent task, research shows that individuals converge in performance; that is, between-subject variability decreases over practice. By increasing task complexity, there will be a decrease of convergence in performance; general intelligence will moderately correlate with performance. Similarly, by increasing the demand for learning transfer in a task, there will be a decrease of convergence. In other words, correlation of performance in ability measures may increase or decrease upon practice, depending on task complexity, transfer of learning, and task consistency.

To clarify the issue of individual differences, Ackerman proposed a radex model of the structure of abilities, which can also explain skill acquisition. Ackerman's model is a modification of a similar but simpler model proposed earlier by Marshalek et al. (Marshalek, Lohman, and Snow, 1983), which gave a two-dimensional spatial representation of the structure of abilities.

The Radex Model of Structure of Abilities

Ackerman's improved version is a three-dimensional radex (see Figure 2.6) in which he divided complexity into two continua, complexity and speed. Thus Ackerman's model has three dimensions: content (figural, numerical, verbal), complexity (from simple to complex), and level-speed (from slow to fast and from general ability to perceptual speed ability to psychomotor speed ability). "Complexity of processing is reflected in the distance from the centroid, the most complex test requirements located close to G. As one moves to the periphery, less complex abilities are located" (Ackerman, 1989, p. 181). Ackerman's radex cylinder is most applicable to the explanation of skill acquisition because it has taken into account three abilities, general, perceptual speed, and psychomotor speed, which are all required in skill acquisition. To justify his model, Ackerman did some data re-analysis: he transformed 31 tests of 351 subjects by R. B. Allison's large-scale ability-learning study in 1960 into a three-dimensional scale and fit them into the radex cylinder. While Allison (1960) identifies 14 factors, Ackerman transformed them into three dimensions: content, complexity, level-speed.

In line with his radex model, Ackerman divided the stages of skill acquisition into three phases. Phase 1 is predominantly related to cognitive understanding, so that general intelligence is more correlated with performance at this phase. Phase 2 is one in which associative linkage and networks are established. It is a compilation and tuning phase in which perceptual speed is correlated with performance. Finally, phase 3 is reached when the skill is fully acquired in automative processing, where performance is a function of psychomotor speed, such as reaction time, which measures the upper limits of human physical constraint. Ackerman further applied his theory to the study of task complexity and memory load and found the model predicts about the three phases well.

Figure 2.6
Ackerman's Radex-based Model of Cognitive Abilities

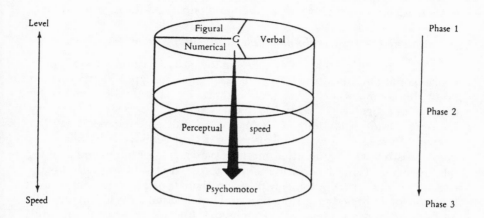

Source: From "Determinants of individual differences during skill acquisition: A theory of cognitive abilities and information processing," by P. L. Ackerman, 1988. *Journal of Experimental Psychology: General*, 117: 288-318.
Copyright 1988 by American Psychological Association. Reprinted by permission.

Is Intelligence Equivalent to the Ability to Learn?

This brings us back to a more basic and perennial question: Is intelligence equivalent to the ability to learn? Ackerman's answer is a qualified yes, if learning is defined as the initial stage (phase 1) of skill acquisition. In fact it is at that phase that general intelligence is correlated with performance. Earlier, D. Zeaman and B. J. House (1967) pointed out that intelligence is moderately associated with speed of learning in simple concept attainment and discrimination learning tasks as well.

On the other hand, if learning is defined by some achievement index, such as some final, asymptotic performance level attained, a more qualified answer to the question of the intelligence-learning equivalence appears necessary. To the degree that the skill acquisition tasks discussed here are those within the ability repertoire of nearly all members of the subject population (albeit with different levels of initial performance), general intelligence does not strongly limit final level of skilled performance. Instead, other abilities determine individual differences at skill phase three. (Ackerman, 1989, p. 207)

In other words, general intelligence seems to have a dynamic interplay with learning. If we look at performance outcomes, general intelligence is not so much a determinant as perceptual speed and psychomotor speed. What is important is that, through practice, skills could be learned and the general intelligence effect will diminish. Alternatively put, abilities will change; and general intelligence, being not a fixed entity, will be transformed and enhanced through learning.

Recent Theory Development on Adult Intelligence

More recently, Ackerman (1994) made a distinction between intelligence-as-maximal-performance and intelligence-as-typical-performance. From this distinction, Ackerman substantially expands the scope of his theory and proposes, with Maynard Goff, a "Process, Personality, Interests, and Knowledge Theory of Adult Intelligence" (PPIK). (Ackerman & Goff, 1995). Ackerman and Goff reviewed the history of mental testing and argued that modern paradigms of intelligence taking intelligence as typical performance are too restrictive, especially for the case of adults where intelligence lies in their typical performance as a function of knowledge acquisition and intellectual development. The authors offered an alternative framework for the assessment of adult intellect in terms of process, personality, interests, and knowledge structures. Instead of going the factor-analytic way, they proceed with meta-analysis to discover correlations among these variables. Their attempts have been formidable (903 items reviewed, 88 items taken, 1,148 independent samples included, 1,716 correlations computed with a total N of 58,522!). Their conceptions will hopefully change our previously restrictive view of adult intelligence.

PITFALLS IN CONTEMPORARY RESEARCH OF INTELLIGENCE

The above review draws on the theories of 23 scholars from four major paradigms in the contemporary study of intelligence. Their major themes are presented in Figure 2.7. In the next section, I will discuss some pitfalls in contemporary research.

The Colonization by Information-Processing Paradigm

Starting in the 1970s and progressing into the 1980s, we saw the colonization of intelligence research by the information-processing paradigm in all fronts and aspects: intelligence is being reconceptualized and measured in terms of information-processing terminology and conception. Seeing intelligence this way, more intelligence means speedier and more accurate processing of more information. Thus we have John Carroll's (1976) new structure of intellect, Earl Hunt's (1980) information-processing concept of intelligence, and Sternberg and Powell's whole set of information processing terminology on cognitive competencies (1982, p. 997).

Figure 2.7
Major Paradigms in the Contemporary Study of Intelligence

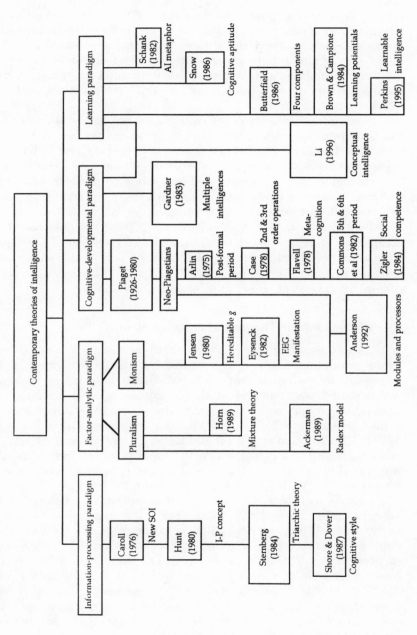

Moreover, most research questions are formulated in terms of how cognitive tasks are related to processing speed, processing accuracy and so on. (For example, Hunt, 1978). Under the influence of the information processing paradigm, even Gardner (1983) adopted the "symbol systems" approach: different symbols are treated as different kinds of information to be processed. Even the factor-analytic approach and human abilities are conceived in information processing terms of scanning, inspection, retrieval, and so on. (Horn, 1989; Ackerman, 1989).

Intelligence researchers are culpable for not having a consensus on the conception of intelligence, thus there seems no common point of departure for doing intelligence research. Sternberg and Powell (1982) mentioned explicit and implicit theories of intelligence. Explicit theories are untenable (see arguments below), while implicit theories, being informal notion of intelligence rested in experts or laypersons' heads, are no solid ground for conceptualization of intelligence. While Sternberg's triarchic theory of intelligence (1984) has gradually gained acceptance in recent years, his definition of intelligence—"purposive adaptation to, shaping of, and selection of real-world environments relevant to one's life" (Sternberg, 1984, p. 271)—is too abstract and general to serve as guidelines for intelligence research.

Where Lies the Theoretical Foundation of IQ Test?

As a convenient alternative, some researchers (e.g. Jensen, Boring) try to ground intelligence in IQ tests, but this is a conceptual error because IQ test is a measuring tool, not what intelligence is. Taking the tool as the phenomenon itself is confusing measurement with conception. Again, as we penetrate further by asking what conception of intelligence there is about in IQ test, say Wechsler's Intelligence Scale (WISC-III), we obtain an a prori and rather general notion: "Intelligence as an aggregate and global entity, the capacity of the individual to act purposefully, to think rationally, and to deal effectively with his or her environment" (Wechsler, 1944, p. 3; WISC-III, 1991, p.1).

First, a considerable number of intelligence scholars (notably Gardner, 1983, Horn, 1989) do not agree that intelligence is a global entity; instead they take intelligence as a collection of overlapping abilities. Second, WISC-III in no way measures how an "individual act purposefully" or "deal effectively with environment." What WISC-III does is to test children on a collection of mental abilities, such as verbal skills, vocabulary, general knowledge, memory, perceptual skills, comprehension, processing speed and so on and come up with a standardized index. IQ is thus an weighed average score of various tests that lack a unified theoretical foundation.

Consensus of the Professional Community

On the other hand, if we follow Horn's conception of intelligence as a collection of multiple abilities (Horn, 1989) such as Gv, Gs, Ga, Gr, Gc, and so on, how are we to justify this conception? Basically, it is by external validation, that is, to find relatively high correlation between each of these abilities and full-scale IQ score and low correlation among these abilities to justify their relative independence. In that case IQ is used as an external criterion. But then how can IQ itself be justified? We have a serious problem of circularity here. I can only see a very flimsy justification: IQ measures as agreed by the community of practicing psychologists of what intelligence is. In other words, since these psychologists are practicing intelligence testing, the consensus of what intelligence is ultimately rests upon this professional community.

Exactly what underlies those consensus? My tentative answer is that these psychologists receive the same professional training; thus they share the same conception of taking IQ as intelligence, where intelligence is defined in terms of, say, 13 subtests of WISC-III, presumably to tap a child's cognitive abilities in the collection of mental tasks. Thus a child is deemed to have more intelligence than her peers if she knows more vocabulary, gets her mathematics right, possesses more common knowledge, is more susceptible to see similarities and differences, recalls senseless digits more accurately, works speedily, and so on. In addition, they would also agree that intelligence has to do with cognitive processing. They would see intelligence in the prevailing information-processing paradigm. Moreover they would measure intelligence by conducting IQ tests in an objective and standard way where some obviously questionable assumptions are:

1. Time is important in measuring intelligence. Higher response speed would be given higher score and thus higher intelligence.
2. Idiosyncratic or creative responses are irrelevant to the processes going on, so that testees' wrong answers are not the testers' concern.
3. Objective, detached mode of questioning is appropriate. No hints should be given. A child is supposed to be capable of handling test anxiety.

The Measuring Euphoria

There are historical antecedents for the interest in the measurement of intelligence. Galton, the founding father of the study of intelligence and giftedness, was the first to set up a laboratory for the measurement of mental abilities in 1896. The measuring tool was later refined by Binet, Terman, and others. There are practical reasons for the interest in measuring intelligence: IQ testing is a useful tool for the initial screening and diagnosis of mentally retarded and learning disabled. Throughout the history of intelligence research, there has seen a very strange phenomenon: we keep trying to measure intelligence although we are not sure what intelligence exactly is and are so much divided in our conception of intelligence. First, we are interested in having a general index of intelligence, an intelligence quotient. Then we get more refined and different score for verbal and performance subtests. In the latest version of WISC-III, there are four factors: verbal comprehension, perceptual organization, freedom from distractibility, and processing speed. The appearance of precision and objectivity is probably the reason that we are so much attracted to measurement.

Apart from measuring intelligence researchers are also interested in measuring cognitive functioning. Basically they are measuring speed and accuracy, and there are statistical techniques for experimental studies to measure them jointly and separately. Tasks for measurement may range from very low-level cognitive tasks such as digit scanning requiring just miniseconds to higher-level reasoning tasks requiring measurement of several minutes. In addition to measuring reaction time and trying to correlate it to IQ, Jensen (1982) and later Eysenck (1986b) also measured brainwave patterns such as EEG and AEP. It is no exaggeration to say that intelligence research is an enterprise dominated by the findings of measurement, mostly in scores (accuracy) and time units (speed). As a corollary, if a concept is found difficult to decompose or measure, it may face the danger of being neglected, not because it is unsound but because there is no known way to measure it. It seems we have failed to ask a very basic question: how far and in what ways are intelligence susceptible to measurement?

Methodological Flaws

There exist many methodological flaws in intelligence research, for example, self-defined intelligence, "theory-based-on-data" fallacy, internal validation fallacy, unjustification of task analysis, and so on. Sternberg's views can serve as an example.

Intelligence Self-Defined

Sternberg tried to delineate intelligence theories into explicit and implicit theories (1985). The former are "based on date collected from people performing tasks presumed to measure intelligent functioning," (1985, p. 3) while the latter refers to people's conception (experts, laypersons) of what intelligence is (p. 31). In other words, explicit theories of intelligence are based on experimental research in information-processing terms while implicit theories are "opinion polls." Such delineation is bewildering because the latter, with its consensus of the professional community, in fact implies the former.

A further review of Sternberg's explicit theories of intelligence shows that it is self-defining. Intelligence is defined in terms of intelligent functioning and intelligent functioning is defined by a presumption of whatever intelligence is. But then this presumption is not defined. Probably this presumption is "to understand intelligence in term of a set of underlying abilities—for example, verbal ability, reasoning ability and the like" (Sternberg, 1985, p. 4). Such is the debate of monism and pluralism in intelligence research and recent recast of mental abilities in information-processing terms, but then the questions of what intelligence is and what underlie intelligence abilities remain unanswered.

"Theory-Based-on-Data" Fallacy

Sternberg seems to assert that theories are based on data collection, a fallious line of thought because theory shapes what counts and does not count as data. Theory determines what kind of data is to be collected. It is entirely a false belief that there exist some objective data that a theory can be based. Rather, data collection is based on theory, not the other way round. Theory shapes our way of seeing, thinking and data collection. In this case, Sternberg may have committed the "theory-based-on-data" fallacy.

Validation Fallacy and Circularity

According to Sternberg, "internal validation involves determining how well a theory accounts for the data" and this can be "the question of what proportion of variance is accounted for (Sternberg & Powell, 1982, p. 976). This way of doing internal validation by statistical calculation of proportion of variance is highly problematic. This is because the proportion of variance accounted for is a matter of degree, not a matter of kind. Even if the proportion variance is very low, say, less than 10 percent, there is no a priori reason to totally reject the theory because by statistical interpretation, the theory still accounts for 10 percent variance of the data. Sternberg's internal validation based on statistical interpretation is very different from designing a crucial experiment to conclusively falsify a theory. Again, here Sternberg elevated the status of data as the criterion of validation of a theory.

Sternberg also talks about external validation by "whatever correlates with external measures of intelligence, functioning" (1982, p. 976). Here Sternberg quotes an example: correlating "verbal comprehension" with "grades in school" or correlating "lexical access time" with psychometric tests. Sternberg called this "atheoretical" because items for some psychomeric tests of intelligence themselves are without internal validation. In other words, psychological tests of intelligence themselves have no theoretical basis. Thus Sternberg saw the need for explicit theory of intelligence to be "theoretically based" and "there is a need to accept some theoretically prespecified criterion of what intelligence is" (p. 977). But then we run into is "the risk of eventual circularity—that is, that one will justify the theory on the basis of correlation with external criteria, only later to justify the choice of external criteria on the basis of a theory" (p. 977).

Task Analysis Unjustified

Sternberg and Powell acknowledge that a theory of intelligence is mostly based on prior task analysis. "In practice the theory has often been derived from prior analysis of the tasks" (1982, p. 976). But then "acceptance of the specifics domain of tasks, however, depends upon acceptance of the theory" (p. 976). If Sternberg's characterization of intelligence theory is correct, then these theories of intelligence are very narrow in scope indeed: they are just about task performance based on task analysis. Furthermore, there is a circular relation between theory and task: theory is derived from task and task depends on theory. They mutually define each other but are not supported or justified by other more elementary factors. The real question remains unanswered: What is the basis or justification of a theory? What is the basis or justification of a task?

In conclusion, Sternberg's explicit theories of intelligence are untenable because it has inverted the data-theory relation, applied statistics to the benefit of theory validation, based the theory on task analysis, which is not further justified, and correlates data with external measures of intelligence, which are again not justified. Simply put, a lot of terms and constructs are not justified. There is thus no justification for explicit theories of intelligence.

This brings me to the final question: What exactly are explicit theories of intelligence? It seems to me that Sternberg is referring to hypotheses within the information-processing paradigm, not to any full-fledged explicit theories. Sternberg has painstakingly shown one point: these hypotheses from the information-processing paradigm cannot themselves be justified by data collection alone: they need to be anchored on some external criteria, but so far no such criteria have been found to be entirely secured and satisfactory.

CONCLUSION: THE EVOLUTION OF THEORIES OF INTELLIGENCE

In a seminal paper by Sternberg and Powell (1982), the authors offered an evolutionary model for theories of intelligence. According to them, the history of theories of intelligence was characterized by three stages, each with its unique research question and problem domain in progressive succession. In Stage 1, it is Spearman's monism (Spearman, 1904, 1927) against Thomson's pluralism (Thomson, 1919). In Stage 2, it is Cattell's (1971) and Horn and Cattell's (1966) hierarchical models against Thurstone's (1938) and Guiford's (1967) multiple models. In Stage 3, the order of units (hierarchy) was combined with the overlap in units (multiple, nonhierarchy) into another integrated theory. In Sternberg and Powell's words:

The present view suggests that different questions are paramount in theorists' minds at different stages of the evolutionary process. At a general level, one might characterize the differences as follows. In Stage 1, the primary question is whether a theory of intelligence should be monistic or pluralistic; in Stage 2, the primary question is whether these two views should be, in some sense, integrated in a hierarchical or a nonhierarchical way; in Stage 3, the primary question is how hierarchical and nonhierarchical views can themselves be integrated in some sense. When Stage 3 comes to an end, the questions of just what intelligence is and how it should be studied are reconsidered, and possible new answers are considered. (Sternberg & Powell, 1982, p. 991)

Two Competing Theories in the 1980s

Such a characterization is a fairly accurate representation up to a decade ago, with the only shortcoming being that the authors have omitted the immense contribution of Piaget and his followers in the cognitive/developmental tradition. Now from the vantage point of the 1990s, I would characterize Stage 3 of the 1980s again with two competing theories: Sternberg's triarchic theory of intelligence (1984, 1985) and Gardner's theory of multiple intelligences (1983).

In summary, Sternberg's theory is an ambitious attempt to reinterpret intelligence in cognitive terms within the information-processing framework. Sternberg seems to have eschewed the monist/pluralist debate. Instead he tries to redefine every domain of intelligence in terms of cognitive competencies, seeing intelligence as a phenomenon/process decomposable into smaller parts of information-processing terminology. For example, the informational aspect of cognitive competencies includes representations of information, contents of representations, information-processing capacities and so on, while the processing aspect includes the executive process and the nonexecutive process, each with its subprocesses. But tacitly Sternberg leans toward the monist camp of general intelligence, employing the Cattell-Horn version of fluid abilities and crystallized abilities in test design and supplementing them with social and practical intelligence.

In contrast, Gardner explicitly espouses the multiple intelligences position. He does not arrive at the conclusion of multiple intelligences through the factor-analytic tradition, as his predecessors did (Thurstone, 1938; Guiford, 1967). Instead, he approaches the issue of intelligence from another route: the biological base and the neuropsychological and clinical evidence, providing fresh insights into and conceptions of the subject. Gardner should be credited with offering different approaches and broadening the scope of intelligence.

Asking Very Basic Questions in the 1990s

In the 1990s we just cannot help asking very basic questions again, "When Stage 3 comes to an end, the questions of just what intelligence is and how it should be studied are reconsidered, and possible new answers are considered" (Sternberg & Powell, 1982, p. 991). Such a reflection is a very fruitful undertaking when we find so many divergent conceptions of intelligence in the field. In addition, the 1990s see some revival of the IQ version of intelligence (Locurto, 1991). Herrnstein and Murray (1994) take it seriously as a measure of intelligence and a major factor polarizing the American society. Perkins, on the other hand, flirts with IQ and tries to outsmart it by his learnable intelligence (1995). Even Mike Anderson's *Intelligence and Development* (1992) has to contain IQ and ends with the observation of the "irony that IQ may turn out to be a valuable empirical tool in the cognitive scientists' methodological armoury" (p. 213). Anderson's theory is an ambitious integrating effort of the 1990s that I will contrast with mine at the end of this book.

The above review draws on the theories offered by 23 scholars from the four major traditions in the study of intelligence. Apart from showing the complexity and vast diversity in theories of intelligence, it also leads to my belief that there is room for further theory development. So far there is still no theory of intelligence based on thinking and learning, despite the strong consensus that the two are major components of intelligence.

CHAPTER SUMMARY

There are four major paradigms in contemporary theories of intelligence. Jean Piaget is the founder and major exponent of the cognitive- developmental paradigm. He offers a very powerful and sophisticated theory of intelligence and learning. It is a system of thought with a whole set of concepts, terms, notions and explanatory schemes, forming a theoretical construct and giving a descriptive account of intelligence in its development and stages. His theory of intelligence can be axiomatized into three premises (functionalism, structuralism, and interacting principles) and one conclusion (intelligence in successive stages). His theory of learning is a general theory of development under four conditions: maturation, experience, social transmission and equilibration. It is hard to deny Piaget's substantive contribution to theories of intelligence. In addition, Piaget's scope of study on the growth of intellect, that is, thinking and learning, coincides with the historical consensus on the major components of intelligence.

Following Piaget's footsteps, there are Neo-Piagetians who try to theorize on the more advanced stages of cognitive development. Some postulate the existence of higher-order operations and further periods in intellectual development (Arlin, 1975; Case, 1978; Commons et al. 1982). Another Piagetian Edward Zigler stresses social competence and motivational factors (1984). Robert Glaser is a cognitivist who proposes a cognitive efficiency theory (1985) with Mitchell Rabinowitz to account for the attainment of competence (proficiency). His theory is an information-processing approach stressing knowledge representation, retrievability, development of automaticity and so on. Glaser is also concerned with learning (attained competence), knowledge structure, and its acquisition.

Howard Gardner's neural-developmental approach (1983) has expanded our conception of intelligence. In breadth, he has introduced many symbol systems into intelligence, such as musical, visual, bodily, and personal symbols traditionally neglected by cognitive psychologists. In depth, he has drawn on neuropsychology to deepen our understanding on the underlying neurophysiological mechanisms of intelligence. Gardner's theory structure is to assert brain modularity, gather evidence, and conclude with multiple intelligences. By taking a brain-map-cognition approach, Gardner presents well-documented cases of multiple intelligences including linguistic, musical, spatial, bodily, inter-personal, intra-personal, and logico-mathematical intelligence. However, the last one is a synthesis of many abilities and looks like an overarching general intelligence, thus defeating the whole notion of multiple intelligences.

For the information-processing paradigm, Robert Sternberg's triarchic theory of intelligence (1984, 1985) aims to explain intelligent behavior in the real world (contextual subtheory), and show the dynamic interplay between controlled and automated processing in its competition of cognitive resources (experiential subtheory). It also theorizes on thinking and learning (componential subtheory), but only partially. His theory is merely a description of the reasoning (not thinking) process with little content. For learning, Sternberg is concerned with the knowledge-acquisition process and its measurement but has neglected its underlying mechanisms, knowledge characteristics and representation, principles of learning and so on.

The learning paradigm has a long history and its contribution to intelligence has persisted. Many contemporary theorists in the 1980s continue to focus on learning and intelligence. When John Horn and Raymond Cattell made a distinction between fluid intelligence and crystallized intelligence (Horn & Cattell, 1966), the latter can be interpreted as an outcome of learning, the acquisition of knowledge, or knowledge crystallized.

Earl Butterfield's treatment of learning from the cognitive and information-processing approach equates learning to intelligent action, which is the creation of novel executive routine (Butterfield, 1986). Such definition has limited his scope of learning to the processing side (executive routine) and neglected the content and nature of learning, knowledge structures, and acquisition principles. The same could be said of Richard Snow who is concerned with the cognitive aptitude of learning (Snow, 1984, 1986), but offers no comprehensive theory of intelligence based on learning. Ann Brown and Joseph Campione propose an interesting notion of learning potential: that learning should be viewed as a fluctuating characteristic that will vary across domains and over time. Thus they are faced with the challenge of developing adaptive testing procedures to measure it. Roger Schank proposes a theory of intelligence by piecing together a few fundamental concepts such as understanding, explanation, and learning (Schank, 1982, 1986), but learning in Schank's theory is treated as a peripheral concept defined in terms of understanding. David Perkins proposes the notion of learnable intelligence (1995), that intelligence can be learned, but he does not theorize on how learning and thinking interact to create intelligence.

The factor-analytic tradition is exclusively concerned with the quantification of intelligent behavior, that is, intelligence test scores. Their methodology is to get a large bank of test items, collect test scores, and apply factor analysis to estimate the common source of variance among tests. Their euphoria of measurement has ranged from Spearman's g to reaction time to evoked potentials in EEG.

Does there exist single or multiple intelligences (abilities)? Researchers within this tradition and applying the same tool have come to entirely opposite conclusions, with Arthur Jensen (1980) and Hans Eysenck (1982) asserting the former while John Horn (1989) and Phillip Ackerman (1989) arguing for the latter. It seems Horn has a stronger case than Jensen and Eysenck.

The factor-analytic tradition has applied a mathematical tool very vigorously to the study of intelligence, but this tool is unable to elucidate the nature and scope of intelligence. Horn admitted the arbitrary nature of factor analysis and that his seven abilities are still tentative. Moreover, Horn has failed to make a conceptual distinction between cognitive and conceptual abilities. By defining elementary cognitive abilities as subprocesses underlying higher-level conceptual abilities, we can solve the puzzle of overlapping abilities in the factor-analytic paradigm.

Since the 1970s we witnessed the explosion of cognitive psychology and the colonization of intelligence research by the information-processing paradigm. Intelligence is broken into smaller and smaller components but we do not have a clear conception of what intelligence is. IQ test itself has no theoretical foundation, and the consensus of the professional community may rest on questionable assumptions. Intelligence researchers keep measuring digit scan, reaction time, and EEG, but there are numerous methodological flaws: intelligence self-defined, task analysis unjustified, "theory-based-on-data" fallacy, and validation fallacy and circularity.

Theories of intelligence have evolved in the 1980s through the competition between Robert Sternberg's triarchic theory of intelligence and Howard Gardner's theory of multiple intelligences. The 1990s has seen David Perkins proposing learnable intelligence and Mike Anderson constructing a minimal cognitive architecture of intelligence. Notwithstanding their contributions, there is still no theory in sight based on learning and thinking, which are the two major components of intelligence researchers have long come to agree.

Intelligent Food for Thought II

This chapter outlines Piaget's theory but does not mention his experiments with children (Piagetian tasks), which are as ingenious as his theory. For example, Piaget would show a preschooler four tulips and two daisies and ask, (a) are there more tulips or more daisies; and (b) are there more tulips or more flowers? According to Piaget, preschoolers will say more tulips in both cases because they cannot master class inclusion. This was challenged by Linda Siegel (1978) who replicated the experiment with M & Ms and other candies to American children. Siegel found that her American subjects can understand that there are more candies than M & Ms. She thus concluded that Piaget's is a language problem.

Wouldn't you believe that an adult Chinese may fail in a class inclusion problem? The case is that the Chinese may not take a tulip as a flower. An ancient Chinese philosopher held a theorem that "A white horse is not a horse!" Another Chinese premier publicly named "a horse as a deer!" For details of reasoning, see Fung (1948).

3

The Thinking Dimension of Intelligence: Language and the Emergence of Thought

INTRODUCTION

In this chapter, I will venture into neurophysiology and linguistics, pointing out the primacy of language in human evolution. Then I will argue how language leads to the emergence of conceptual thought, the defining characteristic of human intelligence.

Competing Definitions of Intelligence

In chapter 2, I point out that there were two competing theories of intelligence in the 1980s: Gardner's theory of multiple intelligences and Sternberg's triarchic theory of intelligence. Their respective definitions of intelligence are:

Gardner: Intelligence is the ability to solve problems, that are valued within one or more cultural settings. (Gardner, 1983, p. x)

Sternberg: Intelligence is the mental capability of emitting contextually appropriate behavior at those regions in the experiential continuum that involve response to novelty or automatization of information processing as a function of metacomponents, performance components, and knowledge-acquisition components. (Sternberg, 1985, p. 128)

Note that both definitions stress the importance of adaptation and intelligence within a culture where Gardner pointed to problem solving and creation of new products, while Sternberg stressed on response to novelty. However, Sternberg's definition is a summarizing account of his theory rather than a working definition. The terms within his definition, such as "contexual," "experiential," "novelty," "automati-zation," "metacomponents," and so on are only definable and meaningful within his theory. It seems that Sternberg first formulates his theory and then regresses it to a definition.

Intelligence as Mental Capacity for Thinking and Learning

My own working definition of intelligence is:

Intelligence is the mental capacity for higher-order conceptual
activities of thinking and the acquisition of knowledge.

Here some explanations are necessary. Firstly, intelligence is a mental capacity and not some physical acuity such as body prowess or keen eyesight. It is the use of the human mind, not the body per se, that I consider as intelligence. Second, intelligence is concerned with higher-order conceptual activities and not with lower-order cognitive abilities, such as Horn's Gv (visual and spatial abilities) or Ga (auditory abilities), though the latter may serve as the basis for the former. Third, through thinking and learning, the human species solve problems, create products (Gardner's definition), respond to novelty, and attain automaticity (Sternberg's definition). Yet these are the results of intelligence and not intelligence itself. To study intelligence, we have to focus on the thinking process and the learning process. Fourth, this working definition is the consensus viewpoint, among social scientists and educators, of what intelligence is all about (See chapter 1.) Hence, I take this as my starting point.

With this working definition, the immediate question is: How does intelligence come about and what makes the human species intelligent? In other words, what makes humans capable of these higher-order conceptual activities? What has led to the development of such capacities? More specifically, what makes thinking and learning possible in the human species? While other lower animals may have rudimentary thinking and problem-solving abilities, it is the complexity and sophistication of our thinking and learning abilities that has separated humans from animals. So, what is so unique about human thinking and human learning?

The Symbol Systems, Language, and the
Emergence of Intelligence

I believe that intelligence has a strong link with symbolic systems, and the conjecture is that intelligence is the unintended consequence of using symbol systems that facilitate thinking and learning. According to Gardner (1983), the ability of human beings to use various symbolic vehicles in expressing and communicating meanings distinguishes them sharply from other organisms. The commonest symbolic systems are language, music, gesture, mathematics, and pictures (Gardner 1983, p. 25). Based on this "symbol systems" approach, Gardner formulated his theory of multiple intelligences, with each symbol entailing each intelligence, and thus linguistic intelligence, musical intelligence, logical-mathematical intelligence, spatial intelligence, bodily kinesthetic intelligence, and personal intelligence.

Among the various symbolic systems that human beings invent, I think that language is of primary importance. It has led to the creation of concepts which further enhance thinking and learning. In this chapter, I would argue that human language has led to the creation of a symbolic world while the mental occurrences have brought about a mental world. The interactions of both worlds have transformed rudimentary thought into concepts. Once concepts are formed, thinking and higher-order conceptual activities come into being and, hence, the emergence of intelligence (see Figure 3.1).

THE PRIMACY OF LANGUAGE IN HUMAN EVOLUTION

How Unique Is Human Language?

Language is a system of arbitrary sounds or written symbols to convey meaning and for the purpose of communication. Broadly defined this way, language is not a unique characteristic of the human species. Many other species possess language and communication systems as well. For example, bees can communicate through dances. Whales are capable of making very low-frequency sounds that can

Figure 3.1
The Growth of Human Intelligence

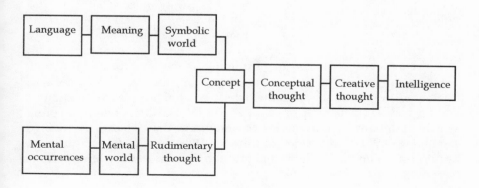

communicate through water to a very long distance. In observing animal communications in their natural habitats Jane Goodall (1971) discovered that chimpanzees have at least 14 identifiable calls and cries (vocabulary) in their speech. But what is unique in humans is our capacity to use language for different functions. According to Karl Bühler (1934) and Karl Popper (1972), human language has four functions:

1. **Expressive function.** To use language for the expression of emotion, such as fear, excitement, anger, and so on.
2. **Signaling function.** The sender uses the language to signal to the receiver and tries to bring about some reaction, such as the case of a bird's alarm call signaling danger to the flock.
3. **Descriptive function.** To use language for the descriptions of objects, actions, events, and experience.
4. **Argumentative function.** To use language in critical and discursive discussion.

Many species can use language for expressive and signaling functions; that is, they can make sounds or communicate by other means to express their feelings or make signals to other members of their species. But they are incapable of the descriptive and argumentative functions. The human use of language is unique in that it can attain all four functions. Undoubtedly, the human species is capable of description and argumentation. But how can we be sure that other species are incapable of doing so? Would birds not be describing or arguing with one another when they produce bird songs? Research in ethnology does not indicate any species capable of using language or speech as we do. Many species do make sounds to express or to signal, but they do not have the capacity to describe or to argue (Walker, 1985).

Can Chimpanzees Be Trained to Use Human Language?

The human species, belonging to the primate family, is a near relative of the ape. The interesting question is: Can apes or chimpanzees be trained to use human language, or at least to use some symbolic communication systems that people can understand? There were many attempts to teach apes to speak when they were brought up in a human family. After years of training in one case, the ape was only able to produce four words—papa, mama, cup, and up. The failure was attributed to the vocal apparatus, which has limited the articulation of certain vowels (Lieberman, 1975). In 1966, the Gardners taught a young female chimpanzee, Washoe, to communicate through American Sign Language (ASL). After years of training, Washoe was able to master a vocabulary of about 130 signs and arrange them in a string of up to four words. With such apparent success, researchers begin to ask what Washoe wanted to communicate with human beings.

It was found that Washoe used ASL predominantly for requests for food or attention. Washoe demonstrates no "curiosity" and does not use ASL to inquire about her surroundings. This is very different from a human child, who spontaneously uses language to inquire and learn about the world around him/her. There is no doubt that Washoe can convey intended meaning, but she has difficulty in mastering syntax. Moreover, Washoe, in communicating with her offsprings, did not use sign language. In effect, Washoe's capacity to use ASL was a training effect by behavioral and reinforcement principles limited to the trainer and trainee. It seems Washoe took advantage of the training to get more food and attention without regard to the value of flexible communication through ASL.

There are further efforts to teach apes to communicate with humans. Most notably, D. Premack in 1976 developed a system of plastic chips with different shapes and colors to represent objects, actions and positions. The ape, Sarah, was trained by operant conditioning with reward for success. In 1980, D. M. Rumbaugh designed a computer keyboard with 25 keys to represent words and phrases. The chimpanzee, Lana, had to use it for requesting food, drinks, and services, and it has to be done in correct grammatical form. "For Lana, language is an adaptive behavior of considerable value for achieving specific goals not readily achieved otherwise" (Rumbaugh, 1980, p. 250). In other words, Lana has to use this means of symbolic communication to get food for survival.

Chimpanzees Cannot Master Syntax

It must be pointed out that all the trainings of apes to speak were in artificial and experimental settings. The attempts to teach apes to employ human speech were utter failures because of neurophysiological misfit. By teaching Washoe to use ASL, researchers have shown that she has the capacity to use signs and symbols to represent objects and actions, for the pragmatic purposes of requesting food and attention. But such capacity is not a natural behavior but a contrived behavior for adaptation. Having reviewed the literature in this field, a biologist concluded:

There is no doubt that apes are adept at learning symbolic languages at level two, i.e., as signals, but it is doubtful if they ever manage to rise to level three, descriptive language, and of course level four is not in question. These characteristic features of human language have not been displayed by apes, even after the most painstaking teaching procedures. Apes can use language semantically, particularly in ASL, but there is no clear evidence that their linguistic expressions have syntactic form. (Eccles, 1991, p. 80)

In the same vein, Chomsky pointed out:

Recent work seems to confirm, quite generally, the not very surprising traditional assumption that human language, which develops even at very low levels of human intelligence and despite severe physical and   social handicaps, is outside of the capacities of other species, in its most rudimentary properties, a point that has been emphasized in recent years by Eric Lenneberg, John Limber and others. The differences appear to be qualitative: not a matter of "more or less," but of a different type of intellectual organization. (1980, p. 439)

In the development of human language, speech precedes written symbols. The first primitive speech probably occurred in Homo habilis that appeared on earth some 2 million years ago (Tobias, 1983, 1987). When Homo erectus appeared on earth some 1.3 million years ago, it had a large increase in brain size and speech area (Eccles, 1991, p. 95). The Neanderthal man that inhabited the planet 100,000 years ago had presumably attained speech ability more or less similar to that of modern man, the Homo sapiens. While writing may be an invention as recent as 5,000 years ago, as witnessed in Sumerian cuneiform, the human ability to draw, to use written symbols for expression or record keeping, may date back as early as 30,000 years ago (Marshack, 1985). Nevertheless, speech was the dominant form of language until about 4,000 years ago. Before then, our ancestors lived in oral cultures passed down by oral poets (for example, Homer) who could recite and memorize thousands of lines before the dawn of writing (Egan, 1988, pp. 50-74).

The Physiological Basis of Human Speech

Many physiological factors converge to produce human speech. The first factor is the vocal apparatus. Apes are unable to speak because of the structure of their vocal apparatus   (Lieberman, 1975).   For humans, there is the nasopharynx that opens up a vocal tract so that air can come in through both the mouth and the nose.   Without that structure, apes are limited in their production of vowels. The second factor is the speech area in the human brain. Briefly stated, Broca and Wernicke are major speech areas.   The posterior speech center of Wernicke (Broadman areas 21, 22, 37, 39, 40) is involved with the semantic processing of speech.   The anterior speech area of Broca (Broadman areas 44, 45) is related to the motor aspect of speech, or control of speech muscles.   The superior speech cortex at the supplementary motor area is related to the initiation of speech movements. It is the complex coordination of these areas that makes speech production a unique human achievement. The third factor is that there are auditory pathways. Speech is dependent upon the feedback from hearing.   Human sound first reaches the primary auditory area (Heschl's gyrus, area 41) and planum temporale (area 42).

It is then projected to the Broca-Wernicke area, as well as the frontal lobe (area 8, 9, 10), prefrontal cortex (areas 6, 8, 9), and parietal cortex. Then there is simultaneously some unexpected activity on the right hemisphere. Thus speech must have involved more areas of the human brain than researchers initially believed. In fact our understanding of the cerebral mechanism of speech is still at a very crude level. Take the example of reading aloud. From the visual areas (17, 18, 19) the pathway goes to area 39 (the angular gyrus). Then semantic interpretation takes place in the Wernicke area, which are then transferred via the arcuate fasciculus (AF) to Broca's area for processing into the complex motor patterns, leading to the activation of the motor cortex to produce reading (Eccles, 1991, p. 83).

There is thus physiological explanation of why the chimpanzee, being a close relative to the human species, fail to utilize speech. Eccles's review of neurophysiological evidence suggests that the chimpanzee has a vocal apparatus sufficiently developed for making speech sounds (phonemes), at least at a crude level (1991, p. 94). But something is missing in its brain structure. An equivalent map of the brain of an anthropoid ape showed that most of the speech areas are missing. There are areas 21 and 22, but area 39 and 40 of Wernicke is missing. Also Broca's area (area 44, 45) is entirely unrecognizable (1991, p. 92). Area 39 is especially important here, as Geschwind (1965) has suggested that it may be the convergent point for two or more sense modalities. If sensory information of vision and touch converge onto the same neurons, these neurons can then signal the identity of things and hence in the naming of objects, which is a basic component for the descriptive function of language. This is hardly achieved by chimpanzees and apes.

Another striking difference is the incessant babbling sounds made by human babies. They not only imitate sounds but keep practicing their vocal apparatus spontaneously, as in some kind of self-learning. By contrast, chimpanzee babies are remarkably silent and do not practice their vocal apparatus. Their silence is attributable to the missing of speech areas in their brain structure.

Summary and a Perplexing Question

From the above neurophysiological and experimental evidence, we can come to the following conclusions:

1.   Different species have different means and symbols of communication.
2.   Many species possess language, and they employ language for expressive and signaling functions.
3.   The human species is unique in its use of language for two other functions: descriptive and argumentative functions.

4. The training of apes for human language indicates that apes can convey simple intended meanings, but there are few evidences that they can master syntax.

5. Apes' failure in human speech is attributed to the structure of their vocal apparatus, the missing parts in their brain structure, and the utilization of the auditory pathways.

6. Naming is the basic component for the descriptive function of language, where chimpanzees fail while human babies succeed.

A perplexing question thus becomes apparent: Why are humans capable of higher-level language functions (descriptive or argumentative) while lower animals are not? What in the human evolutionary history has led to this jump? And what are its consequences? Some evolutionary pressure must be at work to press for naming, communication, and team effort that lead to the development of higher-level language functions. Imagine one hunter-gatherer tribe goes without language. Here we can start to appreciate the evolutionary advantage of language. The mystery has to be unveiled by evolutionary biologists. My task here is to explain how language, with its higher-level functions, brings about concepts, conceptual thought, and subsequently intelligence, which transforms the human species and planet Earth. I can give only a rather broad picture and a sketchy account. Many more scholarly works need to be done in order to uncover this complex developmental process in which concepts, conceptual thought, and intelligence are inseparable from higher-level language functions.

LANGUAGE AND THE SYMBOLIC WORLD

Chomsky and Vygotsky on the Nature of Human Language

Human language is a system of arbitrary sounds and visual symbols to represent meaning (Pei, 1966; Brown, 1987). It has an enormous creative potential in thought and communication (McArthur, 1983). It is a social product that evolves over time. It is social in two senses: first, it has shared meanings made intelligible only in a social context of communication between members of a community. Second, it is passed along through a social process: language has to be learned again and again and generation after generation. Thus, for example, if we isolate a newborn infant, he/she will not develop any languages on his/her own accord, though he/she can make use of his/her vocal apparatus to make less differentiated sounds meaningless to us. At the same time, human language is both a human invention and a convention. It is an invention because it is created by humans. It is also a convention because it is handed down by tradition, with implicit rules governing its usage (grammar). These are not explicit rules that people will sit down, discuss, and make, for with what language can they use to discuss these rule in the first instance? Rather, its rules evolved over time as a result of fulfilling the human communicative and expressive purposes.

Seen in the light that sounds and symbols of language are just arbitrary, it is not surprising to find that languages all over the world differ so significantly from one another. They differ not only in sounds and shapes, but also in meanings and rules. However, linguists such as Noam Chomsky have speculated upon the existence of universal grammar, that is, a set of underlying, universal rules that govern all languages. Chomsky further distinguishes surface structures from deep structures, competence from performance in the study of languages. Chomsky (1965, 1970) also postulates the existence of a language acquisition device, some sort of a "little black box" that makes the child's mastery of his/her native language possible. At the same time, McNeill (1966) also described the properties of the language acquisition device.

Lev Vygotsky (1934, reprinted 1986) postulated that language is a vehicle for thought. Language facilitates and speeds up thought, bringing thought to a new plateau. Vygotsky traced the development of language in four stages and that of concept formation in three phases. He pointed out that with the help of language in the socialization process, concepts gradually form, and so thought becomes verbal and speech becomes rational. In order to appreciate the power of language, let us try to use a thought experiment. Imagine yourself thinking without the use of language. What can you come up with? Can we still think? No matter what you can come up with, you cannot articulate it because you are not supposed to use language. Probably without language we may still be able to think, but in great difficulty and hindrance. We can still have mental activities such as rotating an object, noticing some special features, changing visual/spatial position, but we cannot give names to objects or articulate features, directions, relative positions, and so on. Higher-order conceptual thinking without language is entirely impossible and out of the question.

Language and Meaning

Under the behavioral paradigm in the 1950s, language was seen as a verbal behavior learned through operant conditioning (Skinner, 1957). This was challenged by Chomsky (1959), who pointed out that the behaviorist account cannot explain novel utterances in language usage and acquisition. Eric Lenneberg (1967) further proposed that language is "species-specific" in that the modes of perception, categorizing abilities, and other language mechanisms are biologically determined. Going deeper into the essence of language, Brown (1987) pointed out that it is the convergence of meaning which is the most important function of language.   Lois Bloom's studies of child language development (Bloom, 1973; 1978; 1991) can be seen as outlining the cognitive underpinnings of language development and focusing on the mastery of increasing semantic complexity.   Specifically, Dan Slobin (1971; 1986) demonstrated that semantic learning depends on cognitive development, where the sequences of development are determined more by semantic complexity than by structural complexity.   It is clear that language cannot be separated from its meanings or from the context of its usage (Bruner, 1983).   Thus, Mathilda Holzman proposed a "reciprocal model" to explain the function of language in discourse (Holzman, 1984).   Also Eric Wanner and Lila Gleitman (1982) pointed out that children tend to map each semantic idea with a word in their learning of a language.

The Power of Language

The power of language lies in its flexibility. It is not a concrete object like a stone, nor is it a flexible object like playdough. Rather, it is a flexible abstract entity, upon which we can manipulate: to add, to delete, to move around, to lengthen, to shorten, to give negation, to give interrogatives.   And there are things that we can do with language units: making phrases and sentences.   Language is so flexible that we can create any abstract entity through it as long as we can conceptualize.

Another power of language lies in its communicability. We can use language to represent reality, to express feelings and intentions, to analyze plans and actions.   Language is invented for the purpose of communication within a social group.   While lower animals have tremendously ingenuous ways of signaling and communicating, their communication fails to have the flexibility of a human language.   The power of human language is like this: a social group understands the language, identifies with the language, follows the language instructions to collectively do something creative, such as the making of tools and hunting.   It far transcends the instinctual behavior dictated by our genome.   There is no doubt about the cohesive power of language, which cements a social group and directs it to social collective action. Language is not only the vehicle for thought.   It is also an objective platform for thought.   Without language, thought cannot be shared, reified, and objectified. It is quite true that we can only observe actions and events, not thoughts.   But we can put our thoughts in languages so that others can listen to them, share them, understand them, and talk about them.   Otherwise, thoughts cannot be shared by a community.

Language also possesses immense condensation power, which facilitates more higher-order and complex thoughts.   Language representation, in fact, expands our cognitive resources and helps to focus our attention.   The human cognition is characterized by its limited attention span, limited short-term memory, limited working memory, limited focus of attention, and so on.   Contemporary cognitive psychology demonstrates these limitations again and again. There is no way we can change this genetic limitation of human cognition. But through language, the human species is able to overcome these limitations and enormously expand its limited cognitive resources because language, through representation, has enormous condensation power. Each term in a language can encapsulate a lot of ideas and meanings. For example, the term "student" may encapsulate the idea of a male or female, who has to sit quietly to learn, who has to go to a place called school, who has to do homework, who may have to put on school uniforms and so on. Now, a sentence is made up of many terms, for example:

A student is reading an encyclopedia.

The U.S. government has issued an ultimatum to Iraq.

Considered separately, each term can represent a lot of ideas, implications, and meanings. But in language, we can condense these ideas into a few terms and put them into a comprehensible sentence, so that our attention span, short-term memory, and working memory can handle them. In other words, we can avoid the problem of mental overload by means of the condensation power of the language. A complex problem with lengthy ideas can be condensed into a limited number of terms that is within the manageable size of our working memory. Through the use of language, we can consider more complex problems and issues than our cognitive resources can initially permit us.

Let us also consider the structural problem of our short-term memory and working memory. Since working memory is working so fast and information is decaying so rapidly in our short-term memory, language can be used as a vehicle for rehearsal, for keeping them in short-term memory and working memory until they are fully understood and processed.

The Emergence of Meaning and the Symbolic World

But the most important consequence of language is the emergence of meaning and the symbolic world. In fact, meaning is at the core of a human language. Human language is not meaningless, random sounds and utterances. It means something. This brings us to a very tricky question: What is the meaning of meaning? The analysis is that when we ask "What does x mean?" we are in fact talking about three levels of meanings:

Level 1:   Representational Level
            What does x stand for or represent?

Level 2:   Ideational Level
             What's the idea behind x? What's its conceptual implication?

Level 3:   Experiential Level
             What sense does x make to my experience and why?

Let me illustrate these three levels with an example. You are driving and see a red light ahead. You pull the car over and stop. At the representational level in this example, red stands for stop. Here red is an arbitrary symbol. Red may stand for stop, for danger, for go ahead, for warning, in short, for whatever we assign to it. It is a matter of social convention. Next at the ideational level, there are two definitions: the correspondence definition and the operational definition. The correspondence definition is that the language term has to correspond to the state of affairs of reality as well as correspond to what one wishes to express. Thus "to stop" means to stay still, to be motionless, or to bring an object from moving to nonmoving. The operational definition is the procedures or steps implied by the language term. Thus the operational definition of "to stop" is to proceed with as operational routine that would bring the car to a stop: remove foot from gas pedal, put foot on brake, add force slowly until you see no more car movement and so on.

To appreciate the meaning of level 3, the experiential or subjective level, imagine a person from an ancient tribe sitting next to you in your car. Your stopping the car in front of a red light does not make sense to him. He does not know why. But it makes sense to you and you know why: You have to follow the traffic codes, or your license will be suspended; in fact all drivers implicitly agree to follow this rule so that pedestrians can walk across the road and another car may pass through the junction without being hit by the car from another direction.

The Significance of Meaning

Now let us examine the significance of these three levels of meanings. At level 1, representational level, it is where the power of the flexibility of language lies. A language is an arbitrary sign in which A can represent B, C, or D; X, Y, and Z can all represent K and so on. This gives us a lot of power to manipulate with the symbolic world: The physical world exists as it is and cannot be changed easily; the symbolic representation is very flexible and can be readily changed.

Another importance of the representational level is that it leads the human species to see one step more, to look one step ahead. Show a red sign to a dog, and it may have a red sensation, nothing more, nothing less. Show the same red sign to a man, and he may see red as implying danger, and he may respond by making a move to safety. A man-made symbol can inspire any meaning, such as idea, fear, excitement, and so on, that the social group agrees arbitrarily. In other words, we have penetrated deeper and deeper into the phenomenal world.

More importantly, levels 1 and 2 add up to a symbolic representation of ideas. It is the use of a symbol (red) to represent an idea (danger). This is a very rudimentary and yet the basic form of representation. We do not even need to write the word "D-A-N-G-E-R" to represent danger. In fact, by representing an idea through a symbol, we can anchor an idea and are able to manipulate it and to operate on it, such that a symbolic world of ideas and meanings can be created.

Level 3 of meaning, or the experiential level, is also intricately related to levels 1 and 2 and the symbolic world thus created. Notice that the symbolic world itself cannot have its own existence. It can only exist in people's minds. The symbolic world is not like a physical object, say a stone, that has an objective instance of existence. Instead, it is a mental representation whose existence is contingent upon the existence of humans, without which the symbolic world simply cannot exist. Imagine that all humans have died after a catastrophe while other lower animals still survive. The earth is left with libraries and books written in human language. What is the use of those books to monkeys, chimpanzees, or snakes?

At the experiential level, we frequently ask questions of meaning that are related to our own experience, such as the following:

- What does x mean?
- Why and how does x happen?
- How is x related to me?
- What are the implications of x to me?
- Does x relate to me in any of my past experience?
- What should I do in response to x?

In fact, this experiential level of meaning is about how to relate the symbolic world to oneself. We relate it by asking how it relates to our past experiences. It is how the human species tries to make sense out of the symbolic ideas and attempts to relate it to past experiences. In other words, the human species is trying to construct a coherent and consistent picture of the world based on its former experiences by taking into account of this symbolic world of ideas and meanings. The symbolic world would not be operative if it is not elevated to this personal level of meaning. This is because, until then, the symbolic world is still an outside, detached world. However, once it is elevated to this personal level, the idea has undergone a rapid change: it is not just the question of the idea or meaning itself, but a question of how it relates to one's past experiences, how a consistent picture can be established, and what action a person may take in face of this new idea/meaning. The symbolic world is no more external to oneself, but is directly related to one's own experiences. It has direct bearing on one's understandings and future actions. At the same time, one's own experiences and thoughts can now be encoded, through the medium of language, to be understood by others in the same social group sharing the same language and the symbolic world. In other words, the symbolic world can now become a shared and public world within a social group.

As mentioned earlier, a language helps to anchor an idea. Our working memory moves so fast that some form of anchoring will help to understand and manipulate an idea. By seeing red we think of danger and can anchor our thought on it: red reminds us constantly of danger. A red card is a stable instance of physical existence that can remind us of the fleeting idea of danger. Another important outcome is that a red card and "danger" differ qualitatively, the former being a concrete physical object while the latter is an abstract, mental construct. You can locate a plant, a predator, or an insect; but you cannot locate a "danger." It is a quality not inherent in the physical object itself but that exists in terms of our relation with the object. As an example, predators, some insects and plants are not dangerous in themselves but are dangerous in our relations with them. More generally, then, danger is a "mental" construct, an idea to express our feelings about a situation. Primitive people know what danger is: they feel it, they experience it, but it is through language with meaning that danger is articulated and clearly expressed: danger means one may have physical pain, may lose one's life, may mourn, may experience anxiety, fear, psychological tension, and so on.

The most important consequence of the use of language, then, is the creation of a symbolic world with meanings and ideas. Now the human species is no longer living in one world only, but is instead living in two worlds, the physical world and the symbolic world. We now operate in two worlds, and we can operate beyond the "here and now." We can think of the past as well as the future, this immediate spatial field as well as that beyond the immediate spatial field. There is no longer any need to act out all outcomes with the concrete physical world. We can operate by thinking, imagining, and planning. We become more flexible and we live in open possibilities.

Three Levels of Meaning at Work

Let me summarize how this symbolic world of meanings works by an illustrative example. You hear an alarm bell and see smoke coming from your neighbor's house. At the representational level, alarm and smoke mean fire. At the ideational level, fire means its attributes—burning, hot, bright, red, dangerous, and so on. At the experiential level, you make sense of the situation that this is a fire, and it triggers a lot of actions and emotions on you: fear, escape, bang at your neighbor's door, shout for help, call the fire department, and so on.

The above example may seem trivial, but imagine we are in a world without language. What will happen? We will still hear the alarm, but can we associate alarm with fire so efficiently? It probably depends on the extent of training and conditioning. We can still see smoke, but we cannot articulate the word "smoke," which means that we may not be able to represent it in speech. Without the representational level, we can only recall the immediate physical event which is fast fleeting away—the smoke that comes and goes. We may have immediate visual image, but we do not know what it means. It is impossible to anchor a physical event to the meaning or implication of the event, that is, to anchor the phenomenon of smoke to the meaning and implication of it. Then how can we efficiently and flexibly associate smoke with fire? We can only have fixed association without meaning. At the ideational level, how can we spell out the attributes of fire without language? The flash of ideas may be too fast to be captured and processed by our working memory. Finally at the personal level, how can we make sense out of the situation, not to say relating it meaningfully to our past experiences or planning for future actions. All we can have is just pure conditioned response—fleeing for safety, like lower animals. It is thus no exaggeration to say that language has transformed the human species.

Language is an artifactual device created by the human species. It is like an additional appendage equipped to humans so that they can deal with the world more effectively. With language we suddenly enter into a symbolic world of vast complexity. We use the symbolic world to represent the physical world. We extract properties from the physical world and express them through categories and constructs. These categories and constructs form the backbone of our symbolic world, which we take as real and live in. We not only live in the physical world, but also in the symbolic world which we have created.

MENTAL EVENTS AND THE MENTAL WORLD

Philosophers and psychologists have for centuries been very much interested in the issue of mental events. Extreme positions such as the denial of the existence of mental events altogether on the one side to the embracing of mental events as the essence of humans on the other side has characterized the history of debate known as "mind-body" problem in philosophy (Hospers, 1967). I will first outline the nature of mental events and the emergence of the mental world. In the next section I will argue how the interaction between the mental world and the symbolic world has led to the creation of concepts and subsequently the development of intelligence.

Essential Features of Mental Events

The time-honored tradition of dualism tends to characterize mental events with the following essential features: First is the privacy of mental events. Mental events are private. They can only be experienced by the person. When a person feels a pain or has a color sensation, it is his/her private experience inaccessible to others. The privacy of mental experience dictates that it is logically impossible for one person to feel the pain of another person, or vice versa. As a corollary, mental events cannot be observed.   No matter how much progress we make in neuroscience, we can only observe the physical event, that is, the stimulation of nerve fibers. We can never in principle observe a mental event; this makes it distinct from physical events (Matthews, 1977).

Second is the nonspatiality of mental events.   Physical events and objects occupy space, but mental events do not.   One cannot locate mental events in the physical world. The typical example is that when a person hears a sound, neuroscientists can locate, in principle, the stimulation of auditory nerve responsible for the hearing of that sound, but they cannot locate the auditory sensation. The auditory sensation, a mental event, is nonphysical, nonspatial; any attempt to locate it will end up locating a physical stimulation of nerve fiber inside the physical brain, not the auditory sensation itself (Shaffer, 1963).

Third, mental events have intentionality.   Intentionality comes from the Latin verb "intendo," meaning "to aim at" or "point toward" (Flanagan, 1991, p. 28). It is broader than "intending," and it denotes the idea of meaningful intentional content.   Basically this idea sprang from Franz Brentano (1874), who proposed distinction of the mental act and mental content.   According to Brentano, mental act such as think, believe, hope, desire (similar to our concept of thought) must have intentionality, that is, meaningful intentional content.   Every mental act must be about something (aboutness).   For example,

I think this is good wine.

The thought is about good wine, but the good wine itself is not about anything else.   In other words, every thought or mental act must be about something and have meaningful intentional content. Brentano's distinction between knowing (consciousness) and things known (content) and his thesis that one is irreducible to the other can be termed epistemic dualism (Flanagan, 1991, p. 28).   As a collorary, mental events cannot exist without the mental act performed by a subject, and that mental events by nature possess subjective, meaningful content.

Dualism Under Attack

The dualist's position has been severely attacked from different perspectives. Aldous Huxley, for example, takes mental events as epiphenomena—mental phenomena are like the shadow of a body which is caused by the body (brain) but cannot cause it (Jackson, 1982). Gilbert Ryle attempts to reject mental phenomena altogether by linguistic analysis, showing that the concept of mind is a linguistically confusing and mistaken concept (Ryle, 1949). Idealists accept the privacy of mental experience. This, they claim, leads to the impossibility of knowing and therefore the impossibility of the study of mind. Materialists take an opposite route. They argue that mental concepts are idle, that nothing of mental activity ever exists. By grounding mental events in a physical object—the brain, they try to dissolve dualism (Feyeraband, 1963; Rorty, 1979). The program of identity theory is to map or identify all mental events with physical activities in the brain, so that we may abandon mental terms altogether, based on Ockham's razor principle (Smart, 1962; Lewis, 1966). The latest functionalist approach accepts the use of mental terminology but redefines them in functional terms such that there is no longer any need for a distinct, "mysterious" mental entity and thus marks the end of dualism (Fodor; 1968, Dennett, 1978). Even William James, a pioneer in the study of mind who developed the idea of conscious mental life into a rich taxonomy, naturalizes the mind and gets rid of its ontology: "the mind is a process, like breathing, drinking; it makes sense to ask how the mind works, but not what the mind is, as according to James." (Flanagan, 1991, p. 45).

As for the notion of privacy of mental events and experience, I agree that they can hardly be observed. But it does not follow that one cannot study mental events or phenomena. In a seminal experiment, psychogists (Shepherd & Metzler, 1971) studied the properties of mental images and their rotation and found that mental rotation has many characteristics similar to physical rotation. While it is true that in studying mental phenomena one has to rely on verbal reports or observed behaviors of our subjects, it does not mean that one cannot derive regularity of patterns or reliable laws about them. The privacy of experience does not indicate that every individual's experience is idiosyncratic and different in kind: since humans are born with the same genetic endowment, live in the same social world, use the same language and under the nurturance of the same culture, it follows that quite a substantial part of this private experience can be studied and made intelligible to others.

Mental Events as Representing Physical Events

The dualists, following René acute Descarte's route, make a physical/mental distinction in which the physical world and events are spatial-temporal, but mental events are nonspatial. Take the example of a red apple. A mental event of it, or a mental representation means

1. Sensation of certain hue and intensity of color;
2. A certain shape and size;
3. Meaning in relation to a network of concepts.

A mental representation here is to represent the concrete, the reality, while itself by definition is nonconcrete and nonspatial. It is not the real physical thing but is just a mental representation of color, shape, attributes, and so on. It cannot be spatial. The dualist is right that even if one opens a person's brain, all one can find or locate are sensory cells responsible for red sensation; one cannot find the sensation-of-red. This being so, the dualist is merely stating the obvious: The nonspatiability of mental events is so notoriously obvious that arguing for or against it does not lead us anywhere.

Suppose one talks about concrete representation in a child's world. In a child's play, a four-year-old pretends himself/herself to be a doctor and takes his/her dolls as his/her patient. In that case, would the representation be concrete and spatial? The answer is no because here the representation is through the mediation of concrete objects, that is, a doll and himself/herself. The concrete objects symbolize what the child imagines, which is another mental representation of concrete instances of human interaction. The child necessarily has mental images of what a doctor looks like and does, how a patient would respond and so forth, before he/she can play and act it out. The concrete object merely serves as a vehicle for mental representation, which is itself nonconcrete and nonspatial. In fact, the marvels a child can do in mental representation in comparison with other species further supports the notion of primacy of mental representation in the human species.

What exactly is inside this mental world? I postulate that there are two kinds of mental events: mental images and rudimentary thought. Inside the mental world are mental images—visual and auditory. For visual images, there are images of objects, images of actions on objects, images of immediate events, and image of past events, that is, sequence of happenings with objects and actions, and so on. For auditory images, there are sounds, voice, utterances, as well as background noise. As for rudimentary thought, there are some very preliminary ideas distilled from experiences, such as the idea of relation between objects, relation between objects and actions, mean-end relation, cause and effect, and so on. Consider the case of a mouse pushing a lever to get water, or a monkey making use of a stick to get food. These are problem-solving activities involving rudimentary thought of mean-end relation and cause and effect.

Characteristics of the Mental World

Based on the above analysis, one can thus postulate the existence of a mental world with the following characteristics: it is private, nonspatial, nontemporal, distinct from, and irreducible to the physical. It arises from a person, has subjective meaningful content, and represents meaning in the physical as well as the nonphysical world. It is true that one cannot observe mental events directly, but one can study them indirectly. Take the example of object permanence. A child is said to have had a mental world of his/her own when he/she could master object permanence.   In that instance one can infer the existence of mental images in his/her mind. Without the stability of mental images and by implication the existence of a stable mental world, there is no way to explain object permanence. Another example is an eyewitness account of, say, a robbery. The eyewitness is simply recalling the whole sequence of events which he/she has stored in his/her memory. These were once physical events that have occurred; they have been observed, remembered, and stored: They become mental events when being recalled. In other words, one can indirectly know of the existence of mental events.

Mental events are private. Thus every individual has a private mental world of his/her own, populated by mental events. Some of these mental events may be commonly shared among individuals, while others are very idiocycratic. Take the example of an apple. Individuals sharing the same culture and eating the same kind of apple would have the same visual mental image of an apple. However, they may have different past experience with apples and have different thoughts about them.

INTERACTION AND THE EMERGENCE OF THOUGHT

Similarities Between the Two Worlds

The symbolic world and the mental world share many similarities. They are both nonspatial, nontemporal and nonphysical. They both arise from the physical. Take the example of human language that makes up the symbolic world. Without the physical vocal-aural apparatus there could hardly be speech. Even speech itself has its physical existence: the utterance can be measured physically in terms of frequency, pitch, tone, volume, and so on. But it is the nonphysical side of it, the symbolic meaning, that is most essential in the characterization of speech. As for the visual images of the mental world, they also arise from the physical brain, manifested in stimulation and firing of neurons, but it is the mental side of it, the visual and auditory images, that reminds us of certain mental events that are of significance. We are more interested in the idea, meaning, and implication of a mental image than its physical manifestation of firing of neurons.

Both the symbolic world and mental world are grounded in the physical world and the human species. Without the external physical world to serve as input, there would be no visual/auditory images and hence no mental world; without a physical world to serve as an edifice and reference point, it would be impossible to create a system of symbols to represent it, for what could symbols possibly stand for? Also, without the existence of the physical brain, there cannot be any existence of the mental or symbolic world. At the same time, both are grounded in human experience. For the symbolic world, we get the experiential meaning only through our experience in contact with the physical world. For the mental world, the beginning of mental images are just mental representation based on our experience with the physical world. Not surprisingly, however, they both transcend the spatial-temporality of the physical world. They go beyond the "here and now" and bring the human species to a new plateau of existence.

Difference Between the Two Worlds

The most glaring difference between the symbolic world and the mental world is that the former is public while the latter is private. That mental events are private has been elaborated earlier. The privacy of mental experience is a key feature of mental events and the mental world. The mental world is a private and subjective world. It belongs to the individual in question. As a corollary, mental events cannot be observed. So are thoughts and feelings. The case is that one can observe overt behavior of an individual, but not his/her thoughts and feelings. On the other hand, language (and the symbolic world it creates) has an opposite character: it is objective and public. The symbolic world is objective because the symbols in oral or written form can have an objective existence. Suppose one writes a sentence or says something and then disappears. The written sentence or the spoken words can still be an instance of one's objective existence: Its meaning can be decoded, studied, interpreted, and understood by other individuals independent of oneself, the originator. The symbolic world is also public because the oral or written symbols are passed down from generation to generation. A language system is a public heritage. Because it is public and is a system of shared symbols, any individual can make use of it to communicate with others, to express oneself, and be understood by others.

Interaction Between the Two Worlds

Thought Becomes Objective

The above glaring difference has led to the dynamic interaction between the two, resulting in profound changes in the transformation of the human species. When the objective, public, symbolic world meets with the subjective, private mental world, something important happens. First, a person's subjective mental events or states, while remaining private, can now be expressed through language and be understood by others. A person seeing a predator can now shout and warn others instead of just showing instinctual behavior of flight. In other words, a person's private mental world is now made public. Second, inner feelings and thoughts can now be expressed through language. Thoughts, while still cannot be observed, can be expressed through language. Language becomes a vehicle of thought. Thought is no longer a flimsy, unarticulated, muddled, and rudimentary entity, but it is expressed in narratization, in arguments, in reasoning, and in logic. Third, once thought is objectively expressed through language, a thought becomes an objective instance and is capable of being evaluated, criticized and improved upon. The objective character of thought is instrumental to the growth of knowledge and development of culture.

In summary, through the use of language the public, objective symbolic world is able to penetrate into the private, subjective mental world and transform it into a world with public character. The subjective experience of the mental world is expressed in an objective way through the use of language, hence the integration of the subjective and the objective. Without an objective language, there is no way one could express one's thoughts and ideas, or the inner, subjective mental world within oneself, in order to let others know what one thinks or feels. On the other hand, if there is no inner mental world, there is no need for the use of language because there would be nothing to express. In other words, the mental world serves as a starting point while the symbolic world serves as a stepping-stone for the human species to take off to a higher plateau of thoughts and knowledge.

Language Acquires Meaning

Another important interaction between the symbolic world (language) and the mental world (thought) is related to meaning. Language, after all, is a system of arbitrary sounds. Most lower animals can make a lot of sounds. What distinguishes the human species from them is that those arbitrary sounds represent meaning. But where does meaning come from? Meaning is not an inherent property of language. Meaning is given by the human species itself. Meaning is human dependent. Without the human species, language will have no meaning

of its own.   In other words, the human species assigns meaning to
arbitrary sounds that make up language.

As stated earlier, one characteristic of mental events is its
intentionality; that is, every mental event has a meaningful intentional
content. The mental world is composed of mental act (such as think,
feel, love) and mental content (idea). Mental content is an idea or a
mental representation which is nonphysical and has meaning. In other
words, the mental world is a world of ideas and meaning.   In the
interaction between the symbolic world and the mental world, the idea
and meaning of the mental world is now represented by language. The
unique characteristic of the mental world, which is meaning, is now
passed onto language. Language is transformed from the utterance of
sounds to a system of arbitrary sounds to represent meaning. Thus the
final outcome after interaction between the two worlds is that language
partakes meaning as its unique characteristic.   Thus William Stern
(1928) noted that intentionality (meaning) is an important characteristic
of language.

Beginning of Imagination

Another difference between the symbolic world and the mental
world (mental image) is their nature of representation. Language is a
symbolic system in which A represents B and there exist three levels of
meaning: representational, ideational, and experiential. Mental images,
on the other hand, is just a copy of an instance; for example, a visual
image of an apple is just a stable and faithful copy of the real apple. It is
not a transformation of an apple into anything else. Similarly, a mental
event of hunting is the sequence of actions taken collectively for the
capturing of a prey. It is just a replay of what actually happens. Seen in
this light, language has more flexibility than mental images in its
representation, and this power has passed over to mental images in the
interaction between the two.   Take the example of a mental event of
hunting. It is a sequence of mental images involving a lot of actions,
movements, and so on. Through language these mental images can be
expressed and be known by others not having participated in hunting.
By talking and discussing it, we can think through it and try to improve
it. Because of the flexibility of language, we can create new scenarios
that have never happened before. In other words, we need not only
reproduce a faithful copy of what has happened but can change it to
represent a new sequence of events of an improved version of hunting.
Such creation of new make-believe events is what imagination is all
about. In fact, the power of imagination has now been gained by mental
images through its interaction with the symbolic world.

CHAPTER SUMMARY

My working definition of intelligence is: Intelligence is the mental capacity for higher-order conceptual activities of thinking and the acquisition of knowledge.

Language occupies a pivotal role in human evolution and intelligence. The training of apes to speak fails due to their inability to master syntax and their physiological misfit in vocal and brain structure.

Language has four functions: expressive, signaling, descriptive, and argumentative. Lower animals are capable of only the first two functions while the human species has advanced to all four functions as a result of strong evolutionary pressure.

The power of human language lies in its flexibility, communicability, and condensation. It has led to the emergence of meaning in three levels: representational, ideational, and experiential. It also creates a symbolic world of human speech.

Mental events are private, non-spatial and intentional. They can represent physical events and come in two kinds: mental images and rudimentary thought.

The interaction between the symbolic world of language and the mental world of mental events has led to the creation of concepts and the emergence of conceptual thought. The public, objective symbolic world penetrates into the private, subjective mental world, integrating the subjective with the objective.

Language and mental events are the precursors of thought. Once thought becomes objective and language acquires meaning, we witness the beginning of imagination and the dawn of human intelligence.

Intelligent Food for Thought III

In this chapter you have seen that chimpanzees were given human names—Sarah, Lana, Washoe—and trained to speak the human language. So far it was not successful. Can you think of other more successful training such as the following:

Can you train a	dog crocodile bee bird ox plant	to	stand yawn dance chew read sleep	?

If this still doesn't appear anthropocentric to you, report your findings in a scientific journal.

4

Intelligence in Progress: The Growth of Conceptual Thought

In chapter 3, I argue that language and mental events are the precursors of thought, which is, without doubt, the essence of intelligence. In this chapter I will first review previous researches on thinking and point out their inadequacies and limitation in scope. Here I venture into the state of the art in thinking research and review the complex findings. Next I will outline Piaget's theory of adolescent (formal) thought. Contrary to most researchers, who tend to neglect the central role played by language and concept in thought, I will argue that language and concept facilitate thought and that thinking through concepts (conceptual thought) is what intelligence is mainly about. Then I will trace the co-evolution of language and thought, outline the formation and growth of concepts, and examine the nature and characteristics of conceptual thought.

THE SCIENTIFIC STUDY OF THINKING: A REVIEW OF THE STATE OF THE ART

Four Domains in the Scientific Study of Thinking

The scientific study of thinking can roughly be divided into four domains: problem solving, concept formation, creative thinking, and reasoning. The classical study of problem solving was Wolfgang Köhler's ape (1927). Modern studies tend to define problem solving in terms of problem space; psychologists study how subjects devise heuristics and methods in approaching and solving problems. Problem-solving strategies are then formalized to become a production system with rules (Anderson, 1990, chapter 8). Some theorists have extended problem solving to cover all human adaptation with self-regulation (Mithaug, 1993).

The modern study of concept formation has its roots in K. L. Smoke (1933), who designed a laboratory experiment on the learning of artificial concepts: DAX and NOT-DAX. While behaviorists interpret concept formation as discrimination learning, Jerome Bruner, Jacqueline Goodnow, and George Austin (1956) propose that children learn concepts through hypothesis testing. In addition, set theory (negation, affirmation, conjunction, disjunction) has been employed for the description of concepts (Haygood & Bourne, 1965). Basically there are two approaches: one is the experimental methodology which aims to discover attribute learning through the design of artificial concepts, mostly in visual or graphic form. The other is to study natural, everyday concepts by surveying how people classify objects. Eleanor Rosch (1978) proposes the notion of prototype to account for novel object classification while R. T. Kellogg (1983) prostulates a feature-frequency model to explain classification decisions. Some researchers also studied concept formation in children: how they categorize and name objects (Markman, 1989), form concepts (Keil, 1989), and theorize about abstract entities such as the human mind (Wellman, 1990). In addition, readers may be interested to note a pioneering study by Lev Vygotsky (1896-1934), who theorizes about the complex relations among concept, learning and thought and introduces the notion of preconcept, pseudoconcept, and complex to account for concept development (1934, reprinted 1986).

Among the studies and theories on the creative thinking process, the most renowned general theory is the four stages of creativity (insight) proposed by Jacques Hadamard (1949). A recent research approach is the case study method proposed by Howard Gruber (1981), by which the life and work of outstanding creative persons are studied extensively to uncover certain patterns of development in creativity (see chapter 6 of this book for a more thorough discussion of creativity).

Reasoning, the focus of this review, is probably the hottest research area at present. Reasoning is normally divided into inductive reasoning (IR) and deductive reasoning (DR). Inductive reasoning is to reason from the particular to the general, that is, to infer general rules and patterns from particular evidence and examples. The most frequently studied areas are analogy reasoning, serial reasoning, and classification reasoning. Psychologists also study hypothesis formation and evaluation. As for deductive reasoning, psychologists study it under the subtopics of linear, categorical, and conditional syllogism.

The Study of Reasoning

While following logicians' footsteps in the study of deductive and inductive logic, psychologists are not interested in logic itself but in the thought processes that make logical thinking possible. In other words, they want to describe and outline the internal thinking processes that are responsible for logical thinking. There were pioneers such as R. S. Woodworth and S. B. Sells (1935) who found faulty reasoning patterns in subjects working on categorical syllogism (i.e., reasoning from premises to conclusion with quantifiers of all, no, some, not). Woodworth and Sells (1935) proposed an "atmosphere hypothesis" postulating that the premises created an "atmosphere" that predisposed subjects to accept certain faulty conclusions. Their ideas were further refined by P. N. Johnson-Laird and M. Steedman (1978), and L. S. Dickstein (1978). Figure 4.1 is a hierarchical presentation of the various subtopics under study.

Localized Theories in Competition

There seems to be no general theory to account for all types of reasoning, although numerous localized theories have been proposed to account for various types of reasoning, some with more generalizability than others. Take the example of categorical syllogism in deductive reasoning. In a matter of decades, numerous competing theories have been proposed, to explain this particular type of human thinking ability: Woodworth and Sells's alogical information-processing theory (1935),

Figure 4.1
Subtopics in the Study of Reasoning

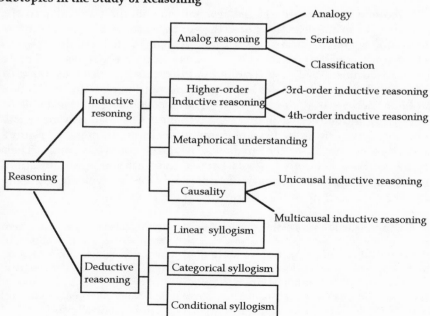

Chapman and Chapman's conversion theory (1959), Erickson's complete-combination theory (1974, 1978), Erickson's random-combination theory (1974-1978), Johnson-Laird and Steedman's mental model theory (1978), Guyote and Sternberg's transitive chain theory (1981), to name but a few. This is indicative of the complexity and sophistication in research in reasoning, where, as in other fields, theories compete, grow on, and build upon one another. Another example is in linear syllogism. There are primarily two theories, Clark's (1969, 1972) linguistic theory and Huttenlocher and Higgins's spatial theory (1971), which were later integrated and represented in a third theory proposed by Sternberg (1980), the mixture theory. In addition, readers may like to take note of these extensive references quoted by Sternberg :

Researchers have engaged in vigorous debate regarding the representation and processes subjects use in solving such problems: (Clark, 1969a, 1969b, 1971, 1972a, 1972b; DeSoto, London, & Handel, 1965; Egan & Grimes-Farrow, 1982; Handel, DeSoto, & London, 1968; Hunter, 1957; Huttenlocher, 1968; Huttenlocher & Higgins, 1971, 1972; Huttenlocher, Higgins, Milligan, & Kauffman, 1970; Johnson-Laird, 1972; Potts & Scholz, 1975; Sternberg, 1980b, 1980d, 1980e; Sternberg & Weil, 1980). (Sternberg, 1985, p. 182)

Theory of Inductive Reasoning

From Philosophy to Psychology

Inductive reasoning is the reasoning from the particular to the general. For example, we witness the sun rises from the east for a few times (particular instances), and then we reason that the sun always rises from the east (general rule). Philosophers such as David Hume and Karl Popper (1972) have pointed out that this is faulty reasoning, or the "induction problem." Psychologists are not interested in induction problem per se but aim to uncover the psychological mechanisms underlying inductive reasoning. They have focused mostly on a few problem types in inductive reasoning, such as analogy, seriation, classification, higher-order analogy, metaphor, and so on. Their researches have led to the speculation that there are similar information-processing components underlying different problem types of inducing structure. According to Sternberg,

Several information-processing psychologists have claimed that the high interrelations obtained between subjects' performances on various kinds of problems of inducing structure are attributable to commonalties in information processing across the various kinds of problems (e.g., Greeno, 1978; Pellegrino & Glaser, 1979, 1980; Simon, 1976; Sternberg, 1977b, 1979b, 1982g). The theory and investigations represent an attempt to make this claim in a precise way and then to test the claim. Essentially, it is argued that the cognitive basis for 'fluid ability' can be understood in terms of information-processing components that overlap between tasks that tap fluid ability. (Sternberg, 1985, p. 132)

In Quest of a General Theory

Sternberg's research on inductive reasoning is, in fact, typical of psychologists' attempt of generalization, that is, attempt to offer a general theory covering all problem types in inductive reasoning. He has proposed two complementary subtheories to account for inductive reasoning—the componential theory of inductive processing developed by himself (1977) and the theory of response choice by David Rumelhart and A. A. Abrahamson (1973).

The componential theory of information processing in inductive reasoning asserts that there exist similar inductive processing processes across such inductive reasoning tasks as analogy, seriation and classification. It further asserts the existence of seven performance components in every task:

- encoding
- inference
- mapping
- application
- comparison
- justification
- response

To test this theory, Sternberg decomposes inductive reasoning tasks in seven performance components and try to measure each. This is done by designing experiments and experimental situations with incremental complexity. For example, an experiment is designed with only one component, say encoding, so that this component can be measured. Then another experiment is designed in which the task calls for two components, say encoding and inference. We can then calculate inference latency by measuring the second experiment and subtract it from latency of the first experiment. In Sternberg's words,

The primary dependent variable was response time (with error rate serving as a secondary dependent variable), and the independent variables were manipulations of various aspects of item difficulty that were needed in order to separate parameters representing duration's of the theorized component processes. (Sternberg, 1985, p. 143)

The theory of response choice in inductive reasoning deals with how subjects make decisions in face of choices in inductive reasoning tasks. It borrows mathematical concepts (in Euclidean geometry and probability theory) to elucidate the decision-making process. Basically, an inductive problem is represented in an mdimensional (psychological) space with magnitude, direction of distance, vector, and so on, and the subject's choice is represented by a probability function where the best choice follows an exponential decay function with increasing distance from the ideal point (Sternberg, 1985, p. 140). Sternberg further extends this to second-order and third-order analogy in semantic space (Sternberg & Downing, 1982).

The Challenge of Generalizability

How far is Sternberg's theory generalizable? Sternberg himself takes up this challenge by adopting the following strategy. He develops specific models for each task testing in accordance with his own theory. There are at least three tasks: analogy, seriation, and classification. Each task can have a variety of forms, that is, various ways of asking questions that may affect response. Then under each form there are different formats, such as pictorial, verbal, or geometric ones, and finally each model can be specified in various levels of detail (Sternberg, 1985, p. 134). Readers may be interested to refer to Figure 4.2 for some sample items.

I contend that this strategy can never conclusively validate a theory. Philosophers of science (for example, Popper) have rightly pointed out that we can only falsify a theory, but we can never conclusively verify a theory. Theoretically speaking, it is impossible to confirm Sternberg's general theory. A more worse fundamental problem is that Sternberg is not directly confirming his general theory. Instead, he is only indirectly confirming his theory by confirming particular instances, which in turn rest upon particular task models, particular formats, and particular forms. Thus Sternberg is merely using a particular format (e.g., geometric), of a particular task model (e.g., series completion) of a particular form (e.g., multiple choice answers) with particular question items to confirm a theory. What is more, each particular instance is confirmed by a case (or a number of cases) of homogeneous subjects (mostly Yale undergraduates).

Supporters of Sternberg may contend that these are standard experimental procedures. After all we have to select samples, operationalize the problem by tasks, and confirm a theory by particular instances. My point is that it is not that Sternberg is entirely mistaken in his strategy. Rather he should not make too strong a claim on theory validation. In his case, readers should be cautioned that as the level of particularity increases, the power of confirming instances weakens. Even if Sternberg is able to confirm every particular case in every particular format in every particular form and every particular task, there always remain new tasks, formats, forms, and so on, to be devised and to be confirmed. Furthermore, the complexity of the problem may lie in the interaction and nonlinear relationship among task, form,

Figure 4.2
Test Sample Items of Analogy, Seriation, and Classification in Pictorial, Verbal and Geometric Forms

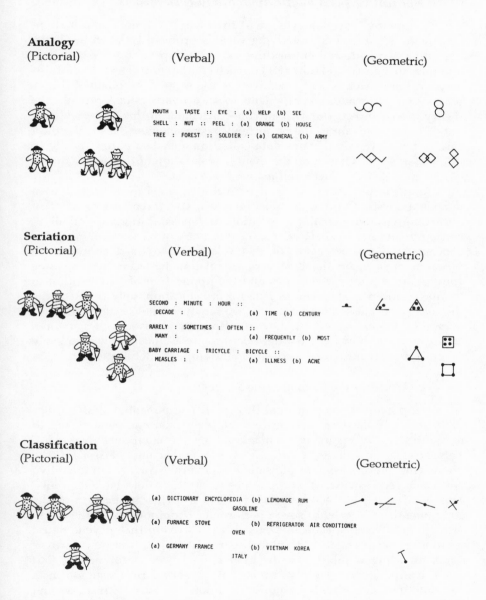

Analogy

(Pictorial)   (Verbal)   (Geometric)

MOUTH : TASTE :: EYE : (a) HELP (b) SEE
SHELL : NUT :: PEEL : (a) ORANGE (b) HOUSE
TREE : FOREST :: SOLDIER : (a) GENERAL (b) ARMY

Seriation

(Pictorial)   (Verbal)   (Geometric)

SECOND : MINUTE : HOUR ::
    DECADE :   (a) TIME (b) CENTURY

RARELY : SOMETIMES : OFTEN ::
    MANY :   (a) FREQUENTLY (b) MOST

BABY CARRIAGE : TRICYCLE : BICYCLE ::
    MEASLES :   (a) ILLNESS (b) ACNE

Classification

(Pictorial)   (Verbal)   (Geometric)

(a) DICTIONARY ENCYCLOPEDIA   (b) LEMONADE RUM
                              GASOLINE

(a) FURNACE STOVE   (b) REFRIGERATOR AIR CONDITIONER
                OVEN

(a) GERMANY FRANCE   (b) VIETNAM KOREA
                ITALY

Adapted from "Unities in inductive reasoning," by Robert J. Sternberg and Michael K. Gardner, 1983, *Journal of Experimental Psychology: General*, 112, pp. 96-98. Copyright 1983 by the American Psychological Association. Reprinted by permission of the publisher.

format, level of difficulty, and so on.   The simplistic view of theory validation by data will not hold.

Empirical Versus Analytic Approach to Task Models

Claims by psychologists that there are common information-processing components underlying various problem types in inductive reasoning can be tested empirically by setting up various task models and measuring reaction time (RT) of each component. The pitfall of this empirical approach is that since we use the same componential theory with seven performance components to set up various task models, the theory in fact directs our way of collecting data, in this case collecting only RT data relevant to the performance components. This is a typical case of how a theory dictates data collection and data automatically fit in the task models based on the theory. Validation of the theory by the so-called "data" is in fact a self-justified outcome.

Apart from testing a claim empirically, we can subject it to a deeper analysis. On a more general level, the three task models of inductive reasoning (analogy, seriation, and classification) are all about concept relations. In analogy, it is the discovery of relation between two concepts and the extension of that relation to a third concept.   In seriation, it is again the discovery of relation between two or three concepts in a progressive series and the application of that relation to the next concept. The same is true for classification, only that it is the discovery of class relations.   If we analyze the issue from this perspective, that is, studying how conceptual and associative networks are formed and how higher-order relations are established, we are likely to make more fruitful discoveries than the empirical RT approach.

The Limits of the Decomposing Strategy

The power of componential theory, or componential analysis, lies in its ability to decompose a process into ever finer components and to measure each by ingeniously manipulating the component variables. This strategy seems to pay off: we now become clearer of the underlying subprocesses responsible for a complex process of cognitive performance. However, this decomposing strategy does have its limits. This is admitted by Sternberg (1977) himself in his application of the componential theory with seven performance components to the study of analogy. More specifically, Sternberg discovers that psychometric reasoning tests correlate with global scores (average response time over items for a given subject, or the total score before decomposing into seven components). He also finds that psychometric reasoning tests correlate far more with response component than with reasoning components (inference, mapping, application, and justification)! Inter-pretation: the better you reason, the faster you press the key-board—but not the better you infer or map. How absurd! In a similar experiment a few years later (Sternberg & Gardner, 1982, 1983) the researchers simply dropped the idea of separating the different components and used a combined reasoning parameter, (i.e., combining inference, mapping, and application) so as to increase the reliability of estimate! With that they found correlation with psychometric reasoning scores!

There are two lessons which we can learn from the experiments. First, decomposing strategy has a limit and may become self-defeating when the limit is overstretched. Researchers aim to decompose reasoning into inference, mapping, and application. Yet the results taken separately fail to correlate with psychometric reasoning scores. Second, if we do not decompose and instead combine different components (inference, mapping, and application) into a single reasoning component, we are back to square one and can never know the relative contribution of each of the components. Regrettably this is the case we have to accept here. One more point is that we should not be too excited to find that the combined reasoning parameter correlates with psychometric reasoning scores. After all, this makes good sense because (1) they share similar test items and (2) they measure more or less the same process, with the only difference that one is in score units and the other is in time units.

Theory of Deductive Reasoning

Types of Deductive Reasoning

Deductive reasoning is the reasoning from the premises to the conclusion. Usually the premises are formed by a general statement and a condition, and the conclusion is a particular statement logically deduced from the premises. Given the truthfulness of the premises, the conclusion is necessarily true according to the rules of inference in logic. Modern set theory gives a mathematical reinterpretation of this Aristotelian logic. For example:

Premise 1 (general statement) :	All men are mortal	All A are B
Premise 2 (condition) :	Aristotle is a man	C is an A
Conclusion	∴ Aristotle is mortal	∴ C is a B

The types of deductive reasoning that psychologists have extensively studied are linear syllogism (A>B, B>C, then A>C), conditional syllogisms (statements of if, then), and categorical syllogisms (statements with all, some, no, not). As pointed out earlier, there is fierce theory competition in each type of deductive reasoning. Moreover, there are also repeated attempts of generalization, such as Sternberg's attempt to extend his transitive-chain theory for categorical syllogism to conditional syllogism on the ground that the latter can be transformed into the former so that the two syllogisms become "structurally isomorphic" (Sternberg, 1985, p. 207).

Issues and Postulates

One interesting, though not surprising, finding is that most subjects in experiments do not know the rules of inference in logic. For example, L. J. Rips and S. L. Marcus (1977) discover that many subjects have faulty reasoning in conditional syllogism, such as the rule of modus tollens, denial of the antecedent, and affirmation of the consequent. There is also faulty reasoning in categorical syllogism among subjects. Woodworth and Sells (1935) propose the "atmosphere hypothesis" to account for such errors; specifically, the premises create certain "atmosphere" that leads to certain faulty reasoning. Another explanation of reasoning behavior has been proposed by Johnson-Laird and Steedman (1978), namely, the mental world model. According to their model, subjects reason by creating an imaginary world with things, entities, people, and so on, that satisfy the premises and by subsequently trying to "see" what conclusion they can draw. Basically, such a theory merely reasserts that subjects tend to thinking in context, in meaning, and in concrete content instead of in abstract structure. When content and context are absent, they will try to create them. On the other hand, Guyote and Sternberg (1981) has proposed a transitive-chain theory with representation of information and combination rules that specify subjects' reasoning procedure in categorical syllogism. Probably it is a simpler heuristic, but more restrictive in application compared with logicians' predicate calculus of quantified proposition. Guyote and Sternberg claim that their theory can account for success and failure (i.e., avoiding or making errors) in performance in categorical syllogism because some terms and forms (e.g., some, not) require more attentional resources and memory capacities than others, where all possible combinations range from 1 pair to 16 pairs of set relations. As a result, more people fail as the number of pairs for comparison increases. To elaborate their theory, Guyote and Sternberg further propose two rules of combination (i.e., forming transitive chains), four stages of transmission, three-tier preference hierarchy, four parameters of information processing, two labels for choice, error indeterminacy, and so on.

A Critique

Does Componential Theory Enhance Our Understanding of Thinking?

Researchers in reasoning are still studying very elementary reasoning processes such as the following in linear syllogism—if A>B,

B>C, which is biggest? By transitive rule a boy at seven or eight can give the right answer, namely A>C. But how does this thinking process take place?

Researchers focus on the processing side of the problem and attempt to isolate various components in the thinking process.   To articulate these components, they bring in a lot of concepts, ideas, and terms that are undefined. Take the example of the study of analogy. Sternberg explains this simple elementary process by at least nine terms, mostly undefined: encode, infer, compare, map, extrapolate, apply, identify, attribute, better. As for categorical syllogism, researchers employ up to 13 parameters (components) to articulate the process. Another example is the above-mentioned problem of linear syllogism. Sternberg's linguistic-spatial mixture theory employs no less than 16 terms, procedures, transformation rules, or principles (see Table 4.1).

Table 4.1
Parameters Employed to Explain Linear Syllogism in Sternberg's Linguistic-Spatial Mixture Theory

Item	Parameters	Nature of Parameters
1	Marked/unmarked continuum	Term
2	Deep-structure proposition	Term
3	Reformulation	Transformation rule
4	Negation	Transformation rule
5	Preferred and nonpreferred seriation	Term
6	Linguistic-spatial transformation	Transformation rule
7	Spatial array	Term
8	Pivot term identification	Procedure
9	Relational tag	Term
10	Distinctiveness principle	Principle
11	Search of array	Procedure
12	Mental traverse	Procedure
13	Congruence	Principle
14	Sharp versus fussy spatial encoding	Transformation rule
15	Premise position	Term
16	Term position	Term

An immediate question that readers are likely to raise is: why use so many complex terms to explain such a simple, at times intuitive, thinking process? Other legitimate questions will probably follow: Does this approach enhance our understanding? How can it be justified? How much progress have we made by working in this direction?

I will try to defend the componential information-processing position as follows. First, it is no sin to solve and explain a simple problem by an array of complex concepts. That is what we do in science. To explain the phenomenon of heat, for example, we have developed the discipline of thermodynamics with laws, principles, and theories. In fact, it is often necessary to explain the innocently simple phenomenon by very complex theories. Second, the components proposed are not empty structures: they are often concepts with high content, deep implications, and vast ramifications. Take the example of Sternberg's linguistic-spatial mixture theory of linear syllogism. It has evidently enabled us to make progress for we have discovered that (1) we use both verbal and spatial strategy, (2) there exist deep-structure propositions, (3) there exists verbal-spatial transformation, (4) negation has to be processed in a particular way, and (5) preferred versus nonpreferred seriation affect performance. In fact, the terms employed are not redundant; they are functional in our approximation of the thinking process in linear syllogism.

The Unanswerable How

The real problem, however, is that some terms are undefined. Some researchers note that the components identified tend to be something like a black box, since labeling something (e.g., inference) does not tell us how it works (Sternberg, 1985, p. 174). This opens the question of the unanswerable how: In analogy, how do we infer? How do we extrapolate? What are the psychological mechanisms behind those process? In linear syllogism, how do we transform linguistic representation into spatial representation? How do we seriate one array with another array? How do we mentally traverse an array? How do we locate a pivot term? How do we put on relational tag? The same questions can be asked in categorical syllogism. It seems that researchers in thinking outline the processes, decompose the processes, measure the processes, describe the processes, but have not yet opened the black box and tell us how the processes work.

How Far Can Mathematical Modeling Be Used to Validate a Theory?

Many researchers in thinking make use of mathematical modeling to validate their theories. Basically what they do is to formulate a theory, say, componential theory of information processing in inductive reasoning with seven performance components, and then design experiments to collect data to validate his theory. Data collected are mostly reaction time measures, which are organized and manipulated by regression analysis (simple and multiple, linear, and nonlinear) to obtain a model of good fit. Regression analysis can help us transform data, discover underlying patterns, and compress information into a regression equation for the best fit. The mathematical tool can lend support to the asserted existence of underlying patterns and theoretical constructs and guide us to the unfolding of the process.

Most of Sternberg's researches and experiments follow this procedure. Data are organized by regression analysis to be fit into a mathematical model. When reading Sternberg's data, readers should be cautioned that they are not raw data, but data transformed and calculated to fit the model. For example, the response component score is *not* a measured value but is estimated as a regression constant in the mathematics model (Sternberg, 1977), with the assumption that response score is constant across different problem types in analogy (Sternberg, 1985, p. 145)!

Despite its scientific appearance, mathematical modeling may not carry us very far. In fact, so long as data collected are not random, there will always be some correlation and patterns. By applying regression analysis on even flimsy patterns, there is still some account of data variance by a regression equation and by implication some explanation by the model (explanation in statistical, not philosophical, sense). At the same time, there is almost always some unexplained variance. After doing all these "scientific experiments" and mathematical calculations, we are still left with the same question of the unanswerable how. It is naive to expect that experiments or mathematical modeling can provide us with all those answers, although sometimes they may give us insight as to where we should look for the problem.

The Problem of Good Fit

Another common characteristic across Sternberg's thinking research is that most of them have high R^2 values. R^2 is the proportion of squared correlation between predicted value and observed data value in the experiment. In inductive reasoning research, Sternberg claims that his proposed theory provides the best fit to the latency data, accounting for .92, .86, .80 of the variance in the schematic-picture, verbal, and geometric group-mean latency data, respectively (1985, p. 144). For another experiment on inductive reasoning (Sternberg & Gardner, 1983), R^2 ranges from .49 to .94 over nine tasks. In studying categorical syllogistic reasoning, Sternberg's transitive-chain model (Guyote & Sternberg, 1981) shows a model fit where R^2 = .92. This gives the impression that Sternberg's theory/model is a close approximation of reality.

As a standard text in statistics tells us, R^2 shows the correlation between predicted value and observed value. That means for each observed data point there is a predicted point predicted by a regression equation. But where does the regression equation come from? In fact, it is derived from the given data and is itself a compressed expression of the data. If the data are relatively uniform, that is, there is small variance among data, the regression equation may fit more closely. Take for example Sternberg's 1983 experiment. Mean response time across nine tasks range from 2.92 to 5.87 seconds. Probably the subjects do not vary much in the latency of summation of the seven components. Variation may be merely in a few decimal points. In order words, R^2 reflects variance of subject performance, and when variance are small, models fit pretty well. This is plausible because Sternberg's subjects are all Yale undergraduates, who represent a homogenous group with similar cognitive and intellectual ability. Seen in this way, good fit is a function of task and subjects and not a criterion for a good theory.

Can We Use Model Fit to Evaluate Theories?

Sternberg has at least tried two times. In evaluating linear syllogism theories, Sternberg (1980) fit data into his mixture theory as well as two other competing theories, linguistic theory and spatial theory. He observes that the median fits (R^2) are .84 for the mixture theory, .60 for linguistic theory, and .58 for spatial theory and thus declares the superiority of his mixture theory over others. By the same logic, Sternberg claims that his transitive-chain model (Guyote & Sternberg, 1981) is far superior to complete-combination model and random-combination model.

Sternberg is not unaware of the difficulties in theory comparison, namely, that some theories have more parameters than others, and that each is conceptualized differently and makes different assumptions. In his words,

The numbers of parameters estimated differed widely across quantified models, an inevitable consequence of the different information processing assumptions the theories make. Thus, the transitive-chain theory involved estimation of seven free parameters; the complete- and random-combination theories involved estimation of 13 free parameters apiece; and the atmosphere and conversion theories each involved estimation of one free parameter. (1985, p. 204)

Yet, Sternberg is confident that meaningful comparison can be made because:

First, our major concern was with comparing the historically important theories in a way that did full justice to the initial conceptualizations, and these conceptualizations differ widely in their complexity and completeness. Second, we always estimated large numbers of data points (at least 100) in comparing theories, thus minimizing the opportunity for capitalization upon chance variation in the data. Third, the fits of the quantified models showed little correspondence to the numbers of parameters in the theories, suggesting that number of parameters was not an important determinant of fit. (1985, p. 204)

I doubt very much the validity of Sternberg's claim and his evaluation procedure. He seems to assume that the three theories in comparison share the same data and that the data in small RT measures can be separated into comparable processing components. But since the three theories use different terms and different components, how can they be compared meaningfully? For example, linguistic theory postulates compression of first premise, end-anchor, long-term memory retrieval, separate storage of two premises, and so on. On the other hand, mixture theory postulates the establishment of congruence option, and spatial theory hypothesizes preferred working direction. It thus sounds improbable that the same set of data can be fit in different models with fundamentally different theoretical constructs and orientations. On the other hand, though we may use different sets of data, how can we establish the comparability among them? Finally, it may be the case that the experiment is designed in terms of mixture theory components, obviously to its favor, making it difficult to measure components of other theories. Theory comparison is possible, but Sternberg's work leaves much to be desired.

Conclusion—What Have We Learned?

(1) Research in reasoning has been making progress. The information processing approach has evidently paid off, as more complex terms and concepts are used to describe and explain simple phenomena. Progress is due more to problem reconceptualization than to the use of mathematics, which merely serves as a supporting and measuring tool. Theory competition has led to the development of more encompassing theories.

(2) Researchers have come closer to the understanding of reasoning, but each component of reasoning (e.g., inference) is still a black box waiting to be unlocked. The decomposing strategy has its limitation and has run its course. More conceptual breakthrough is needed on the question of the unanswerable how. In addition, we seem to need a broader conception and more sophisticated taxonomy of reasoning.

(3) Researchers under the positivist paradigm have encountered numerous problems, for example, random chance, delayed response, inattentiveness in experiment, comparability between data set, and so on. They have overcome these problems by ingenious experimental design and technical advances. How far the positivist paradigm can

carry us remains to be seen. So far we see that some parameters have to be dropped to increase reliability of estimates and some estimated values have been used instead of measured values, both with questionable assumptions.

(4) Theory confirmation remains methodologically unattainable. Despite a ceaseless quest for general theory, it is not easy to make generalization claims. Still researchers should aim to design experiments with higher generality.

In short, researchers have outlined the reasoning process but have not yet opened the black box. With different theories making different assumptions, comparison among them is extremely difficult, if not impossible. At this moment, we are still in need of a better reconceptualization of the problem. Moreover, researchers on reasoning focus too narrowly on reaction time and componential analysis but leave some very basic questions unanswered: What is the nature of thought? How do we think? Do we think in terms of language, concept, images, or a combination of them? What is the role of language in thought, and what are their relations? How do concepts enhance thought? I do not pretend to have all the answers, but I will address some of them in the following sections.

PIAGET ON ADOLESCENT AND FORMAL THOUGHT: A CRITIQUE

Piaget's Experiments

According to Piaget, adolescent thought or formal thought is the final stage of human mental development. To study adolescent thought, Piaget and his colleagues asked their subjects to perform a number of scientific experiments (physics) based on a given problem and some materials. One experiment was designed to study the relationship between the pendulum's frequency of oscillation and length, width, height, and force. Another experiment was designed to study the effect of weights on the bending of rods, based on factors such as material, length, thickness, and cross-section form. These subjects were high school students from Geneva's academically more advanced schools. By observing these youngsters doing experiments and asking them questions on why they performed experiments in such ways, Piaget inferred that their thought processes operated according to two logical models of formal operational thought—the 16 binary operations and INRC group (Piaget & Inhelder, 1958).

Salient Features of Adolescent Thought and Logical Models

The following are some salient features of adolescent thought depicted by Piaget. He observed that younger children at concrete operations would approach the problem unsystematically, for example, comparing a short, light pendulum with a long, heavy pendulum and drawing faulty inference. The adolescent youngsters, however, would plan the experiment systematically, execute the experiments step by step, observe accurately and draw valid conclusions. The adolescents are using a very basic but effective strategy in scientific investigation, varying one variable while holding all other variables constant so as to ascertain the effect of this variable. They would then vary another variable while holding all others constant and systematically observe and record the results. Falsity is taken as nonobserved results. Most important of all, they are able to draw valid conclusions.

Based on such observations, Piaget argued that the adolescent are able to think in terms of all possibilities and reason by hypothesis testing and deduction. They are able to state and discover ideal possibilities, and observation now becomes secondary to reasoning. Piaget called their thinking processes the 16 logical binary operations. He also noted that the adolescent need not know symbolic logic, but symbolic logic depicts the structure of their thought. Piaget further asserted that his logical model can describe the underlying structure of the adolescent's mental activity, as all the thought processes can be translated step by step into his logical model. Thus Piaget is satisfied that his logical model represents the essence of formal thought.

Piaget's 16 Binary Operations as Exhausting Two-factor Relations

Why do Piaget's 16 binary operations so neatly fit adolescent thought? Do they represent the underlying structure of adolescent thought? My interpretation is that it represents the underlying structure of the scientific problems given to the adolescents, not necessarily their thought. Probably Piaget's logical model exhausts all the logically possible relations between two factors and its outcome, such as conjunction, negation, implication, inverse relation, reciprocity, and so on. It should be noted that although the scientific experiments are about multiple factors, these factors are isolated systematically in the study to identify the independent and the dependent variable. Consequently it is about two-factor, or cause-effect relationship. Now Piaget exhausts the logically possible relations between these two factors and comes up with 16 binary operations. In other words, he simply covers everything there is about two-factor relations. (Notice it even includes nonobserved results as falsity.) By covering all logical possibilities of the structure of the problem, Piaget's model necessarily captures and formalizes anything the adolescent have to say on the problem. This explains why all the adolescent thought can be translated into Piaget's logical model.

Narrow in Scope

The question is how far Piaget enhances our understanding of adolescent thought, formal thought, or human thought in general? Supporters such as Neimark (1975) have pointed out that "all of the research reviewed supports the validity of formal operational thought as an empirical phenomenon distinct from concrete operations" (p. 572); (cf. Ginsburg & Opper, 1988, p. 200). While accepting this conclusion tentatively, I have to point out that Piaget's conception of formal thought is much narrower than the spectrum of human thought which we have come to know. First, within the domain of human (adult) thought, there is informal/illogical thought (Kuhn, 1991) as well as formal/logical thought, but Piaget examines only the latter. The former has by now become a vast area for research. Second, within the domain of formal/scientific thought, Piaget focuses only on logical, systematic, and scientific thinking but has neglected the creative aspect of scientific thought. In his experiments, he defines the prototype of a scientific problem such as the pendulum as having only four possible causes (factors) and then tries to discover relations and causes and effects within this narrow definition. Piaget elegantly captures the deduction/inference rules of this narrow problem by his 16 binary operations. But in the real scientific enterprise, creative scientific thought is characterized by a change of the whole perspective, a scientific revolution with a paradigm shift as persuasively argued by Thomas Kuhn (1970). Also, identifying one underlying cause out of nearly infinite causes in a phenomenon is another fascinating characteristic of scientific discovery. Another characteristic is to isolate a few simple principles that underlie the working mechanisms of a complex system (such as Newtonian mechanics). All these are barely touched by Piaget.

Finally, even within the domain of logical scientific thought, Piaget is not as exhaustive as we have been led to think. Notice the adolescents are using one strategy: varying variables one by one while holding others constant. In John Stuart Mill's (1806-1873) methods of experimental inquiry, this renowned philosopher offers five canons for induction of causation: method of agreement, method of difference, joint method of agreement and difference, method of residues, and method of concomitant variations. It looks as if Piaget's scientific experiment is employing only the method of difference. For a fuller description of the thought processes in experimental inquiry, it is necessary to expand Piaget's 16 binary operations substantively to cover all of Mill's canons of induction as well as more recent conceptions on the subject.

Piaget's "Privileged" Subjects

Finally, I want to point out a puzzling aspect of Piaget's findings. Ample evidence has shown that even many college undergraduates tend to reason illogically (Rips & Marcus, 1977; Taplin, 1971; Staudenmayer, 1975; Wason & Johnson-Laird, 1972). Piaget's high school subjects must be very well-developed in their logical thinking for scientific experimentation. It leads even to the speculation that Piaget's high school subjects must be very well trained in the form and structure of the scientific problem they are required to handle so that they are able to reason so effectively and plan the experiment so systematically. Even Piaget himself has pointed out that "we cannot generalize to all subjects the correlation of our research which was, perhaps, based on a somewhat privileged population" (Ginsburg & Opper, 1988, p. 203). Another reason what U.S. college undergraduates fail in logical reasoning and Geneva high school subjects succeed is that there is a human tendency to think on content rather than abstract structure. It is thus reasonable to explain that Geneva high school students do better than U.S. college undergraduates because the latter are given artificial and abstract problems while the former are given realistic and practical ones.

THE CO-EVOLUTION OF LANGUAGE AND THOUGHT

In the foregoing sections reviewing the state of the art in thinking and Piagetian theory, I find that most researchers tend to neglect the central role played by language and concept in thought. My contention is that language gives enormous power to thought, and the interaction between the symbolic world (language) and mental world has elevated thought to a high plateau. Now let me examine in greater depth the coevolution between language and thought.

Two Contrasting Positions on Language and Thought

The relationship between language and thought is a complex one. Basically there are two contrasting positions. The first is that language directs thought. Proponents argues that language guides or even shapes thought. Benjamin Whorf (1956) argued that different cultures have different languages which emphasize different aspects of reality. For example, the Eskimos have 60 words for snow, but the English have only one. Thus a language causes the speakers to perceive and to think about the world differently. Moreover, without language, how can we talk in an abstract way, or how can we express our thoughts? Therefore language guides and directs thought.

The other position is that thought directs language. This opposing view just argues the other way round. Language merely reflects our thought. Since we are capable of thinking in an abstract way, we conceptualize our ideas and express them in language. Eleanor Rosch (1973) points out that the Dani and English speakers classify focal color in much the same way. In other words, we perceive (or think of) color in more or less the same way but only express it differently in language. Given our similar cognitive structure, perceiving apparatus, and the existence of a stable uniform reality, it is natural that we think in more or less the same way. Another evidence is from word order. When we think about an event, we usually start from an agent (the subject) that takes an action (verb), with effect on an object. This thinking structure is captured by and reflected in most natural languages, which almost invariably take either the subject-verb-object or subject-object-verb word order. In other words, our thinking directs and structures our language (Anderson, 1990, p. 345).

It is not easy to decide which side is correct. However, I wish to point out that neither has conclusive evidence. For example, Whorf merely shows that language causes speakers to see and classify snow differently, but this is only at a perceptual and visual discrimination level. It can never prove that people in different culture think differently at a conceptual level with different logic. Even if we can prove this, we still have to explain how this is caused by language because it may be caused by other factors as well. Similarly Rosch's study of color is at a perceptual, not a conceptual level. Finally, if thought matches langauge on word order, it cannot serve as evidence for either position, because it may be merely due to a third factor, the existence of reality that both language and thought correspond upon. In other words, it may be the case that both language and thought correspond with reality, giving the impression that they match with each other.

The Relative Independence of Thought and Overlap with Language

But I wish to point out that there are overwhelming evidences that thought can exist independent of and without language. The following are some important findings of this century:

1. Lower species such as the ape (Köhler, 1927) were able to "think" and solve problems although it possesses no language.
2. S. M. Smith et al. (1947) demonstrate that thought is not subvocal speech. Thought is an internal, non-motor activity.
3. Thought in the form of memory exists as an internal propositional network with nonverbal, semantic representation (Rumelhart & Norman, 1975).
4. Reasoning (thinking) can be carried out without language, as evidenced by nonverbal reasoning tests. Roger Shepherd and Jacquline Metzler's (1971) mental rotation is a classic example of mental operation (reasoning) without language.

Thus, it is possible that thinking can be carried out without the use of language. In other words, thought can exist independent of and without language. Moreover, in my view, language and thought are not identical entities. Rather they overlap with each other, so that thought can be carried out with as well as without the medium of language. When thought is carried out without the medium of language, let me call it rudimentary thought. When thought is carried out through the medium of language, let me call it conceptual thought.

Rudimentary Thought

What is rudimentary thought like? How does thought without language operate? As stated earlier, without language we probably may still be able to think, but in great difficulty and hindrance. We can still have mental operations such as rotating an object, noticing some special features, changing visual/ spatial position, but we cannot give names to objects, or articulate features, directions, relative positions, and so forth. As we shall see, such rudimentary thought in prelinguistic stage is capable of certain problem-solving activities.

Prototypical Image and Manipulation

I postulate that the capacity of rudimentary thought is not unique in humans but is shared by lower species such as the ape. I further postulate that rudimentary thought operates on prototypical images, which are not just an exact copy of the physical object. Rather, the ape or early humans have encountered many instances of similar physical objects, such as stones, rods, apples, and have created a generalized, "prototypical" image of these objects. Thus a prototypical image is already generalized from many similar physical instances, and it represents the physical object itself. I further postulate that these prototypical images are mainly about objects and actions and that they are mostly visual images. In other words, a prototypical image is not just a reflection or faithful copy of the physical object, but a generalized image of it. Prototypical image carries the major characteristics of the physical object, but is already a mental representation distilled from perceptual experience of many physical objects. An auditory image can also be prototypical; it is not a copy of a physical object or action but is part of an associative network related to many other objects and actions.

In this prelinguistic stage, we still possess some cognitive/thinking abilities for problem solving. We can form visual images of objects, and even manipulate this visual image, such as mental rotation. Most important of all, we can create prototypical images of objects and manipulate them. By visually imagining and visually manipulating objects, we can do some problem solving. This can be achieved because a prototypical image, while originating from physical objects, is not just a static copy of the physical object. It is a mental construct so flexible that it can be manipulated: lengthened, shortened, changed, moved from position to position by our imagination. So long as we are capable of performing mental operation (thinking) on manipulating our visual image, we are able to do some problem solving. For example, in Köhler's ape, it may be able to imagine a rod that is lengthened and expanded to touch an object. With this imagined image, it may help the ape to move toward the goal by searching for a longer rod to do the job.

Thought must operate on some content, without which it cannot exist, while memory is the storage of content. Given the existence of long-term memory, we can postulate the ability of free association and random recall in rudimentary thought. By recalling from long-term memory, we can form many prototypical images of objects and actions; then we can manipulate and operate on them. Also, we can recall that we have solved the problem in a similar way before. We can recall the steps and actions we have taken. Based on this retrieval, we apply it in another situation. In other words, we may retain a prototypical solution in our long-term memory and retrieve it to solve immediate problems.

Anchoring Rudimentary Thought on Objects and Actions

Rudimentary thought is already a very rich mental operation with a lot of prototypical images of objects and actions. In other words, rudimentary thought is anchored on prototypical images which are further anchored on objects. In Köhler's experiment with apes,

He showed by precise experimental analysis that the success of the animals' actions depended on whether they could see all the elements of a situation simultaneously—this was a decisive factor in their behavior. If, especially during the earlier experiments, the stick they used to reach some fruit lying beyond the bars was moved slightly, so that the tool (stick) and the goal (fruit) were not visible to them at one glance, the solution of the problem became very difficult, often impossible . . . Köhler considers the actual visual presence of a sufficiently simple situation an indispensable condition in any investigation of the intellect of chimpanzee's, a condition without which their intellect cannot be made to function at all; he concludes that the inherent limitations of imagery (or "ideation") are a basic feature of the chimpanzee's intellectual behavior. (Vygotsky, 1986, pp. 73-74)

In other words, rudimentary thought is very much dependent on the visual presence of physical objects. Without physical objects entering the visual field of Köhler's ape, rudimentary thought would probably not be triggered to perform a problem solving behavior. It seems rudimentary thought is a passive way of problem solving depending heavily on the presence of visual clues. Also, rudimentary thought is limited to operation on physical objects and actions.

The Limits of Rudimentary Thought

Without language, our rudimentary thought can still have mental representation, and the prototypical image of many objects and actions, such as cat, dog, rod, hit, jump, run, and so on. But what is lacking is concepts such as longness and shortness. These higher-order concepts are not about physical objects or actions themselves, but are relations between objects and qualities extracted from generalization of objects. Thus we can see a rod but not longness, which is an abstract quality. In fact, these concepts do not rest on objects themselves but in our understanding of objects. These concepts cannot be operative without the use of language. In rudimentary thought, that is, thought without language, we can only handle problem solving of physical instances by representing them in prototypical images, then manipulating and imagining them. Conceptual problem-solving activities are out of the question.

The Advent of Language and the Advantage of Conceptual Problem Solving

With the advent of language growth in concepts is possible. With concepts we can talk in a very general way. We are no more bound by the immediate physical event but can apply concepts to express deeper relations between objects and actions and have deeper understanding of how to solve problems.

Let me illustrate how problem solving by concept is much more efficient than problem solving by rudimentary thought. Let me go back to the Kohler's ape experiment. To solve the problem by rudimentary thought, the speechless ape has to form a prototypical image (visual image) of the stick. Then it has to manipulate the visual image in many possible ways. Only one way, lengthening the prototypical image of the stick, is instrumental to solving the problem. Then the ape realizes that it can abandon the short stick and search for a long stick to get food. Imagine a young boy doing the same experiment. He may exclaim and say to himself, "The stick is too short to get the food. Let me get a longer one." Notice even in this speech a mean-end relation (short stick and get food) has already been established. A solution is immediately made transparent by using abstract concepts such as longness and shortness.

When rudimentary thought and conceptual thought (thinking in concepts) are compared, it is obvious that the former is much slower than the latter. For rudimentary thought to operate, a prototypical image has to be formed first, and then the image has to be transformed/manipulated to match the solution. For conceptual thought, the process is much faster, and the solution is immediately made transparent. By using language, we can skip the steps of visual image and its manipulation, go immediately to thinking through concepts. We can think by jumping from concept to concept. Thus it is a much more efficient way of problem solving.

How Language Transforms Thought

It is no exaggeration that language transforms the nature of thinking. Formerly we may possess rudimentary thought, and we think by imagining and manipulating prototypical images. With the advent of language, we begin to think through the medium of language, jumping from concepts to concepts. Since concepts are higher-order mental constructs expressing multirelations, richer understanding of the situation is made available to us. Since concepts are also condensed ideas, a lot more ideas are available to our manipulation at the same time. In theory, an infinite number of concepts can be created to enhance our thinking. Abstract thinking now becomes possible, thanks to language.

Thinking through language and concepts is a more efficient way of thinking. It now becomes the dominant mode of thinking. Consider the case that when we think, we speak to ourselves internally through the medium of language. Also in many psychological experiments in thinking, subjects are required to verbalize aloud their thinking processes. In fact, verbalizing thought helps to clarify thought. Language has clarified and verbalized thought, and now thought can be made explicit through language.

Language also transforms thought by anchoring it. It is characteristic of conceptual thought that a thought jumps from concept to concept. Since conceptual thought is so abstract, they have to be anchored, remembered, and applied in mental operation. Language is the vehicle to anchor those abstract thoughts. Without language to anchor them, it is doubtful if we could reach this level of abstraction. Even if we can have a vague thought of cause and effect, the fleeting thought may move so fast that it is impossible to pin it down, capture it and operate on it. Thus language may help to slow down thought and anchor thought in concepts so that we can operate on it.

With the advent of language, we go beyond prototypical images and create a lot of concepts. With more general concepts, we are better equipped to describe reality: we can describe more dimensions of reality, we can see deeper relations and have richer understanding of reality. We are no more bound by the unique, the here and now, but represent reality with general concepts whose implications are generalizable to various situations. It even changes our perspective of the world into an orderly world. In other words, language gives order to reality, and now our thoughts can operate on an orderly reality.

How Thought Transforms Language

In the co-evolution of language and thought, it is not only the case that language transforms thought; it is also the case that thought transforms language, as shown in the following analysis. Consider the following sentence structures in the English language:

(1)   If <u>a</u>, then <u>b</u>   (condition)

(2)   <u>a</u> lead to <u>b</u>   (cause and effect)

(3)   <u>a</u> so as to <u>b</u>   (reason).

These are examples of the abstract structures of language that express thought. In those cases, language already embodies thought. Language as we now know it today has evolved with many structures that facilitate thought. It is so natural now that we think in terms of those language structures. But the question is: where do those thinking structures come from? They do not come from language itself because in describing reality language need not evolve those abstract structures. Rather, these thinking structures may come from our thought. We think in terms of cause and effect, condition, reason, and so on, and we create those linguistic terms to represent our thought. Our language has evolved in such a way that it is prepackaged with a lot of thinking tools and thinking structures. Thought has transformed language in such a way that our thinking structures have been incorporated, represented, and manifested in language. In other words, our language today is not only a descriptive language but also a thinking language. Our language today is probably different from some early primitive languages that incorporated fewer thinking structures.

Language is a very powerful tool for communication, expression, and argumentation. But it is after all just a tool. Underlying language is meaning, and meaning or ideas originate from thought. Thought is expressed in this language tool, and in the process thought sharpens, improves, and transforms that tool. Remember an occasion you have a thought but cannot think of a right word for it. Maybe there is no such right word in our vocabulary, and you may have to invent it. This is a typical case of thought creating language. In every domain of intellectual inquiry, we create new terms, concepts, or even an entirely new vocabulary to represent our thought. The case is that the cutting edge of thought keeps expanding our language horizons and creating new concepts to represent newly discovered phenomenon or reality. In this sense, thought is constantly shaping and improving our language.

Karl Buhler (1934) postulates that language has three functions: expressive function, signaling function, and descriptive function. Karl Popper (1972) further elaborates it and adds yet another function, namely, argumentative function. It is now clear that human thought is the pivotal force transforming human language from lower to higher functions. This is because if our thought had not grown to a point that there is a need to describe reality and to argue for its validity, there would not have been a corresponding development in language for those higher functions. To describe and to argue implies to think in a conceptual way, and to think implies that there must be some mental content. It is this thinking process in a conceptual way with mental content that elevates human language to higher functions unparalleled among other species.

THE NATURE, FUNCTION, AND TYPOLOGY OF CONCEPTS

The most significant consequence of the interaction between the symbolic world (language) and the mental world is the emergence of conceptual thought. With the advent of language and the symbolic world, the private mental world has undergone qualitative change. First, although it remains private, it can be made public. Second, a mental event is no longer seen as a single unique instance but is to be expressed in langage through the use of concepts. Mental events are no more just perception and sensation but are expressed in concepts.

The Nature of Concepts

Concept as Generalized Category

A concept is a mental construct to denote a class of physical or nonphysical occurance or reality. For example, a mouse denotes not only that single mouse but the class of small dark, furry animals. Also a stone denotes not only that single stone but the class of solid nonmetallic mineral matter. In other words, a concept is a generalized category denoting a general case instead of a particular case. In the English language, all the common nouns and verbs are generalized categories. In fact, our language is full of such generalized categories.

Understanding Through Concepts

Language, concepts, and ideas are nonspatial and nonphysical. They are just mental representation; their essence lies in their meaning. They are important because they help us to understand the world, both its physical and nonphysical aspects. What is surprisingly counterintuitive is that we understand physical objects by highly abstract concepts. Concepts are the product of language and thought: they are mental constructs. In other words, we understand the physical by the mental. For example, we humans understand the physical apple by means of a lot of mental constructs, such as shape, size, weight, color, and so on. But for lower animals such as a monkey, or for an infant, understanding is achieved by action. Their understanding of an apple is limited to the direct experience of holding it and eating it. What a monkey "understands" about an apple is far more partial and superficial than what we do. Moreover, through abstract concepts we begin to understand the nonphysical aspects of the world, such as relations between objects, number concepts, causality, and so on. All these are unattainable without concepts. In other words, concepts or mental constructs have carried us a long way in our understanding of the world around us and have shaped our way of knowing it.

How do all these concepts come into being? How do they grow? Do lower animals have primitive concepts? Why have they been unable to develop intelligence? To answer this question, let me try to briefly compare the human species with lower animals in terms of their mental events. Our question may be reformulated as follows: Do lower animals have mental events? This philosophical question can be recast into a scientific one, namely, a question to be answered empirically by ethnologists broken down as follows:

(1)   Do dogs have visual sensation?

(2)   Do dogs have olfactory sensation?

(3)   Do dogs have color sensation?

(4)   Do dogs have "sensation-of-red," an instance of color sensation that is an instance of mental occurrences?

The answer is a qualified yes, though in a very broad and rudimentary sense. Note that a dog's olfactory sensation is much better developed than humans. In a well documented book on animal thought, an animal psychologist concludes that mental organization and awareness occur in animals without the involvement of language (Walker, 1985, p. xiii). Animals surely have sensations and rudimentary mental occurrences, but if mental events stand for higher-order mental representation that calls for the use of language and concepts, then the dualist is right to insist that it is unique in humans.

Characteristics of Concepts

If sensation is a vague and passive form of knowing, concepts are active reconstruction of the external world and a strong and clear form of knowing. A concept possesses the following characteristics:

First, a concept is a mental construct and is more than a mental image. Remember that a mental image such as a visual image or an auditory image is just a faithful copy of reality. A concept is a mental construct in the sense that it is constructed in the human mind to represent reality, but it is not a copy of reality. For example, the concept of table is not the copy of any particular table but a generic instance of a prototypical table. Since it is just an idea and not a fixed copy of a real thing, it is very flexible and can readily be changed. Also it has a wide range of applicability to any imaginable situation.

Second, a concept is formed in a network of related concepts. For example, the concept of table has a family of related concepts such as flat surface, certain minimum size, degree of hardness, functional use (such as putting things on it and setting people around it), and so on. In other words, a concept is definable in terms of a family of related concepts.

Third, concepts and categories have different levels. At the most elementary level, we use a term (category) to denote an instance of occurrence, such as a stone to denote solid nonmetallic mineral matter. Then these categories can be grouped for the representation of a higher-order concept, and higher-order concepts can again be grouped for representation of still higher-order concepts, ad infinitum. For example, mouse, cat, horse, and so on can be grouped under the concept of animals. Look, find, and examine can be grouped under the concept of search; spears, stones, arrows can be grouped under the concept of tools. These second-order concepts—animal, search, tools—can be grouped under the third-order concept of hunting and so on.

Mental Representation and Concepts

I have talked in some detail about mental events, mental representation, mental constructs, mental images as well as concepts. At this juncture, let me clarify their relations using Figure 4.3.

Mental Events and Mental Constructs

Mental representation is a very broad term for any nonphysical representation of either physical entities (such as table, cup) or abstract entities (such as length, family). Mental representation comes in two broad categories, mental events and mental constructs. The two are different in

Figure 4.3
Types of Mental Representation

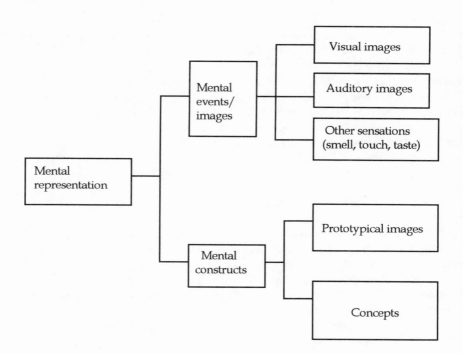

their ways of knowing. Mental events are a relatively passive way of knowing while mental constructs are a more active way of knowing. Mental events are sequences of happenings that are processed in our visual, auditory, and other modalities. We can liken mental events to the replay of a videotape. A visual image is like a frame of a videotape while an auditory image is a string of utterances or sequence of sounds. Generally, a mental event (visual or auditory image) is not an exact copy of physical reality. Instead we process the physical event by selecting salient features from it and retaining them as visual/auditory images.   Naturally, there is simplification in this selection process, as we select what is relevant to usand what interests us.   Quite often what we retain as visual image is a simplified version of the physical event. As for auditory image, we retain the semantic rather than phonological version of the event. In short, these visual images and auditory images are simplified reflection of the physical event.   Other sensations such as smell, touch, taste, pain are all mental events, but they are less important to our thinking process.

Mental constructs are different from mental events in that they are creations/products of the human mind. Unlike mental events, they are not reflection of the physical reality; nor are they simplified versions of physical reality. Rather they are constructed by the human mind to represent ideas or reality. They come in two types, prototypical images, and concepts.

Prototypical Images and Concepts

Here I have to postulate the existence of the human mind's ability to generalize from similar experiences and to extract common features from them. Take the example of a book. Suppose a child encounters a few different books at different locations (e.g., at school, at bedtime, at the library).   Her ability to generalize from similar experiences and extract common features will lead to the creation of a prototypical image of a book. This prototypical image is a generalized image. It is not about any specific book or a visual image of any booklike physical object but the prototypical image of it. It is not a reflection of any physical object but an abstract image of it. It is an active construction to represent external objects. They are mostly about objects and actions.

Apart from prototypical images of physical objects (such as book, apple, etc.) and actions (such as jump, run, eat), concepts are also mental constructs.   As generalized categories, concepts are nonspatial and are defined in terms of certain salient abstract features. Take the concept of a book. It has salient abstract features such as thickness, size limits, front and back cover, printed ink, and so on. They are mental constructs, and their meaning lies within a network of related concepts. Apart from representing physical objects, concepts can represent abstract ideas that do not correspond with any physical instances. Take the example of the number concept. It is not an attribute of any object, but a result of counting objects. Take again the example of size (big or small). It is not an attribute inherent in an object, but the result of a comparison between two or more objects. All concepts are constructed by the human mind for a richer representation of reality. A concept is the product of interaction between language and thought.

Progression from Visual Images, Prototypical Images to Concepts

There seems to be a progression from mental events to mental constructs, or, more specifically, from visual/auditory images to prototypical images to concepts. Let me illustrate their difference and progression.

Take the example of a dog. Suppose this is the first time you see a dog and hear it bark. Now close your eyes so that no other visual image enters your visual field. You may form a vague visual/auditory image of the dog: your visual image is about its physical characteristics and is naturally a simplified version of the dog. Moreover, your visual/auditory image is a mental representation of one single event, that is, the dog you have just seen, and a simplified copy of it.

Higher up in the progression is the prototypical image. Here you have had encounters at different times and places with dogs of different size and race. Your generalization ability helps you to organize your perceptual experience of dogs into a single unified prototypical image of it: it is a construct from your experience, and the outcome is a visual image not reflecting any specific dog, but representing a general case with major common characteristics shared by all dogs: a head, a tail, a body, four legs, a protruding mouth, and so on. The auditory image is also a generalized case of string of barking sounds. As I argued earlier, prototypical image is a construct mainly about objects and actions. It is very instrumental to the operation of rudimentary thought. Thus the fine difference between visual image and prototypical image is that the former is just a simplified reflection of a single event, but the later is a mental construct derived from the generalization of many similar experience and events.

Still higher up is the stage of concepts. Now think about the concept or idea of a dog. What do you come up with? I think there are two aspects, the commonsense idea and the formal abstract concept. The commonsense idea of a dog flashes in your mind: Unlike visual image or prototypical image, it is nonvisual, nonaural, nonimagistic; first, it is a name tap of an object named dog, and then the idea is immediately spread/activated to a family of related concepts and experience: you have played with one, you have been bitten by one, a small dachshund is cute, and so on. Notice all along that it is the association from idea to idea, no visual image. The formal abstract concept of a dog refers to the defining attributes of the dog: its physical appearance, its race and species, biological characteristics, and so on. In neither case do you need to visualize an image of a dog. In fact the visual image of a dog need not even surface in our consciousness when we conceptually talk about dogs. The main point is that a concept is nonimagistic. It is ideational and semantic. It is a higher-order mental construct. It goes beyond our visual understanding of the world and leads us to a stage of conceptual understanding of the world in which understanding is achieved by the representation and configuration of ideas.

The Power and Function of Concepts

Improving Our Way of Knowing

With the advent of concepts our way of knowing has undergone a qualitative change. Formerly, for lower animals, the most basic way of knowing is recognition and recall. For example, a dog is said to "know" its master by recognition of him/her through its visual, auditory, and olfactory sensations. The problem with this primitive way of knowing is that it can only apply to physical objects. You cannot know anything beyond the physical, such as relations between objects, relations between relations. If sensation is a vague and passive form of knowing, concept is an active reconstruction of the external world and a strong and clear form of knowing. Through concepts, we can know not only physical objects but also more abstract relations and ideas. For example, humans are now capable of understanding the concept of "family." A family is the members of a social group belonging to the same kinship: they live together, they have specified relations, they play different roles, they can be considered as a whole unit. Notice that the concept of "family" entails a lot of abstract ideas (role, live, belong) and relations. Yet we are capable of understanding it without much difficulty. To conclude, knowing through concept is a qualitatively more advanced way of knowing than knowing by recognition and recall.

Breaking Up and Ordering Reality

Let me explain how concepts break up reality. The reality, or physical/phenomenal world we live in can be viewed as a totality superimposed with sequence of events. The phenomenal world is continuous and eventful, everything is unique and is available to our immediate experience. Suppose there is a girl out there eating an apple. The phenomenal world would be a discrete instance of one female person, putting one red round object called "apple" into her mouth, which is a unique event occupying a sequence of a few minutes at a particular location. By using concepts to describe this event, we simply say:

That girl is eating an apple.

Notice we are using categories to describe the situation. We are using generalized terms to describe a unique event. "Girl," "eating," "apple" are all concepts. They are not about this single girl, this single apple, that single act of eating, but about a general case of girls eating apples. If at another time and place another girl is doing the same thing, we can use the same sentence to describe it again. We need not take every instance of occurrence as a new and unique experience, but can group similar experience and express them in concepts. As a result, concepts reduce our mental load; they help us organize the unique world into an orderly world, unify repetitive experience into intelligible representation, and extract certain properties and dimensions from the world for our attention. As a corollary, we ignore other aspects of the reality: we break up the total reality by extracting only a few dimensions for our attention. We order the reality by concepts (Schultz, 1932). Our limited cognitive resources dictate that we cannot see everything all at once through their spatial temporality. By using concepts we can extract certain properties of reality for our attention. We can express a certain aspect of reality through categories and constructs, thus going beyond the unique, the here and now, and the ostensible, immediate reality. We are no more "submerged" in a "total reality," but live in an "orderly" reality, where the order is given, represented, and articulated in concepts.

Accumulation of Knowledge

Why are concepts so powerful? It is because they revolutionize our relations with the physical world. Formerly we lived in the physical world and acted on it by primitive instinctual behavior and response. We had some rudimentary thought and problem solving abilities, but they were primitive, private, and could not be shared by others or passed down to the next generation. Probably only the more gifted members of the species could use thoughts, but could not "tell" others. Now with concepts we suddenly begin to understand the physical world. We see through the physical world with the lens of our symbolic world—we invent concepts and categories to see the physical world. Put it another way, we create language, concepts, and categories to understand the world. By creating concepts to sharpen our understanding of the world, we are able to share at the same time these concepts and knowledge through our language. Thus knowledge becomes accumulative through the objectification of concepts and thoughts. Now with our ever-accumulating understanding of the patterns of regularities of the physical world we become detached from it and begin to work toward gaining more control over it.

Naming and Updating Experience

One function of concepts is to give names to our abstract experience and entities. Feelings such as fear, anger, hatred, excitement can be expressed by concepts. Linguists discover "performatory verbs" such as command, promise, agree, refuse, and so on, which are words to describe the relations of human communicative interaction. They are abstract entities that were given names to facilitate our understanding. Another function of concept is that it guides us to see and express relations between things and us and relations between things themselves. Existential concepts (no more, gone), spatial concepts (here, up, down, in, on), reoccurrence (more), negation (no, not, don't) are very abstract but fundamental concepts to express relations: surprisingly they are mastered by infants 18 months of age.

Concepts by themselves are static entities expressive of the physical world or mental state. Because of the flexibility of language, the concepts we form can constantly be updated, reformulated, and reconstructed. A static concept, when applied to the understanding of the physical world, may turn out to be incomplete. Take our example of hunting. It has three concepts: animals, search, tools. It has left out the concepts of catch and kill. But even more important is that it has left out cooperation. Note that hunting is a cooperative effort and cooperation is a much higher-order concept than just catch and kill. By constantly reflecting on what we do and reflecting on what reality is, we are able to constantly update and improve our concepts to better approximation of reality and improvement on what we are capable of doing.

A Typology of Concepts

So, is there one kind of concepts, or are there many kinds, and how are they organized? The standard point of departure for this issue is from philosophy, where Saul Kripke (1972), Hilary Putnam (1975), and Willard V. O. Quine (1977) studied natural kinds (natural entities such as lemons, tigers, trees), while S. P. Schwartz (1980) studied nominal kinds (entities in existence only by pure definitions, such as circles, triangles). Later, psychologist Robert Sternberg (1982) suggests that there are three kinds: natural, unnatural, and supernatural concepts. Ellen Markman (1989) proposes a concept continuum that ranges from natural kind categories (natural objects such as "rabbits," "trees") to highly arbitrary categories (terms to describe objects such as "yellow," "tall"). In the same vein, Frank Keil proposes a natural–nominal continuum with biological kinds (lions, dogs), artifacts (cars, pencils), social nominal kinds (uncles, news), and one-criterion terms (circles, odd numbers) (1989, p. 56). As for levels of classification, Eleanor Rosch and her associates (1976) distinguishes three levels of categorization: the basic level (chair), the superordinate level (furniture), and the subordinate level (armchair, rocking chair, sitting chair). L. W. Barsalou (1983) further argues that the superordinate level is an ad hoc category implicitly represented and less accessible in memory. So far researchers seem to have neglected argumentative, spatial-temporal, and affective concepts.

I argued earlier that concepts exist in different levels. I also wish to point out there are many different types of concepts. Concepts are the product of language and thought for the purpose of description and argumentation. The most basic and primitive concept is probably the naming of objects and actions. By using our capacity to think, we expand the domain of concepts from the mere naming of objects and actions to higher levels and richer scope of representation, creating concepts of almost any imaginable kind. There are at least seven types of concepts.

Object and Action Concept

This is probably the most basic type of concepts. This type represents physical objects (such as apple, ball, rod) and physical actions (such as eat, run, hit). They are physical and concrete by nature. Thus they are mastered very early in an infant's life, as the baby begins to understand the world by touching and acting on objects. While objects and actions are different in nature, they are both very elementary in our early understanding of the world. In fact, the ability to name objects and actions begins very early in an infant at his/her single word utterance stage about 12 months old (Bloom, 1973). In the beginning, naming is just to give a name tag to an object or action. It is just an abitrary name, a verbal representation. But as a child's understanding of an objects or actions increase, the name not only represents the object but also his/her experience of it. Finally, the name becomes a concept to represent the physical attributes (e.g., size, length, appearance) of an object within a family of related concepts (e.g., apple is related to the concept of red, round, edible and so on).

Quality Concept

These concepts come in two classes: quality concepts descriptive of physical attributes and quality concepts descriptive of mental states. The former are represented in words such as long/short, big/small, hot/cold, while the latter are represented in words such as happy, angry, need, wish.

Notice that these quality concepts are much more abstract than concepts of naming objects and actions. For example, from physical instances of rods we can generalize and create the concept of a rod. Now from these physical instances of rods we can also extract and generalize attributes and qualities such as hardness, length, and so on. These concepts are not attributes exclusive of a rod itself but are attributes descriptive of many objects in general. Hardness is a concept generalized from many different objects such as rod, stone, tree, and so on. They are much more abstract than the rod itself and are higher-order abstract concepts. Also they are relational concepts. Consider the concept of long and short: a rod is long only in comparison with a rod that is short. They are relational concepts and are meaningful only when making comparsion between objects.

Quantity Concept

These are number concepts such as the natural number, quantities such as no, none, all, or expression for comparison: more, less, least. They are what Piaget called logico-mathematical knowledge. Piaget is quite correct to point out that this high-order abstraction is much removed from physical experience. Quantity concept does not come from the objects themselves. It comes for the human mental activity of discovering abstract relations such as correspondence, identity, equivalence, class, and so on.

Classification Concept

This type can be best illustrated by Table 4.2. Note that only the last row in the table can exist in the physical world, thus apple, eel, compass are real objects. Beyond that, they are just classification concepts. Point at an apple and you can call it a fruit, some food, and an object, depending on your level of abstraction. These classification concepts enable us to express different aspects of the world at different levels of abstraction.

Non-Physical Concept

In contrast to object and action concepts which are physical and highly concrete by nature, there exist lots of constructs that are nonphysical and nonconcrete. These nonphysical concepts can be grouped in two subtypes: entities and performance: the former corresponds to objects and the latter to action. Nonphysical entities are those constructs that express symbolic relations on artifact, such as family, money, component, motion. Non-physical performance concepts are action and description such as permit, agree, formulate, guide, and so on, which are performative words in speech acts.

Table 4.2
Three Levels of Classification Concept

Third level classification ↑	object	living organism	direction
	↑	↑	↑
Second level classification ↑	food	marine life	north
	↑	↑	↑
First level classification ↑	fruit	fish	instrument
	↑	↑	↑
Physcial object	apple	eel	compass

Spatial-Temporal Concept

Every person lives in a spatial-temporal zone. Concepts are thus created to represent this fundamental human condition. Basically spatial concept denotes direction, location, position within a three-dimensional space, such as north, south, left, right, front, back, up, down, on, in. It also includes relative proximity denotation such as near, far, close, distant, and so on. Temporal concepts are time-reference points (such as morning, noon, evening) as well as duration (such as hours, intervals, season). There are also relational temporal concepts such as before, after, sudden, simultaneously, and so on.

Argumentative Concept

Our language structure quite often reflects our thinking and argumentative structure. For example, our language of If-then reflects a thinking structure of conditional reasoning. In fact, language itself has captured many of these thinking structures that I classify as argumentative concepts, such as "so as to" (mean-end), "lead to" (cause-effect), "but" (counterargument), "while" (constrast), "for" (reason), and so on. Also, question openers such as why, what, how, would initiate a thinking process and can be viewed as a derivative of argumentative concept.

THE NATURE OF CONCEPTUAL THOUGHT

Thinking is such a natural phenomenon for the human species that it often escapes our attention. It seems not an easy task to pin down or define such a natural phenomenon. Philosopher William James proposed the seductive notion of stream of consciousness (James, 1890), while John Dewey identified four types of thinking—thought streaming, scenario thinking, belief thinking, and reflective thinking (Dewey, 1933). Contemporary researchers tend to define thinking in term of a group of diverse mental activities such as problem solving, deduction, induction, classification, hypotheses formation and testing, inference, and so on (Johnson-Laird & Wason, 1977). Others try to define thinking in terms of concept and language (Shweder, 1977; Rosch, 1973). The first approach eschews the problem of the nature of thinking and how a unifying thought process underlines various mental activities. The second approach is unwarranted because it presupposes that the essence of thought is language. In the tradition of Dewey and Bruner, and under the influence of Kahneman and Tversky, Jonathan Baron (1985) proposes a prescriptive model of "rational thinking," which he takes as the major dispositional components of intelligence (1986). For Baron, rational choices and plans under the scheme of decision-theoretic analysis will lead to intelligent decision and action. Obviously the subject of human thought is so broad and complex that it requires the writing of another book. I will only focus on the modes and scope of conceptual thought here.

Modes of Conceptual Thought

Bruner (1984) suggested there are two modes of thought: narrative and paradigmatic. Narrative mode of thought refers to storytelling, drama, myths, and so on for the depiction of human situation focusing on values of good or evil. Paradigmatic mode of thought refers to formal thought of reasoning that requires verification, proof, argument, and so on with truth as criterion. To these I would add a third, imaginative mode of thought which has some transitory relationship between the two.

Narratization

Narratization if a very elementary mode of thought. Basically it is the presentation of sequence of events in an orderly manner. Narratization implies the clear grasp of objects and action concept, the ability to name objects and action, and the understanding of relations between objects and action. In order to narratize, a person must also master some simple narratizing structure such of sequencing (e.g., first, then, next, later, etc.), development (e.g., and so he becomes, changes to, etc.), object-action pivotors (e.g., by, in, on, etc.) Moreover, narratization usually includes description, that is, outlining salient features of subjects, objects, and events, specifying attributes and characteristics, and so on. The description must be done in an orderly, consistent, and coherent manner, indicating that the thought is also organized and systematic. Since the subject of narratization is not only on objects, actions, and events but also on our relations with them, the success of narratization depends on the abstract understanding of human relations and the ability to use concepts to describe them.

Narratization seems to be a more primitive mode of thought. Young you have a natural thirst for stories. They enjoy listening to stories and can learn through stories. Human oral culture before the invention of writing is mostly in the form of narratization. Narratization is largely a more concrete and empirical mode of thought, with most of the description and narratization done in physical and concrete terms. However, narratization can also be in metaphors which exploit the similarity and difference between concepts, thus widening our scope of conception.

Imagination

If narratization is a recall and retell of a sequence of events and our relations with them, imagination is a special form of narratization that calls for the more flexible use of language and thought. In narratization, the presentation is real and empirical. In imagination, the presentation is surreal but logically possible. Imagination is the creation of make-believe stories, possible situations, and scenarios. Imagination need not correspond with what has happened before. Imagination need only be sensible and intelligible. Imagination is a landmark of which thought is no more grounded in empirical reality but has gained its relative autonomy. By exploiting the flexible use of language, thought has also become highly flexible, describing something a person has never experienced before.

In order to imagine successfully, that is, to describe what might have happened in a make-believe story, a person has to master some general abstract features and structures of a story or an event, such as sequencing, development, coordination, and then fill in details. Again the story has to be orderly, consistent, and coherent.   If these conditions exist in narratization because narratization simply depicts an orderly, consistent, and coherent reality, they are not given in imagination. In fact, imagination requires that the person internalizes these conditions and applies them effectively in making up a story. Thus a very young child in creating an imaginary story may fail in some of these conditions of abstract structures/features. Imagination is a more demanding task than narratization and probably develops at a later stage in human history.

Argumentation

Argumentation is the outgrowth of imagination. In imagination, we have seen the mastery of abstract structures and relations of events and stories. In argumentation, we not only master those abstract structures and relations, but we also evaluate them. Argumentation focus almost exclusively on abstract relations and logical structures. We make explicit those abstract relations by constructs such as cause-effect, means-end analysis. In imagination, we have to make sure that the story is consistent and coherent. In argumentation, we have to make sure that the arguments are sound, that we follow the rules of logic in our steps of reasoning. Argumentation operates on more abstract concepts, trying to uncover underlying relations, by analysis, deduction, induction, inference, comparison, generalization, explanation, and so on. Thus, argumentation is a mode of thought qualitatively distinct from narratization and imagination.

Content and Scope of Conceptual Thought

Thought cannot exist in itself alone. It must be operating on some content. In fact, this position has been championed by Brentano (1874), as I mentioned earlier. Take the example of a statement, "I think this is an easy problem." The thought is about an easy problem, but the easy problem is not about anything else. In other words, every thought or mental act must be about something and have meaningful intentional content. Thus, "I think" cannot qualify itself to be a thought. The immediate question is "you think *what*?" Similarly if you say, "I hate," the immediate question is "You hate *what*?" Without specifying some content, the thought is itself incomplete. In general, no thought can exist independent of meaningful content. By corollary, no meaningful content can exist outside thought.

A thought as simple as a statement of reality (e.g., I am eating) belongs to the narrative mode of thought. Also when thought is just expressing our feelings, intention, or desire, it is the narrative mode of thought. On the other hand, we may apply the argumentative mode of thought to problem-solving situations. In those situations, we try to think through a problem or argue for a position. Generally, conceptual thought can be divided in two categories: to describe and to argue (Figure 4. 4).

Critics may point out that to reason (know, remember, analyze, argue) is a part of thinking, but to feel is not. Thinking is to apply the analytical mind while feeling is to apply one's emotion. Thus feeling is not a part of thinking. I tend to argue otherwise. While it is entirely possible for one to feel, say, to feel angry without being aware that one is angry, it is equally possible for one to be angry and is fully aware of it. In the latter situation, one is thinking about one's feeling. Thinking is to bring to the consciousness or awareness of something. If I want to go cycling but this sublimal desire is not expressed in a conscious thought, then feeling is deep inside (unconscious) and is not thought. But if I can express it by saying it out, saying it to myself, or rehearsing it in my mind, then it is a thought about a feeling. In summary, thought includes both reasoning and feeling. To reason is to apply our cognitive capacity to a problem-situation. To feel is to form an attitude and express this attitude in thought. No matter we describe or argue, we feel or reason, it is the domain of conceptual thought so long as it is operating in concepts.

This chapter is a very preliminary consideration of conceptual thought. I only hope that readers can appreciate the complexity of conceptual thought, and its significance in thinking and intelligence. By opening this Pandora's Box, we face the challenge of a more comprehensive theory to account for some basic issues, such as the linguistic-semantic-spatial transformation, the formation of associative network, the stages of conceptual development, the relation between conscious and unconscious thought, the rules of thought, to name just a few.

Figure 4.4
Two Categories of Conceptual Thought

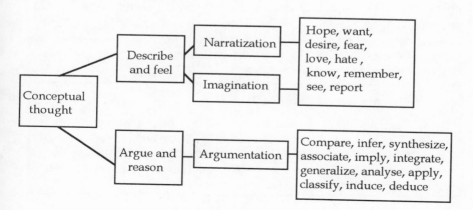

CHAPTER SUMMARY

The scientific study of thinking can roughly be divided into four domains: problem solving, concept formation, creativity, and reasoning. Reasoning is the hottest research domain with inductive and deductive reasoning in various types. There is strong local theory competition and quest for generalizability. Researchers mostly use task models and componential analysis to break reasoning down into many subprocesses and measuring each in precision. Despite such effort, psychologists still fail to unlock the black box of how we reason.

Researchers under the positivist paradigm have encountered numerous methodological problems, and they try to overcome these problems by ingenious experimental design and technical advances. However the decomposing strategy has its limitation and we need conceptual breakthrough for further progress.

Piaget's logical model on adolescent (formal) thought is a subset in scientific inquiry, which is a subset in scientific thought, which is again a subset in human thought. His logical model of 16 binary operations fit neatly in adolescent thought because the model exhausts two-factor relations.

The co-evolution of language and thought can be seen as a progression in which language transforms thought by enhancing it, anchoring it and giving it order, and thought transforms language by creating new concepts and elevating it to higher functions.

Mental representation can be classified into mental images and mental constructs; the former including visual and auditory images, and other sensations and the latter including prototypical images and concepts. There exists a growth process from visual images to prototypical images to concepts. By then we are free from images and concentrate our cognitive resources in meaning, thus speeding up thought.

Concepts are mental constructs formed in a network of related concepts with different levels of generalization. They improve our way of knowing, help us break up and order reality, accumulate knowledge, and name and update our experience. There are at least seven types of concepts: object and action, quality, quantity, classification, nonphysical, spatial-temporal, and argumentative. The three modes of conceptual thought—narratization, imagination, and argumentation—develops one after the other. Conceptual thought must have content and its scope covers description, feeling and argumentation.

Intelligent Food for Thought IV

Readers may find it amusing to try this brain-teasing example by L. J. Rips and S. L. Marcus. If a ball rolls left, green light is on. Now, green light is on. Conclusion: the ball has rolled left. Is this always true, sometimes true, or never true? (For solution see Anderson, 1990, chapter 10).

5

The Conceptual Learning
Dimension of Intelligence

INTRODUCTION

Many scholars see learning as an important subset of intelligence (Glaser, 1986, Ackerman, 1989). Even a major factor-analytic theorist agrees that learning is the cause and result of intelligence (Horn, 1989). In Horn's words, "Human abilities are simultaneously outcomes of learning and determinants of learning" (p. 61). In my view, intelligence is a broader concept than the capacity to learn. But few would deny the central and indispensable role of learning in intelligence.

Traditional Learning Theories

Regrettably, however, traditional learning theories tell us very little about how learning makes us intelligent. Traditional learning theories under the influence of behaviorism focus almost exclusively on behavioral learning (Bigge, 1982; Phillips and Soltis, 1985; Hill, 1985). The enterprise of behaviorism, from classical conditioning to operant conditioning to modern behavioral modification, discovers important learning principles for all species but fails to account for human learning, which in many cases is qualitatively different from that of other species. The recent development to incorporate cognitive research into learning, such as memory, association, retention, and so on (Houston, 1986), does not lead to any new or comprehensive learning theory to account for intelligence. While there have been recent concerns for the psychobiological explanation for learning, learning theorists have retreated from the quest for global theories to the mere discovery of more specific learning principles (Klein, 1991, p. 47).

Human Conceptual Learning

What is so unique about human learning that makes us intelligent? I think the answer lies in conceptual learning, the capacity for which distinguishes us from other species. Conceptual learning is learning through concepts. Learning is achieved through the medium of concept facilitated by language and the mental operation of conceptual thought. Conceptual learning is the learning of knowledge, that is, the acquisition of new knowledge. Here the criterion of success in learning is understanding, or the conceptual mastery of a piece of knowledge. This is in sharp contrast with behavioral learning, whose criterion of success is the development from trial and error to successful physical performance. Behavioral learning is the learning of skills, motor learning, and perceptual learning. All species have some capacity of behavioral learning, which is learning to change a behavior in face of a changing environment. In fact, different species have different capacities and predisposition for learning different types of behavior. But only the human species is capable of conceptual learning. It is the acquisition of knowledge and its application that makes us intelligent.

I will start this chapter with a survey of major learning theories. Then I would advance a definition of learning and postulate the scope of learning by a learning continuum. Next I would venture into the philosophical assumptions of knowledge acquisition and briefly outline the debate between Piaget and Chomsky on this issue. I hope to resolve their debate by my notion of cognitive residues, a subtheory to supplement Piaget's constructivism. After that I will discuss the content of conceptual learning, that is, the structure of knowledge. Here I discover the asymmetrical relations between knowledge and cognitive characteristics which lie at the very crux of learning.

Now I am in a position to outline a typology of conceptual learning. Then I briefly review the issue of concept learning. Principles of acquisition are proposed. Afterward I would outline the factors underlying learning: human experience, predisposition, and the affective domain. Such a treatment, I hope, will explain how conceptual learning makes us intelligent and distinguishes us from other species.

A SURVEY OF MAJOR LEARNING THEORIES

There are three historical traditions and two contemporary rivals in learning theories, namely, mental discipline, natural unfoldment, apperception, behaviorism and cognitivism.

Mental Discipline

With its origin traceable to Plato and later Descartes, mental discipline sees the mind as a nonphysical substance that lies dormant until it is exercised. Faculties of the mind such as memory, will, reason, and perseverance are referred to as the "muscles of the mind." Like physiological muscles they are strengthened only through exercise and practice. Mental discipline thus stresses the importance of strict discipline and learning, where rote memorization, repetitive computation, and mental practice are seen as mental exercise for the development of the mind.

The notion that exercizing the muscles of the mind has positive effect on learning has been empirically disputed by Thorndike and Woodworth (1901), Thorndike (1924), Wesman (1944), and others. Empirical studies show that drilling to memorize specific items do not lead to improvement in memory in general. Nor does the mental exercise or practice of a specific subject lead to improvement in intelligence. While the earlier view of muscles of the mind is considered scientifically untenable and subsequently abandoned, contemporary exponents of mental discipline take a more humanistic and liberal view and stress the importance of the development of the human mind in education, as witnessed in Maxine Greene's call for rational and emancipatory education (Greene, 1978, p. 22).

Natural Unfoldment

According to Jean-Jacques Rousseau (1712-1778), the French Enlightenment romantic philosopher, all people are by nature good, free, and autonomous, but they are suppressed by authority and battered by corrupted influences of society. Hence the ideal education is the natural enfolding of a child's natural impulses, instincts and feelings, and learning is a process of self-discovery of the world, oneself and truth, in which the teacher is just a facilitator who should provide guidance without imposition. Rousseau's emphasis of different training at different stages of development had found some parallels in and gained support from Piaget's theory of child development; his humanistic concern of total development is the forerunner of Abraham Maslow's concept of "self-actualization" and A. Harry Passow's total learning experience (Passow, 1986). However, while Rousseau's view of man and education may have touched the inner psyche and the emotional layer of the human species, it has not enlightened us on the cognitive side of learning and intelligence.

Apperception

Navigating through the empiricist tradition (David Hume, John Locke) and the rationalist tradition (René Descartes, Immanuel Kant), Johann F. Herbart (1776-1841) attempts to build a science of the human mind that would parallel the physical and biological sciences. Herbart sees the human mind as an aggregate of mental states resulting from a person's previously received ideas. A mind is a battleground and storehouse of ideas where ideas would associate, organize, surface, or submerge in a state of consciousness. Herbart proposes a highly sophisticated theory of mind—the apperceptive mass—the stock of mental states at any given time. Every new idea has to build on and associate with this apperceptive mass through a process of experiencing and associating. A mind is like an iceberg, mostly submerged below the level of consciousness, and the submerged mass has to be called upon through a threshold of consciousness for association of new ideas. For Herbart, ideas (conception) and experience (sensation) are intricately related as a unity in the mind.

Apperception is a process of a person becoming consciously aware of an idea and assimilating it into one's apperceptive mass. As a result, apperception is idea centered learning, where Herbart outlined it in three stages: sense activity, memory, and conceptual thinking. Herbartians are convinced that the learning process should proceed through an ordered series of five steps initiated by a teacher:

1. Preparation
2. Presentation
3. Comparison and abstraction
4. Generalization
5. Application

Herbart's view on the human mind has inspired the development of structuralism in psychology, which studies human consciousness through introspection. When introspection was later considered unscientific and replaced by experimental psychology and behaviorism, most of Herbart's ideas were forgotten. Nevertheless his five steps became a standard in classroom teaching plans, and there is some revival of interest in Herbartian tradition: Paul Hirst argues that the school curriculum should be based on the nature of knowledge and that there are seven forms of knowledge for the development of rational mind (1974).

Behaviorism

For decades behaviorism emerged as the dominant paradigm in psychology of the early twentieth century. Behaviorists study observable behavior and its relationships to observable stimuli in the environment rather than unobservable contents of the mind. The core of behaviorism is its disregard of unobserved mental events, thus termed "behaviorism." Its research program starts from lower animals and simple tasks, such as mice in the running maze, and aims to make progress in generalization for higher order human behavior. By varying the nature and degree of stimuli in a well-controlled environment, it hopes to discover laws of behavior in a stimulus-response framework. In learning theory Edward Thorndike studied hungry cats and formulated a number of laws for learning: law of readiness, law of repetition, and law of effect (1913). Following his footsteps, John B. Watson and later B. F. Skinner developed the notion of learning as stimulus-response conditioning. Two major processes were put forward to account for learning: classical conditioning and operant (or instrumental) conditioning. Learning is seen as the forming of a habit (response) through conditioning (application of stimulus) by reinforcement principles.

From Clark Hull's (1943) drive-reduction theory to Edward Tolman's (1959) purposive behaviorism, we saw the transition from behaviorism to cognitivism. Hull theorizes that drive motivates behavior, and he introduces the notion of incentive motivation (1952). But Hull's motivation postulates nothing inherent in an organism; it is only a mediating unit between stimulus and response, so that he can formulate laws, for example, larger reward produces greater conditioned incentive motivation and so on. On the other hand, Tolman maintained that reward is not necessary for learning to occur; our behavior is goal oriented, and the environment conveys information about where our goals are located (Klein, 1991, p. 42).

Cognitivism

The behaviorist paradigm of ignoring the unobservable mental states proved fatal: it failed to explain purposive behavior in learning. In the 1950s Chomsky attacked behaviorism for its failure to explain the learning of human language (1959). In the 1960s Saltz criticized its failure to account for concept learning. With the growing interest in Piaget's work and the development of cognitive psychology and cognitive science, a new information-processing paradigm begins to take shape.

Whereas behaviorists talk about the environment in terms of stimuli, cognitivists talk about the environment as conveying information, which is then "processed." The 1960s boom in computer technology provided cognitivists with a much better metaphor and terminology than the telephone switchboard underlying much behaviorist thinking. Cognitivists thus emphasize internal processes rather than external responses and are correspondingly more willing to study the human mind and its cognitive functioning.

The concern for the cognitive aspect has led to the change of subjects and content of study: the study of mice running mazes gives way to the study of human subjects responding to verbal or auditory stimuli/information. The former is pairing speed with food while the latter is pairing nonsense syllables with words, thus paired associate

learning in the 1960s.   Edwin Guthrie's (1942) contiguity theory of
stimulus-response association in learning also gives way to a more
comprehensive approach by Robert Gagne (1970), whose eight
conditions (types) of learning go beyond mere association but include
(1) signal learning, (2) stimulus-response learning, (3) chaining, (4)
verbal association, (5) discrimination learning, (6) concept learning, (7)
rule learning, and (8) problem solving.

Two Streams of Cognitivism

Cognitivism does not come in one single, neat paradigm.   There
are at least two major streams.   One is the developmentalist view that
argues that with growth and critical experiences, the mental structures
of children (through which they process information) grow increasingly
complex, thus helping them to extract deeper and richer meanings from
the world.   This stream outlined by Piaget treats learning as cognitive
development.   Following his line of research is Jerome Bruner's goal-
directed learning, active acquisition of knowledge, interactive learning
and theory of instruction (1960, 1966). Bruner, Jacqueline Goodnow, and
George Austin (1956) are also the forerunners in the study of concept
formation and concept learning as hypothesis testing.

The   other   stream   is   the   information-processing   paradigm.
Learning   is   now   understood   in   terms   of   information   processed,
acquired, retained, and retrieved.   Learning is no more conditioning,
but is paired association, free and serial recall, pattern recognition,
lexical priming, and so on.   Subjects are now students pressing the
keyboard bar for visual images instead of mice pressing iron bars for
food.

In reviewing learning research of the past 20 years, Gagne (1989)
pointed out that the information-processing paradigm has made
available many "conceptual weapons" with which to tackle the problem
of learning relationship to human abilities (1989, p. 5). These are all too
familiar to cognitive psychologists: treating learning and memory in the
framework of information acquisition/decoding, encoding, rehearsal,
storage, retrieval, schema, associative network, semantic and episodic
memory, spatial and visual storage, and so on. This is in sharp contrast
with classical/behavioral learning studies with independent variables
such as temporal rate of presentation, amount of material, distribution
of practice, task similarity, and so on.   Learning speed and reinforcement schedules now give way to simple RT and choice RT measures.

Strengths and Weaknesses of Major Learning Theories

All the above theories have their insights as well as misgivings.
Mental discipline is an untenable theory, but its modern version has
broadened its scope into a conception of self, with the components of

mind, will, and conscience. It merely asserts an educational ideal for the development of self, to which no liberal educator would object. As for natural enfolding, it starts from the ideal of eighteenth-century romanticism and postulates human innate goodness. Natural enfolding is antilearning and, from a contemporary perspective, naive about the complex learning process. Nevertheless, it is imperative to assert the significance of self-directedness in learning. Rousseau himself advocates an education that takes into account a child's developmental stages, a surprisingly modern and cognitivistic stance (see his *Emile*, 1762). As a result, these two traditions can be seen as more similar than different, for they can be merged into a humanistic perspective and serve as guiding principles for personal growth and value acquisition in learning.

As for the two contemporary rivals, the strength of behaviorism later became its weakness: to be scientific and to focus only on the observable, the behaviorist methodology has limited its scope of inquiry on the S-R bond in learning, an important paradigm that nevertheless fails to explain complex learning process. Thanks to the work of Chomsky, Bruner, Piaget, and many other cognitive psychologists, we saw a resurrection of cognition in the study of learning.

What progress have we made in the past 20 years? We know deeper about our cognitive functioning and memory structure. We witness an explosion in cognitive psychology. We have "more detailed and technically sophisticated analysis of information processing" (Gagne, 1989, p. 8), but our understanding of higher-order learning processes remains limited. Cognitive psychologists are studying simple tasks such as letter-matching task, sentence-picture verification task; higher-level tasks such as analogy task and word fluency ability still appear too complex and involve too many sub-processes. If we go the information-processing way, we still have a long way to go. In fact recent development of the computational metaphor (Jackendoff, 1987) may not bring us too far: the information-processing model remains too narrow to capture the richness of human mind and the complex process of human learning and intelligence (Churchland, 1988).

By far the most fertile is the Herbartian research program, which springs from the synthesis of the two powerful traditions: empiricism and rationalism. It has a much broader conception than the two contemporary rivals, and its notion of knowledge interacting and realigning with mind—the apperceptive mass—is the most insightful. The irony is that its sophistication and richness turned into misunderstanding and superficial adoption, for the Herbartian conception becomes a watered down version of Herbartian method of five steps in preparing a class lesson.

It seems the problem of learning theories today is the problem of reconceptualization. I propose to make a distinction between behavioral learning and conceptual learning. It is the latter that makes us intelligent and distinct from other species. I further postulate that the two may follow different principles. In fact, psychologists today are still uncertain whether there exist distinct types of learning or just one single underlying learning process (Houston, 1986, p. 22).

THE CONCEPT AND SCOPE OF LEARNING

A Commonsense Notion of Learning

Let me begin by giving a commonsense notion of learning: learning is the acquisition of new behaviors, skills, ideas, or knowledge (Biggs & Telfer, 1987, p. 147). I wish to further point out that a behavior or skill is generally acquired through practice while ideas and knowledge are acquired through understanding.

Notice in this notion the terms "acquisition" and "new." The first condition is that the behavior must be acquired. The behavior is not inherent in the child, but she has to learn it. For example, a reflex such as the sucking reflex is a genetically endowed, and not a learned, behavior. Second, the behavior must be new: the child does not possess it before; she possesses the behavior only after the process of learning it. For example, a math ability of adding two numbers is new to a child; she does not possess this knowledge at birth. She has to acquire it knowledge through learning and practice.

The All-Pervasive Learning Phenomenon

By conceiving of learning in this way, we can say that learning is an all-pervasive phenomenon with the human species. In fact, learning takes place within a child in every imaginable situation all the time. A child is born with physical structures, reflexes, and some general tendencies. These genetic endowments are transformed through her acting onto the environment into schemes such as shaking, holding, grasping, looking, attending, and so on. These basic schemes are further coordinated to form higher-order schemes such as walking, running, singing, and so on. A new behavior is acquired through practice, so that a child can get around the world. A child learns most behaviors in order to function efficiently in dealing with the environment around her. It is no exaggeration to say that a child is engaged in learning, consciously or unconsciously, in almost every minute of her time. When older, children use language as a tool for learning about the environment around him. They have incessant urge for new vocabulary, with a vocabulary spur at 18 to 24 months of age. They keep asking questions to understand the world and for the discovery of new things. Language no doubt facilitates learning even at a very young age. Treating language as verbal response is a gross misunderstanding of the significance of language. With vocabulary, language, syntax, and the formation of concepts, learning takes us to a new plateau beyond other species.

Distinction Between Behavioral and Conceptual Learning

The initial commonsense notion of learning remains too restricted. First learning should include not only acquisition, but also retention and transfer, that is, application of new behavior or knowledge to new situations. Second, a distinction has not been made between learning behavior and learning knowledge. In fact, we may divide learning into two major types: behavioral learning and conceptual learning. Behavioral learning is the acquisition of new behavior and its application. It includes skill acquisition, motor learning, perceptual learning, and habit formation. Conceptual learning is the acquisition of knowledge and its application. It includes the formation of concepts, knowledge network, and representation. Different principles govern the two types of learning. In behavioral learning, it is the principle of operant conditioning and reinforcement. In conceptual learning, it is the principle of internal reorganization of mental network for meaning, efficiency, and simplicity. The process of behavioral learning involves trial and error, imitation, and approximation of key features, finally leading to automaticity of behavior. The process of conceptual learning involves the use of language, acquisition of meaning, mental rehearsal, conceptual reorganization, understanding, and addition to existing mental network.

The Learning Continuum

The current thinking on learning, under the influence of Piaget and Bruner, has favored the constructivist nature of the learning process (Piaget, 1971; Bruner, 1966; Bruner et al., 1966). I wish to broaden this conception by a continuum in which construction is just a midpoint.

Imitation

The most rudimentary form of learning is that of imitation, which is represented on one extreme of our continuum. Imitation involves approximation and repetition. The child has to first conceptualize the basic features of the items to be learned, then approximate and imitate them. For example, infants as young as four months old are capable of voice imitation in "vocal contagion" as described by Piaget (1951). Older children are capable of delayed imitation of an action, a fact that implies that they are able not only to imitate but are also in possession of stable mental images and a well-developed long-term memory (Piaget, 1951). In a classroom setting, a student repeats what the teacher says, a student copies what a teacher writes, a student tries to memorize and recall what a teacher teaches: these are all basic learning by imitation. This kind of learning need not involve understanding: the learner simply imitates and tries to anchor the learning item into his memory network, mainly phonological or kinesthetical but not semantic ones for future recall. Imitation learning is most predominant in the first stage of skill acquisition.

Imitation is the most elementary and pervasive form of learning. In order to acquire something, one has to imitate, to repeat, to try out, and act out by approximation. We learn a lot of skills this way. Understanding is not important here. What is important is the amount of practice. Generally, the more practice one has, the stronger the association to recall and closer approximation to the learning item, but the learning curve will soon level off. Ackerman has provided an information-processing interpretation about skills learning (1989).

Understanding

Next in the continuum is learning with understanding. Here we may divide understanding into two broad categories: passive understanding and active (constructive) understanding. Passive understanding takes place when we come to notice what incidentally comes across our conscious mind but take a passive posture in receiving it. Active (constructive) understanding is what has been described by Schank as understanding by relating the new item to the old, similar knowledge structure and by supplying a script to form a coherent picture, thus coherency explanation (Schank, 1986). In fact most knowledge acquisition is active (constructive) understanding, relating the new to the old. I find Piaget's concept very useful here: assimilation is the acquisition of new information into an old structure, accommodation is the altering of old structure in face of new information. In school learning, the instance of learning by rote is that of imitation while the instance of learning by meaningful representation is that of active (constructive) understanding. Learning by rote or imitation is just learning of the surface, physical, phonological features of the learning item, while learning by understanding is a deeper learning of the semantic, meaningful aspect of the learning item. To acquire understanding is the same as acquiring meaning. A meaningful representation is stored much deeper in a memory network in long-term memory than a physical, phonological representation. Also the mode of acquisition is quite different. In imitation learning, the more repetition, the more secured will be the anchorage of the learning item. But for understanding, the number of repetition does not matter. Whether a student masters a learning item depends on whether he achieves understanding, or the successful internalization and formation of a meaningful network.

Routinization

At the other end of the continuum is the end point of learning: routinization and attaining automaticity. The former levels of imitation and understanding will be the precondition for learning to attain this level. In other words, only when a learning item has been successfully repeated, and understood will a student move toward automaticity of performance. The important point to note here is that every instance of learning is a move in the direction from imitation to routinization in the continuum. A learner is said to have attained approximation if she can successfully imitate, to have attained understanding if she has formed a meaningful network, and to have attained routinization if she can perform a learned behavior almost automatically and without much need for paying attention or monitoring the progress of it as everything is done smoothly and automatically.

The development from imitation to routinization is a natural process. In the very beginning, it is the learner's capability to recognize novelty. Then there is the tendency to incorporate this novelty into himself. In doing so, the learner progresses from imitation to understanding and then to routinization. The changing variable is the decrease of attention and cognitive resources to the learning item. In the beginning the learner has to pay a lot of attention to what the key features are to be imitated. Then attention is focused on understanding and the formation of a meaningful network. Finally when the learner is able to perform the learning item effortlessly, without much attention, the learner's cognitive resources are once again freed to explore and incorporate the next learning item.

THE PRECONDITION OF CONCEPTUAL LEARNING: PHILOSOPHICAL ASSUMPTIONS

Knowledge Acquisition Presupposes What Knowledge?

Piaget defines intelligence as the acquisition of cognitive structures, through which a child can begin to acquire knowledge about the world. This leads us immediately to a very basic question: How is knowledge acquisition possible? What knowledge must a child have before she can acquire knowledge? The acquisition of knowledge presupposes what knowledge?

For example, if a child can do multiplication, acquires and possesses the knowledge of multiplication, we must presuppose that she knows the number system. If she knows the number system, we must presuppose she knows counting. If she knows counting, we must presuppose she can differentiate discrete objects. By asking questions this way, we are approaching a perennial problem: whether we have to presuppose any knowledge for the acquisition of knowledge itself.

Another example is transitivity. A child older than seven would find the following self-evident:

If A>B, B>C, then A>C

But where does the self-evidence come from? When and how does a child acquire this knowledge? Bear in mind that transitivity is a very fundamental concept without which we cannot build logic or mathematics. Or, put it another way, if every new learning item has to be related to the old learning item, how do the first few learning items come into being? In the very beginning when an infant does not have a minimal framework, how can a new item be possibly acquired? How can it be related to an old framework when there is no such old framework? Let me call this the problem of initial learning.

Historical Answers

This perplexing question led to some interesting answers by the early Greek philosophers. Plato believed that all learning is a recollection of what we have already known. We need only to be reminded of such knowledge. Knowledge is inborn, or a priori, and we need only to work out the logical consequences of what we have already known (Hamlyn, 1978, p. 6).

Following this line of thought, Aristotle believed that scientific knowledge depends intimately on certain first principles such as transitivity from which the truths of each science are derived. These truths can be demonstrated from the first principles by logic, such as syllogism. The validity of these first principles has to depend on the rational human mind. Aristotle argued that man is a rational being with inborn discrimination potentiality. We can exercise this discrimination potentiality through action and bring out the capacities we naturally possess and thus truth (Hamlyn, 1978, p. 15).

Piaget's Constructivism

Piaget's answer is that there is no need to presuppose any a priori knowledge. He argued that it is through experience and interaction with environment that children are led to the growth of ever-encompassing cognitive structures, which includes this very fundamental concept of mathematics. The roots of this very basic knowledge, or logico-mathematical structures, cannot be located in either the subject or the object, but in the interaction between them. Piaget in fact traces the developmental process of cognitive structures, one following the other, with its roots going back to their elaboration as early as the sensorimotor stage. According to Piaget, the child, within a space of a few years, spontaneously reconstructs operations and basic structures one upon the other, of a logico-mathematical nature, without which she would not understand what will be taught at school. In other words, Piaget's position of constructivism dictates him to dismiss a priori knowledge of any form, because what he sees is a child's action on environment and construction of knowledge, not a priori knowledge.

Chomsky's Preformatism

Chomsky, on the other hand, takes up the position of preformatism (innatism), which postulates the existence of a priori knowledge in the child. This is because Chomsky saw one striking fact about the human language phenomenon: the enormous disparity between the input and the output. That is, there is an enormous disparity between the poverty of the stimulation on the one hand and the highly articulated and precise character of what comes out on the other.

Language output from the average child is so novel and diverse that no learning in the Skinnerian sense would account for it. Thus Chomsky is forced to postulate that there is some innate ability in the child, which is "prewired" in the child's head. Chomsky called it generative grammar, some kind of system of rules that determines the properties of expression over an indefinite range. Briefly it is a system of faculties, in the form of a finite set of rules and principles that compute and create representation of various kinds and produce an infinite variety of correct utterances. A child is said to possess a "language acquisition device," which is most sensitive to the language environment and is triggered to acquire the system of specific language. In other words, Chomsky claims that a child's brain contains certain innate characteristics which "prestructure" them in language learning: it needs only a moderate or even minimal environment to trigger such inborn capacities to unfold themselves.

The Debate Between Piaget and Chomsky

Piagetians and Chomskians had a heated debate on the nature of innateness in language and learning in the late 1970s. Putting the debate in historical perspective, we have seen a shift tending toward apriorism of some kind with its historical roots as far back as Plato and Aristotle. Ever since Descartes and Hume, the problem of innate knowledge has been cast in terms of rationalism versus empiricism, with Kant synthesizing it and proposing the existence of "synthetic a priori" in our knowledge system. Building on the tradition and spirit of Kant but rejecting the existence of a priori knowledge, Piaget can be said to have resolved the rationalist/empiricist controversy by proposing the middleground position of constructivism. For Piaget, empiricism is genesis without structures, and rationalism is structures without genesis. His own position emphasized the strong interplay between the environment and the knowing subject, who actively explores and exploits the environment through action, thus gaining experience and creating cognitive structures for knowledge acquisition.

Piaget's position of constructivism is being challenged less from empiricism than from the side of rationalism. Thus we have seen the debate shifting from empiricism versus rationalism to constructivism versus rationalism, with innatism/preformatism as the modern version of rationalism. Simply put, the Piaget-Chomsky debate is: Are there innate cognitive structures in the human species? Piaget's answer is no: there is only basic biological tendency, general and specific heredity, through which action and adaptation are the impetus leading to reconstruction and the growth of cognitive structures. For Chomsky, the answer is yes: there is the unfolding of the "innate fixed nucleus," the "language acquisition device," and the "universal grammar" through which language acquisition becomes possible. Chomsky cites the phenomenon of language acquisition as support. It is inconceivable that a language learner would produce utterances that have such underlying intricate and delicate structures. Since these structures do exist and since we cannot account for them any other way, we are forced to postulate that they are innate, that they come from some mental organ, in the sense that linguistic rules are prewired in a child's head. Hence innatism holds.

Piaget's and Chomsky's Weaknesses

Neither Piaget's nor Chomsky's position is without problems. For Piaget, how can a child construct a richer cognitive structure from the hypotheses of weaker cognitive structures (Fodor, 1980)? In other words, how is constructivism possible? For Chomsky, the question is even more complex. Language is the product of man. How can a product of an organism be innate to the organism itself? Language is a tool for communication, and like other tools, it is made by man and is culturally shared products. Can we ever imagine a sharp spear, or the making of it, innate to the human species? How can we explain it biologically? In other words, how can biological mutation render the human species to learn to articulate a language with rational linguistic structures? While it is entirely possible that selective pressure may lead to the use of speech for communication and favor linguistic pre-disposition and development, it is inconceivable that rational, abstract linguistic rules can be part of innateness. Likewise, can we think of the system of law, the judicial rules to be innate?

My position is that both Piaget's and Chomsky's theories have their weakness and that the truth may lie somewhere in between. I would accept Piaget's constructivism as a starting point and try to resolve the challenge by Fodor, namely, how can a child construct a richer structure from a weaker one? I will reject Chomsky's position of "innate fixed nucleus" and argue that unconscious learning and internal reorganization of external input has made language acquisition possible.

Constructivism is Piaget's strongest point because it is a synthesized, improved position over the traditional position of empiricism and rationalism. It also stresses the dynamic interaction between action and environment. Piaget's theory is also well grounded in empirical observation: scientific experiments can be designed to confirm/refute them. But in view of Fodor's challenge, I propose to strengthen Piaget's theory with a subtheory, the theory of cognitive residues, and hope this can meet Fodor's challenge.

THE BASIS OF CONCEPTUAL LEARNING: COGNITIVE RESIDUES

Background Information in Knowledge Construction

Let us start by studying how a child constructs knowledge. Take the hypothetical example of a two-year-old who has an age-appropriate vocabulary. Suppose the child has never seen a cat before. She points to a cat and asks her mother, "What's that?" and her mother replies, "A cat."

What does a child see and hear? She sees a four-legged furry animal—a cat—and hears the word "cat." Now suppose the cat gets out of the room and the child said, "no cat." This means the child has already had the image of a cat and is able to relate it to a phonological representation. She has also had the idea of "no" and now relates the two concepts together to represent reality. All along this is the process of active construction of knowledge.

But even in this simple learning situation, there exists a lot of background assumptions that the child possesses:

1. Every object can have a name;
2. The name is given by an adult;
3. The name is not the same as the object;
4. The child can ask for a name;
5. An object exists independent of the child.

The Sea of Unconscious Learning

Where does a child learn all these? How and when does she realize that every object can have a name? Surely it is not the adult who told her this rule; she may not be able to articulate this rule anyway. How can she discover it and actively make use of it? The puzzle can only be solved by postulating that a vast sea of unconscious learning is operating in a child.

I postulate that a child receives more information than she can attend to. She normally selects a small part of the external input, attends to it, and processes it. A vast amount of information is screened out, but some information is captured and unconsciously processed.

In our example, the child sees not only an object—the cat—but many characteristics related to it: whiskers, crawling, skin color, shape of tail, meowing, color of eyes, and so on. It is not easy to decide how much information a child has captured unconsciously. But surely in this experience, a cat is more than just a four-legged furry moving object.

Unattended Information Processed

Take also the example of an apple. A child may be attending only to one aspect: edible. But other unattended information may pass through her visual field and enter her neural network. The information is passively received and unconsciously processed and may include redness, roundness, shape, size, weight, and so on. Most important of all, the child realizes the following: (1) an apple is a discrete object occupying space; (2) it will not move by itself, nor will it suddenly vanish.

My point is that we see and hear more than we are aware of or know of. Take the example of vision. We see the total frame of a visual field, not just an object. Normally within a visual field we will focus on an object, but we are aware of the background of the visual field. In other words, we see the total picture, or, to put it differently, the total picture enters our mind.

Our attention is always attracted to novelty. While we focus only on the novel, on the immediately relevant and respond to it, it is likely that other sensory and perceptual inputs as residues keep coming in and are processed in our neural network. They are residues because they are not immediately and actively made use of. Nevertheless they are kept in our neural network and become important background knowledge and ideas. They are the sea of unconsciousness. Such unconscious processing of unattended information has been going on all the time since a child's birth and in her waking moments. It is no exaggeration to say a child sees a lot and hears a lot after birth, much of it unconscious.

Cognitive Residues

Now I further postulate that there is some internal organization going on with that unattended information. It is processed and distilled. Lots of specific data have been discarded. Probably the long-term memory cannot afford to store so many details. Nevertheless a small portion has been retained and become unconscious concepts and ideas. Let us call them cognitive residues.

Cognitive residues are the deep-rooted cognitive structures that grow with a child. Different scholars have given them different names and have characterized them differently. Immanuel Kant coined it "synthetic a prioris," Michael Polanyi called it "personal knowledge," Jean Piaget termed it "cognitive structures," Alfred Schutz named it "recipe knowledge," and Karl Popper called it "implicit memory."

My characterization is that there are two kinds of cognitive residues: fixed cognitive residues and varied cognitive residues. Fixed cognitive residues are those intuitive concepts shared by the human species: time, space, causality, existence, object concept, transitivity, reversibility, universal grammar, and so on. They are very fundamental concepts that gradually grow with a child. They cannot be learned in the sense of being taught at school. Rather they are slowly realized by the child as her cognitive residues accumulate and slowly form into foundational concepts. Take the examples of time and space. They are common to all human species because they actually reflect the structure of reality we are capable of knowing. Time for a child is the experience of moment to moment, of temporality that defines a child's existence. Space for a child is her whole visual field that confines her spatial experience. It is just impossible for any concrete experience to take place outside space and time. These foundational concepts are not culture dependent. They are species specific in that they reflect how the human species experience reality.

The varied cognitive residues are the part of cognitive residues that depend on culture and family. It is more idiosyncratic in nature, and each child may have her unique version of varied cognitive residues. For example, being held up means feeding time for one child while it may mean going out for another. In one culture, a child being constrained in a seat may anticipate being driven in a car while in another culture it many mean being abandoned for a period of time. In other words, these varied cognitive residues are event association and implication that a child slowly learns through interacting with the environment and interpreting her experience.

Another example is linguistic. Even a two-year-old "knows" the rule that a quantifier can come before a name but not after it. Thus "no cat," "no milk," "no doll," but not "cat no," "mummy no." How does a child learn this?

Surely she does not learn it through being taught explicitly by her parents. She just gets exposed to the English language, reorganizes it into implicit principles and applies them unconsciously. While it is against the English language convention to say "cat no," it is entirely permissible, and in fact legitimate to say "cat no" in the Chinese language. In other words, a quantifier's position before or after a name is a matter of language convention. Different cognitive residues slowly formed in different cultures adhering to different conventions and syntactic rules.

Language acquisition has long been a puzzle to linguists. Simply put, how can a child figure out the underlying rules of a language with so little exposure? It seems my notion of cognitive residues can put this question in a new light. The acquisition of underlying rules is made possible by the accumulation of cognitive residues, which are implicit principles internally reorganized for unconscious application. A child does not only listen to an utterance and respond to it. The utterance in phonological representation is accumulated, reorganized internally, with part of it discarded, and part of it becoming residues. In language learning, the linguistic content is discarded, but the linguistic form and structures is retained. Thus a child is seen slowly acquiring the rules of language.

One characteristic of cognitive residues is that they are realizations only when situation demands. That is, cognitive residues may be there but pass us unnoticed. Certain contradicting experience may demand our attention, and then it leads to the realization of the existence of such cognitive residues, or our underlying assumptions about the world. For example, object permanence would strike a child as part of cognitive residues only when an object suddenly disappears from in front of her eyes. Without this contradicting situation, a child will not realize object permanence although she has already possessed this cognitive residues concept. Another example is object movement. A child will realize something must be wrong when a stone suddenly moves on a flat frictional surface because this phenomenon contradicts with her deeply ingrained cognitive residue that nonliving objects cannot move.

The Physiological and Social Basis of Cognitive Residues

My position is that we are not born with a priori concepts. Neither are we born with cognitive residues. Cognitive residues are the remaining trace of impression in our neural network after undergoing reconstruction. For some still-unclear mechanisms, the content of information is discarded, but the form and structures remain to form cognitive residues. It is our physical structures and cognitive apparatus that make possible the gradual formation of cognitive residues. We are born with the capacity to see and to hear. Going one step further with our perceptual apparatus, we have the capacity to categorize, to order reality, to get at underlying structures, to reconstruct internally for efficiency. Also we have a large long-term memory for storage of cognitive residues after efficient organization. The human condition is that we have created our own social world in which language, value, and culture can be transmitted effectively and efficiently. In short our physiological and social conditions have made the gradual formation of cognitive residues possible.

Supplementing Piaget's Constructivism

Based on my theory of cognitive residues constructed so far, I will now justify how it can supplement Piaget's theory and resolve Fodor's challenge. Piaget's version of constructivism hinges much on his notion of experience: physical experience versus logico-mathematical experience. According to Piaget, physical experience will lead to empirical abstraction, and logico-mathematical experience will lead to reflective abstraction. In my view, these two abstractions belong entirely to the domain of conscious construction. This is to be expected because Piaget stressed the active role of the knowing subject in constructing knowledge. Fodor's challenge is how a child can possibly construct from a weaker hypothesis to a richer one. My answer is to supplement Piaget's conscious construction with the unconscious construction of cognitive residues. With the notion of cognitive residues, we can explain how construction can become more and more powerful. We can explain how unconscious background knowledge come into place and appreciate the significance of their role in knowledge construction. We can further account for the growth of foundational concepts, such as the acquisition of transitivity that Piaget's theory has failed to explain. But I maintain the basic Piagetian framework: there is no need to postulate a priori knowledge. All I suggest is that while a child is born without a priori knowledge, knowledge in the form of explicit and implicit will grow through the process of construction, both consciously and unconsciously.

Is there any "innate fixed nucleus"? I believe "innateness" is a matter of degree and "fixedness" is a matter of interpretation. There is "fixedness" as far as the physiological structure of the human brain is concerned, such as the stages of maturity, critical period, plasticity of the brain, and so on. But there is no fixedness with language acquisition rules. Nor are those rules innate. These linguistic rules are acquired in the process of unconscious reconstruction of cognitive residues. There is internal reorganization and construction going on all the time, working unconsciously in hand with a child's active construction to deal with the world. There is no need to postulate that universal grammar is inborn. How underlying linguistic rules can be acquired is not at all mythical and is a matter of internal, unconscious construction.

THE CONTENT OF CONCEPTUAL LEARNING: ASYMMETRY BETWEEN KNOWLEDGE AND COGNITION

In the long history of epistemology, the philosophical study of knowledge, a lot of issues have been raised about the nature of knowledge, such as the distinction between knowledge and belief (Griffiths, 1967), the ways in which we know how and know that (Ryle,

1949), knowledge by acquaintance versus knowledge by description (Russell, 1912), and so on. In modern psychology, it is common to distinguish declarative knowledge from procedural knowledge (Anderson, 1983). My concern about knowledge here is that there exist some salient features of knowledge that may have significant implications in human conceptual learning. I will first outline these characteristics and then discuss their implications.

Major Characteristics of Knowledge

The first salient characteristic of knowledge is that it is a human construction. Knowledge in propositions or statements is a human cognitive effort to strive for understanding of reality, including oneself. Knowledge products may be manifest in words and books, but it is not the physical instance of books or the phonological sound of words that counts. Knowledge rests in the conceptual or ideational representation of meaning that these words or books stand for. In other words, without human strife for understanding and meaning, there could be no knowledge. Knowledge starts from human beings and is a human construction of conceptual understanding of reality.

Second, knowledge is only a partial representation of reality. Knowledge can represent multiple dimensions of reality. But here I postulate the existence of an inexhaustive reality. We understand reality by using terms and categories. Terms and categories (concepts) help break up reality, but they only depict part of reality. With more terms and categories (concepts) we can sharpen our understanding of reality. Through knowledge we can penetrate more deeply into reality and discover and represent the its multiple dimension. However we probably cannot exhaust reality. This is because as we penetrate deeper into reality and try to exhaust what is "out there," we know more and at the same time discover more unknown terrains. As we try to exhaust those unknown terrains, we enter into even bigger unknown terrains. It is therefore a more cautious position to assume an inexhaustive reality than an exhaustive one.

Third, knowledge is objective. It is true that knowledge is created by the subjective human mind. But once created, knowledge is independent of its creator and has borne an objective existence, like an independent life of its own (Popper, 1972). The important point here is that knowledge, being objective, it can be objectively criticized and assessed and be improved upon. The objective character makes it criticizable and improvable.

Fourth, knowledge is not a belief system. It is a scientific enterprise regulated by truth. There are many criteria for truth; for example, a statement is true if and only if it corresponds to reality. Also in order to be true, the statement must be consistent and coherent, and it must be consistent with our existing system of knowledge. While it has been the case that most scientific statements have been found untrue and refuted (Popper, 1963), our knowledge enterprise thrives because we always aim at truth: we keep discarding untrue statements and keep searching for a better, improved statements.

On these bases I would argue that knowledge is always tentative and is never secured. Western philosophers have for centuries tried to find a secured foundation for knowledge. They have found none. Logical positivism tried to ground knowledge in human sensation or sense data (Ayer, 1936), but this was later found to be fallible. It seems that we may have to accept the tentative nature of knowledge and strive for a better and ever-improving knowledge representation regulated by truth.

Human Cognitive Characteristics and Asymmetry

Given the above knowledge characteristics, how do we acquire them? We necessarily acquire them (learn them) through our mental capacities, that is, our cognitive functioning such as attention, perception, memory, comprehension, retention, and retrieval. In fact, we should be concerned with higher cognitive functioning such as comprehension, concept acquisition, mental network formation, and so on. The question thus becomes how knowledge characteristics are similar to or different from human cognitive characteristics and how they interact to benefit or inhibit learning. In the following I will show that knowledge characteristics have an asymmetrical relationship with human cognitive characteristics and that learning can be seen as a human effort to systematically overcome this asymmetrical relation.

Notice that the first salient characteristic of knowledge is that it is a human construction/creation. But the human mind (cognition) is not a human construction. Rather it is the product of millions of years of evolution and selective pressure. The mind does not create itself; it came into being probably because of evolutionary advantage. Alternatively put, evolutionary pressure has favored the growth of cognition, and cognition leads to knowledge construction and creation. However, knowledge construction is only indirectly related to evolution. Knowledge construction is much related to our human purposes of goals, values, objectives not necessarily survival goals, and is constrained by our cognitive capacity.

The first asymmetrical relation, then, is that cognition is the apparatus while knowledge is the product or final outcome. They belong to two different levels; cognition is more at concrete, operational level, while knowledge is at abstract, ideational level. A helpful metaphor is the hardware/software distinction: the cognitive apparatus is the hardware, and knowledge is the software. Knowledge being a mental construct, it is highly flexible and is capable of constant change, but cognition is a relatively fixed genetic endowment, with physical constraints as manifested in limited memory capacity, limited attention span, gestalt perception principles, and so on.

Second, knowledge is capable of representing multiple dimensions of reality despite its being a partial representation. However, young children's cognition is capable of focusing on one dimension only. In adults, cognition can be extended to consider two or three dimensions at the same time, but the limit will be reached very soon. Take an example of our comparison capacity. Suppose you are given 100,000 faces to remember. Then you are given 1 million faces for identification simultaneously. Such a task is undoubtedly beyond our cognitive limit, but our more powerful computer can do it swiftly. The second asymmetrical relation is that the mind (our cognition) is so structured that it has a limit in simultaneous processing, but knowledge is an open entity that is ever capable of expanding in its representation capacity. It has no upper limit in its representation capacity.

Third, knowledge is independent of its creator. The objective character of knowledge makes it criticizable and improvable. Cognition, however, is dependent on the person in question. The subjective character of cognition makes it inferential. All we can observe are overt behavior such as reaction time measures or introspective reporting. A perennial problem that plagues cognitive psychology is its subjective character. For example, how can one be sure that a subject is trying his/her best to give the fastest response he/she could when the experimenter told him/her to do so and that he/she declared to have done so? When our concern is with higher-level cognitive processing, the subjective character of cognition is even more transparent. In acquiring knowledge, a person has to relate the new knowledge to his/her existing knowledge framework (Schank, 1982) which in fact reflects his/her subjective experience and idiocycracy. In other words, the asymmetry is that knowledge itself is objective but the way it is acquired is inevitably subjective, and sometimes idiocycratic.

Knowledge is regulated by truth. Cognition, on the other hand, is governed by a number of cognitive processing principles. One principle is selectivity, another is interest; still another is moderate novelty. Generally, we select what interests us and process what is moderately novel. We do not select something to learn because it is true; nor could we learn something that is entirely new and incomprehensible to us. In fact, we select what concerns us in learning and processing. We are driven by our purposes and aims, explicit and implicit, which direct our cognition to process external input. The asymmetry here is that knowledge is regulated by truth while cognition is governed by cognitive principles and human purposes.

As knowledge is regulated by truth, we do this by empirical verification or logical reasoning. Basically, we verify the truthfulness of a statement by empirical evidence. Also we can proceed from the route of logical deduction.   From the premise we can deduce a lot of statements and then we can detect whether there is any inconsistency, incoherence, or incompatibility with existence knowledge within these statements. But this is not the case for cognition. Guided by goals and purposes, we will quickly form a coherent picture relative to our goals. We would then see through this coherent picture, or paradigm, in interpreting incoming information.   Instead of doing systematic deduction, we prefer to reduce and generalize from our limited experience to a broad picture of what reality is.

Finally, knowledge is always tentative and is never secured. However, this runs entirely in opposition with cognition and its expectation. Our cognition is so structured that we always look for definite, secured starting points. We have to anchor a learning item in our internal existing knowledge framework before we can acquire it. Quite often, we anchor new knowledge or idea within our internal script so as to understand the new knowledge better, that is, in a more secured sense.   In other words, cognition dictates that we prefer definite, secured knowledge, not tentative knowledge.

Implications for Conceptual Learning

Conceptual learning is the acquisition of knowledge. Given the asymmetry between knowledge characteristics and cognitive character-istics, what are its implications for learning?

First, knowledge is a human construction. In other words, man is the creator of knowledge and knowledge is the product (artifact) of human mind. But our human cognitive apparatus is relatively fixed while knowledge keeps expanding.   In view of the vast sea of knowledge that we have so far created, how can we learn them all? We have invented things that transform us (language, writing), and things that are apparently more powerful than us (e.g., computer, AI systems). Knowledge seems to be a human-created monster, out of our control. What are the prospects of our human mind given its limited cognitive capacities?

One seductive solution is to expand our cognitive apparatus by surgery or genetic engineering techniques. Another is to interface it with a powerful computer with vast memory, processing speed, and capacity. How this interface can be done is still a science fiction (e.g., connect brain neural network with computer network (CD/ROM) by a neural-electronic transformer.) On the other hand, while it is true that knowledge is objective and keeps changing and expanding and our cognitive apparatus is relatively fixed and physically bounded, it does not necessarily follow that we will be overwhelmed by knowledge. Although it is impossible to learn all knowledge, it is possible to master *more* important knowledge. Knowledge has meaningful content and can be represented in different levels. The lowest level is data, which are organized into information and fact, understood as patterns. Higher up are constructs, laws, and theories. Theories can explain laws, which in turn explain patterns, which in term explain facts, and so on. Thus if we can master more high-level theories and laws and learn fewer and data, we end up acquiring more knowledge.

Second, given our limited cognitive capacity and unlimited knowledge, knowledge departmentalization becomes an inevitable outcome. Modern scholars can probably be proficient with one small slice of knowledge at one particular level. Take the knowledge in computer science. A hardware engineer specialized in design of electronic pathways of on-off gates may be ignorant of higer-level AI systems. Knowledge departmentalization is a real danger, but we can try to overcome it by broadening our perspective and by being interdisciplinary. To do so, we should learn about theories, meta-theory, and philosophy of knowledge and be aware of the impact of the latest scientific discoveries on human knowledge systems. To learn a broad picture, to be at the apex of knowledge, is more important than to just learn technical knowledge at any level. Third, knowledge can always be better structured for learning based on human cognitive characteristics. For example, given our limited attention span, we should try to structure our learning to be within this limit. Knowledge should be organized in hierarchy and structured in meaningful network so that it matches with our cognitive characteristics. An orderly presentation with special focus of attention will facilitate learning. Also, since learners learn for interest and prefer to build on a solid foundation, we should avoid dry, tentative knowledge in the initial stage of learning, and challenge the learners' foundation only at a later stage.

Such are some of the implications of the asymmetric relation between knowledge characteristics and cognitive characteristics. Some readers could not help feeling pessimistic about our battle with knowledge; sooner or later, they expect, we will lose and be overwhelmed by knowledge explosion and the product we create. This is not necessarily so. To rephrase the question: Do we direct knowledge or does knowledge direct us? I would argue that the ability to create knowledge rests on our cognitive apparatus. The cutting edge of knowledge production is with us. Knowledge cannot create itself. In fact we direct knowledge and cast it with the image of our cognitive apparatus. Because of our limited cognitive capacity, we create theories to conceptualize and explain lots of facts and data; because of our cognitive network association, we organize knowledge in hierarchy for our easy understanding. Because of our ability to compare new input with previous memory, we are able to evaluate knowledge by a truth criterion of correspondence with previous experience. In fact, we shape and direct our knowledge enterprise as we create it. Before we create new knowledge, we must of course learn existing knowledge, and learning can be enhanced if it matches with our cognitive characteristics. While we cannot learn them all, we can master the more important theories and concepts. Learning is thus a human effort to overcome our cognitive limitation in our acquisition of knowledge.

A TYPOLOGY AND STAGES OF CONCEPTUAL LEARNING

Learning is a very broad concept. Undoubtedly learning knowledge is quite different from learning a skill. School learning is not the same as social learning. Moreover, some learning takes place consciously while others proceed in an unconscious manner. I herein propose a typology of conceptual learning that I hope will cover most types of conceptual learning and be relevant to our discussion of intelligence.

I postulate two important dimensions in learning: one is the intention to learn while the other is the awareness of one's learning. On the intentional dimension, there are active versus passive learning, on the awareness side there are conscious versus unconscious learning, as shown in Table 5.1.

Active Conscious Learning

Conscious active learning includes formal learning of school subjects in a school environment. Both teachers and students are conscious of what they are doing, engaging in a teaching/learning process of knowledge transmission. In an ideal case, students are actively engaging themselves in learning. Each student is actively constructing his/her knowledge. Also, when a student is doing self-study, or when a child has curiosity on a certain topic and actively explores the library to search for more information, it is again active conscious learning. This type of learning has been examined in some detail by Jerome Bruner and Jeremy Anglin, who sees the acquisition of knowledge as an active process involving acquisition of new information, transformation of knowledge, and adequacy checking. This type of learning includes classroom learning, self-study, and second language learning.

Active Unconscious Learning

While active conscious learning is prevalent in formal classroom settings, active unconscious learning is most evident in informal situations. Let me quote an example from Schank:

Consider, for example, the following situation. Imagine yourself going to a Burger King under the circumstances in which you have been to McDonald's on numerous occasions but have never before been to Burger King. You are

Table 5.1
A Typology of Learning

		Awareness	
		Conscious	Unconscious
Intention	Active	Active conscious	Active unconscious
	Passive	Passive conscious	Passive unconscious

confronted with a new situation which you must attempt to understand. (Schank, 1986, p. 122)

Suppose you are going to Burger King to meet a friend for some important discussion. All your attention is focused on the discussion. It is an active conscious engagement in thoughts and ideas. Yet at the same time you are aware of the environment. Your active unconscious learning is at work so that you notice Burger King is like McDonald's and you may say:

Ah yes, Burger King is just like McDonald's except the waitresses wear red and yellow and you can have it your way. A new discrimination in the structure that contains McDonald's is then made, creating a situation in which Burger King is a high-level structure that shares most, but not all, of its properties with the old McDonald's structures. (Schank, 1986, p. 123)

The interesting thing is that this active unconscious learning takes place every day in most informal situation. We are unconscious (not aware) of it, but our cognition is so structured that active incorporation of new experience is going on all the time. The new experience has to be understood in terms of the old and a new knowledge structure is created without our being conscious about it. It is automatic, effortless, unconscious learning. It is active because the human mind is actively engaging itself in memory search, in retrieval of old information, to assimilate the new, which is understood as a coherent event in terms of scripts.

Schank's conception of learning belongs to this category of active unconscious assimilation of information. Schank's version can be seen as a rational account of how informal learning takes place in our daily life. This category also involves the acquisition of cognitive residues: schemes, scripts, linguistic rules, and so on. As stated earlier, cognitive residues such as scripts are important background knowledge and ideas unconsciously acquired. When psychologists talk about scripts or schemes in knowledge representation, they seldom ask where those scripts or schemes come from. Scripts are important, as shown by Schank and Abelson (1977) and others (Bower, Black & Turner, 1979); they form the skeleton for piecing together, narrating, and understanding of an event. Informal learning in our daily life as described by Schank cannot take place without the active application of scripts. Through internal, unconscious reorganization and reformulation, the bare structure of an event becomes a prototype and is stored as a script.

Also, the learning of first language is an unconscious yet active process. It is unconscious because the child is unaware that she is learning; yet she is actively engaged in the use of language. She used the language to communicate, at the same time she is doing hypothesis testing on the language to make sure she is correctly using the rules of language (grammar) that she infers and then applies in use, but which she is never conscious of. In other words, she is actively engaged in the learning process that she is unaware of.

Passive Conscious Learning

Bruner argues that learning is an active constructive process (1966). So the question arises whether there can be any passive learning. I believe so; there are situations when we learn something but we do not actively participate in it. We may call those situations "noticing" or "incidental learning." For example, when we attend a lecture, we are actively and consciously learning the subject matter, but at the same time we learn that the professor is a young man with a British accent. We notice the room is crowded and the professor speaks very fast, and so on. We may notice a lot of things during a lecture; some of them come more consciously while others less consciously into our mind. Yet we take a passive attitude just noticing and not actively engaging. Our goal is to actively engage in the subject matter, not the peripheral, trivial incidentals. Thus what distinguishes active from passive learning is a matter of goals. The former is a goal-directed behavior while the latter is an incidental outcome. In the case of rote learning, it is also conscious but passive: the learner is conscious of the process and does no construction in learning. He/she merely tries to memorize the learning item. It does not involve any understanding, and the learner does not achieve any knowledge acquisition in a real sense. This category exists because we cannot help passively processing that information as we become conscious of it.

Passive Unconscious Learning

While passive conscious learning may not be of much interest, passive unconscious learning is an important category less explored by learning theorists. We learn the items in this category passively and unconsciously. Take the example of cause-and-effect. A child as young as two years old may have acquired this concept. She understands that many physical events happen in a cause-and-effect chain: kick a ball (cause) and it rolls forward (effect). A child may not be able to articulate it, yet she would be very surprised if she kicks the ball and it does not move, or moves in the opposite direction. How does she acquire the law of causality? To consciously teach a two-year-old this law is futile: she simply does not understand your abstract terminology. Yet it can be shown that she may have mastered the law of causality through a series of experiments. Foundation concepts such as space, time, causality, object permanence are never learned consciously. They gradually emerge in children's cognitive development leading to the speculation that they may be acquired in an unconscious and passive manner. It is unconscious because children are not aware of it. It is passive because it does not seem to involve any active construction. They seem to naturally develop among children by maturity. It is clear the acquisition of more contentful concepts in concept formation involves active construction, but it is doubtful whether these foundation concepts follow the same path of active construction. As stated earlier, these foundation concepts are fixed cognitive residues: they are not culturally dependent: they are species specific and reflect how we experience reality. They occupy a very unique position in my typology of conceptual learning: they are no doubt conceptual; they are in fact foundational without which other types of learning cannot take place. If they are learned at all they must be learned very differently from other types of active learning involving construction.

My typology of conceptual learning has summarized the different types of conceptual learning emphasized by different theorists. Table 5.2 demonstrates them.

The Learning Threshold

In the learning continuum, I pointed out that the most rudimentary form of learning is that of imitation. Imitation is the approximation of key features. It is the quickest and simplest way of acquiring knowledge or a skill. Then there arises a perplexing question: How can an infant learn through imitation? How can she possibly imitate? What are the preconditions for successful imitation?

In order for a child to learn through imitation successfully, she must have reached a certain threshold. For example, she must have developed a stable visual image. She must have developed a stable visual memory. Only then can she begin to recognize key features of a situation or a learning item. Her psychomotor ability must be so developed that she is capable of physically imitating a skill. Thus, an

Table 5.2
Types of Conceptual Learning

	Conscious	Unconscious
Active	* Bruner's version of active learning * Formal knowledge acquisition * Classroom learning * Self-study * Second language learning	* Schank's version of everyday learning * Cognitive residues (varied) * Schemes and scripts * First language learning * Concept formation
Passive	* Incidental learning * Rote learning	* Chomsky's preformatism * Foundational concepts * Fixed cognitive residues

one-year-old cannot imitate running, nor can a two-month-old imitate human speech successfully. In order to facilitate the acquisition of knowledge, she must have developed language because it is most often through language that new knowledge is transmitted. Only through language can conceptual thoughts, ideas, and meaning be anchored and better understood. Here I mean language in the broadest sense: human speech, sign language, written language, or symbolic representation with syntactic rules. Skills probably precede knowledge and action precedes understanding.

Once a child attains imitation, she is capable of learning at a much faster rate. In fact, imitation transforms the speed of learning. With imitation there is no need to reinvent all by oneself the skills and knowledge needed to deal with the world. Learning becomes the efficient transmission of cultural tools and ideas. Instead of inventing the number system by giving names to numbers, we simply learn it through imitation, then master and understand it, and then use it routinely as part of our cultural heritage. Therefore it would be appropriate to say that intelligence rests on our culture rather than on an individual. No matter how intelligent a person is, he/she cannot invent everything individually. The use of others' inventions and the contribution to this common stock of repertoire of inventions are what intelligence and learning is about. Our common stock of cultural repertorie takes generations to develop and accumulate. Stripe a person of his/her cultural repertoire and he/she can hardly deal with the world around him/her.

Concept Acquisition

It seems the learning threshold is directly related to biological maturation. This brings us back to Piaget's theory of development which stresses both maturation and experience. My point is that learning thresholds exist in both behavioral learning and conceptual learning. If physical maturation sets the limit for behavioral learning, such as skills acquisition, where does the threshold for conceptual learning lie? In other words, how does a child first acquire language and concepts to facilitate conceptual learning? All there any initial concepts that a child must learn to make conceptaul learning possible?

Language acquisition is a domain of research that has been going on for decades, from behaviorism to Chomskianism to cognitive-developmentalism. In the 1980s we also witness a growing research interest in concept acquisition. Initially researchers started from Heinz Werner's (1890-1964) theory that children's concepts grow from holistic, diffuse, global, and syncretic to analytic, articulated, differentiated, and discrete (Werner, 1948, Werner & Kaplan, 1963). However, Susan Carey (1985) argued that conceptual change is more like paradigm shift in the Kuhnian sense, with a change in the underlying belief and theoretical system (Kuhn, 1970, 1977). Carey further cited empirical support in children's concept of animals: a shift from a theoretical system based on behavioral principles to one based on biological principles (Carey, 1985). Similarly, some researchers argued that concepts are not just bundles of features, attributes, or frequency counts of occurrences or cooccurrences, but are coherent theoretical constructs (Murphy & Medin, 1985). In support of Carey, Frank Keil argued that "concepts might be embedded in larger belief systems known as theories" (1989, p. 282). He thus set out to uncover lay-theories held by children by asking preschoolers interesting questions about their concepts (shown below in italics) such as:

- Are *taxis* cars?
- Must a *princess* live in a castle?
- Can it be a *saw* if made of plastic?
- Can an *advertisement* appear on the radio?
- Can a little girl be an *aunt*?

It seems children's learning of concepts may be as eclectic as concepts themselves. N. E. Kossan (1981) points out that children use exemplar-based strategy to learn categories defined by family resemblance. Susan Gelman and Ellen Markman show that children use thematic groupings and taxonomic groupings as well (1986, 1987). An one-year-old (at prelinguistic stage) has already acquired superordinate concepts (Ross, 1980). By age three, children's induction for categories shifts from perceptual similarity to conceptaul similarity (Gelman & Markman, 1986, 1987). Quine called it the change from immediate, subjective, "animal sense of similarity" to "theoretical sense" of "scientific hypotheses and posits and constructs" (1977, p. 171). Markman further postulates that children work with the whole-object assumption, taxonomic assumption, mutual-exclusivity assumption, and so on to narrow down hypothesis space in concept acquisition (Markman, 1989). This seems to echo the eclectic appearance of concepts: a concept may be exemplar-based, one-dimensional, discrete featured, a pure belief, or defined in use (Keil, 1989).

So far research seems to suggest that concept learning (the acquisition of concepts) and conceptual learning (to learn knowledge through the use of concepts) are two sides of the same coin. Concepts themselves are constructs embedded with theories; as such, they are themselves part of knowledge. Conceptual learning may come after the acquisition of some initial concepts, but the former may lead to the formation of new concepts that transforms the latter.

The Learning Stage and Principles of Acquisition

Once children pass the threshold of learning, they are at the learning stage and can acquire knowledge through the following.

Approximation of Key Features

Imitation is the most rudimentary and basic form of acquisition. There is no such thing as perfect imitation; rather each imitation is more or less a deviation from the item to be imitated. Generally, imitation is just the approximation of some key features of the items to be learned. Take the example of a symbolic play. A child tries to imitate a plane. She pretends that she is a plane: she runs around the room, with both arms stretching apart and makes a humming sound. We can infer from this symbolic play that a child is able to extract three key features of a plane and approximate it: she imitates flying by running around. She imitates the two wings of a plane by her two arms, and she imitates the sounds of a plane by her own voice. Children are very good at extracting key features and approximating them. But each approximation is necessarily a distortion or simplification. For example, the child does not imitate the climbing and landing of a plane, she does not imitate the steering that changes the plane's direction; nor does she imitate the spinning of the engine and so on. What she really does is to conceptualize and approximate selectively some key features by simplification. This being so, the child has already learned the basic concept of a plane through action.

Growth of Mental Network

Once a child masters a new concept, it is integrated/related to her old repertoire or framework of understanding. In fact, a child learns the new concept by relating it to the old. It is quite often the modification or expansion of the old network to assimilate the new concept. In other words, in order to learn a new item, a child must anchor it on the old concept or repertoire she already possesses. Moreover, the child can only recognize the new and integrate it into the old when the new item is moderately novel relative to the old item she already possesses. If the item is too novel, a child may not be able to recognize it; the item may pass her unnoticed, and she would be unable to learn it. On the other hand, if the item is not at all novel, it may be so familiar to the child that she learns nothing from it. In other words, a child is attracted to a new item by a moderately novel principle. The item must not be too novel or too familiar; something new interwoven with the old is most appropriate for a child to learn. This is because the moderately new item can be readily integrated and anchored into the old network.

Development of Individual Differences

We have seen that every new learning item has to be related with or anchored into the old network. In other words, the old network is constantly growing and expanding as a child learns more and more every day. The important point to note is that every child's network grows in her own unique path. Given the unique experience of each child and the subsequent formation of unique mental network, it is necessarily true that each child learns differently according to her network. Then there exists a situation reminiscent of the adage that the rich gets richer. Since the quality of learning is a function of the existing network, a child with a richer network would learn more and better than a child possessing a relatively improvished network. This is because given a richer network, the child is able to see more and capture more through her old network. She is ready to integrate more into her network as she approaches a moderately novel learning item. A child with a relatively impoverished network, on the other hand, will see the moderately novel learning item as entirely novel and ignore it altogether. She may be unable to integrate/extract anything from it. The richness of a network is domain dependent. A child may be rich in one domain say, linguistic ability, but poor in another, say, science. Thus a child with a richer framework relative to a specific domain may learn faster and better than another child with a poorer framework in that domain. With a even better/richer network, that child can learn even more in the next round. This is a common phenomenon of one-dimensional growth path. Each child's network thus determines and enhances the growth of individual differences among children, even given the same environment and exposure to the same learning item.

Internal Reorganization for Meaning, Efficiency and Simplicity

Whenever learning takes place, that is, when a new item is mastered or acquired by the learner, something new is added to her existing mental network. I assert that the new item is not added to the existing network in a random fashion. Instead it is so arranged that the new item can be readily accessed and that it is adjacent to an old but similar learning item. Suppose a child learns the concept of a "dog." It is likely that the new concept is classified in the set of animals, more specifically the subset of pets and attached near "cat," "rabbit" and so on. It is unlikely that "dog" will be classified with apples! In fact we can infer the organization of network by empirical reaction time research.

On the other hand, I postulate that internal reorganization will be taking place unconsciously. New categories will be created as the network grows from simple to complex. It is likely that initially a child has only a rudimentary concept of animal, which gradually grows into pets and wild animals, that wild animals will be further subdivided into dangerous versus nondangerous and so on as a child learns more and more names and features of animals. We work with the basic principle of meaningful network. An item is classified by meaning and its relations to the child rather than a systematic objective classification. Semantic processing is deep processing in which meaningful information is stored in long-term memory. Two other principles at work for internal reorganization are those of efficiency and simplicity. In other words, a framework will not grow by itself. It grows because new items are added to it, and it grows by a more efficient organization, or, more efficient access. Efficient access is in turn a function of frequency and interest. If a new learning item is frequently encountered and it interests a child, it will be organized closer to the working memory for efficient access. Suppose a father bought a child a dog called dachshund. Suppose further that the child is very fond of that dachshund. The child will not only learn the name type of the dog almost instantaneously; she will also notice a lot of behavioral patterns of that dog. It is not implausible to infer that dachshund is not classified with the category of dogs, but rather with pets, or even more likely, with the child's family members of father, mother, brother, dachshund, and so on. This example illustrates that high frequency and high interest may lead to more efficient access in a network of representation. Rather we classify according to frequency and interest for the purpose of efficient access and organization. Metalearning is to uncover principles of how children learn and to apply these principles to enhance their learning.

THE UNDERLYING FACTORS

Predispositions Behind the Learning Capacity

If we go deeper into the reasons for individual differences in learning, (it is necessarily the dynamic interplay between nature and nurture) we would find that it is a matter of predisposition manifested in:

- Persistence
- Alertness
- Positive response patterns

For example, a child with a higher energy level (nature) is likely to display higher alertness. With higher alertness, she is able to receive more input from her surroundings (nurture). Her mind would form more images, both aural and visual. She holds a positive response pattern in that she is always ready to respond positively to external inputs, quickening her process of assimilation and accommodation. Her learning capacity will grow larger, faster and richer as she internalizes more external knowledge and skills to become her own.

Another child may have a lower energy level (nature) and be less alert. She may respond more slowly to external surroundings (nurture). She may have longer attention spans (nature) to external stimulus and display more continuous concentration and repetition in assimilation and accommodation. In other words, her disposition is manifested in persistence, which helps her form a smaller but more solid repertoire of responses. Another child may be more "emotionally unstable" (nature) than others. She may easily get disturbed, be difficult to calm down, and respond to her surroundings (nurture) with agitation and negative response patterns. Her disposition will lead to a even smaller repertoire of action and responses.

In fact, a child's disposition is a configuration of the several factors mentioned above. One child may be both alert and persistent, another may have a higher level of persistence and less positive response patterns, and so forth. There are a vast degree of quantitative and qualitative differences among children, which interaction with the environment (nurture) leads to a formation of different life world of experience among children. Each child then grows and learns in his or her unique life world. No doubt intellectual and personality differences among children are as startling as they are complex.

The Affective Domain

If we further explore differences in predisposition manifested in persistence, alertness, and response patterns, we would find that they are still surface phenomena. Behind them is the complex interaction of at least two background factors that form the affective domain that underlies all learning behaviors: exploratory instinct and restless potential. Figure 5.1 is a framework of conceptual learning that takes into account the affective domain with these two background factors and a security-risktaking continuum, and a gratification-frustration continuum.

Figure 5.1
Li's Framework of Conceptual Learning

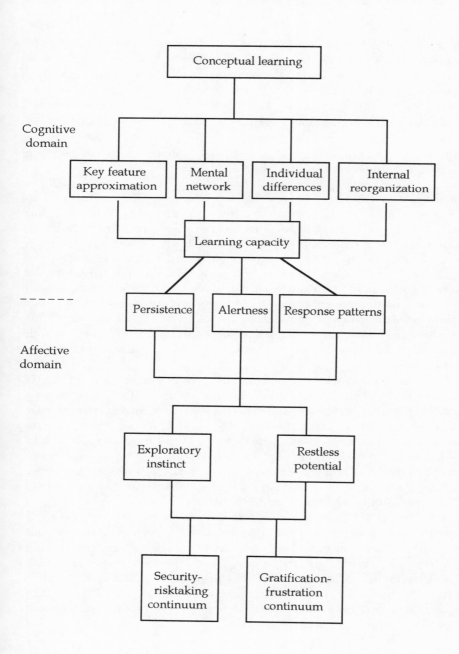

Exploratory Instinct

That the human species possesses an exploratory instinct is without question. For example, the behavior that a baby consistently shows more interest to new objects than familiar objects and keeps exploring them is called dishabituation (Zigler & Finn-Stevenson, 1987, p. 190). Exploratory instinct is most evident when an infant six to eight months old is able to crawl around to explore the environment. But in fact exploratory instinct starts even earlier. As a child's visual and aural senses begin to develop, she starts to make use of her vision and auditory power to explore the environment. One infant reflex indicating this exploratory instinct is rooting—the coordination of head—eye movement with sensory motor responses when being slightly touched at either side of the head. Another reflex is grasping (Zigler & Finn-Stevenson, 1987, p. 178).

Curiosity is a manifestation of exploratory instinct. Every child is more or less curious to her environment, to external stimulus, and to change. Curiosity, being so much a treasured attitude in education and so fundamental to learning, is in fact more or less prevalent in children. An infant starts with exploring her immediate environment, playthings, and nearby objects. When she grows older and acquires language, she explores through ideas, thinking and reasoning, through language and questions, searching for answers, meanings and values. Thus we can say that the human species starts with exploratory instinct, which was manifested in curiosity. Facilitated by the invention of language, this exploratory instinct takes a revolutionary turn and leads to the search for reasons, the development of reasoning, and the growth of meanings and values.

Think of a newborn infant and her environment. Everything is new to her, and she has to explore and get familiar with it. Every move and response of hers is an exploration, a step of venturing into the new and the unknown. As a corollary, the child is taking risks. A new stimulus may be unpleasant, disturbing, or even threatening. If a child explores too much and takes too many risks, she may be risking her life and survival. If she never explores or takes risks, she can never assimilate the external environment and grow up. At the same time, there are competing inputs and stimuli beyond a child's capacity to assimilate. So risk taking is constrained by the sense of security a child needs, and there develops a fine balance between risk taking and security. Study into children's exploratory behavior and risk-taking patterns may throw light on the gradual emergence of curiosity, which has vast impact on learning. A child's response to newness, novelty, or strangeness and the child's readiness to take risks are also of interest to researchers because a child's positive or negative response pattern will have far-reaching impact on learning.

A child gets security by close attachment to her mother/caregiver. One child may show more attachment and less exploratory behavior. Yet another child may need less attachment and security and show more exploratory tendencies. But the most frequent pattern is that, when exposed to a new environment, a child will first need attachment and security before she dares explore it.

Restless Potential

The neuroscience paradigm has postulated about action potential, that state in which neurons with excitory or inhibitory function, which serve as the basis for higher-order cognitive functions such as perceptual, sensory and psychomotor behavior, will discharge (Stevens, 1988). On the basis of this conception I wish to postulate a restless potential as another background factor of the affective domain underlying learning behavior.

A child is often seen as restless while an adult with more self-control can sit quietly and restfully. But such a resting state is not true of adults. Ask what you are doing and thinking now. Then ask what you did a minute ago, then another minute ago, and so on. You may be sitting reading quietly, but a lot of thoughts came to your mind, one stream of thought following another. The conspicuous fact is that your mind, like others', never stops: it is preoccupied in something; it keeps going, thinking, associating. An adult's apparent restfulness belies its restless state of mind.

A child's restlessness is even more obvious. She is always exploring or occupied in some action, such as sucking, moving, touching, crying. For a very simple action such as sucking, for example, it is already a highly complex outcome of interaction between the sucking reflex (nature) and external objects (nurture). It is not inaccurate to describe a baby's drinking or eating as a learned behavior, in which an internally generated restless state leads to that action or learned behavior.

A child is always preoccupied in some action or exploration. We can take this preoccupation as releasing restless potential and tension. A child will simply derive gratification by being occupied in action and exploration. Quite often the action is repetitive, but it is through repetition and practice that a child becomes familiarized with acting on the external world, in the process of which she gets satisfaction. It is likely that such repetition and practices will lead to the formation of certain synapses and the neural network which is the physiological basis of all learned behavior. The restless state leads to action and action leads to automatization in processing, which is reflected in the change/formation of certain neural networks. But an infant does not always get gratified. If an action is successful, for example, approaching an object or responding to a stimulus, it will generate pleasure, interest and further repetition, and in time mastery and automatization in processing. But if the action fails, it may lead to frustration and retreat.

A child's restless state and action is multidimensional. It may be directed in perceptual-motor, sensory-motor, psychomotor, and at later stages, verbal and cognitive functions. Research on the restless state, its processes and emotional manifestation have barely begun. We may investigate how in different ways a child proceeds in learning—how quickly she gets interested, gets familiar, succeeds in learning, later gets bored, and then turns to exploring new things. Also we may study how easily and quickly a child gets gratified or frustrated, how she fluctuates from gratification to frustration, and how quickly she may turn elsewhere to derive satisfaction.

So far I have identified two basic elements that are responsible for learning: security/risk taking and gratification/frustration. These two elements are fundamental to learning and the growth of the intellect. They belong to the twilight zone because they are neither nature nor nurture, but the interaction of background factors affecting human learning capacity. It seems there is a wide range of choices at the continuum of these two basic elements. The child in this schema is slowly emerging as an agent of choice, with a certain degree of freedom and predictability, which more or less leads to a self-directed development in the interaction between nature and nurture. It is likely that the configuration of these two elements are responsible for the uniqueness and the individual difference in intelligence and learning.

CHAPTER SUMMARY

There are five major learning theories: mental discipline, natural unfoldment, apperception, behaviorism and cognitivism. Each has strengths and weaknesses but all fail to satisfactorily explain how learning makes us intelligent.

Human learning is different from learning by other species in conceptual learning, that is, learning through the medium of concepts facilitated by language and the mental operation of conceptual thought. Conceptual learning is the acquisition of knowledge while behavioral learning is the learning of skills, motor and perceptual learning, and habit formation. Different principles govern behavioral learning and conceptual learning

The problem of initial learning is the problem of knowledge presupposition. Piaget's constructivism presupposes interaction between experience and environment without a priori knowledge, while Chomsky's preformatism presupposes innate fixed nucleus and the language acquisition device. Their debate yields inconclusive results.

I propose the notion of cognitive residues to represent unconscious processing of unattended information. They are deep-rooted cognitive structures that grow within a child. The physiological and social basis of cognitive residues can help supplement Piaget's constructivism.

Knowledge characteristics are different from cognitive characteristics. The former are partial, objective, expandable, tentative, and regulated by truth while the latter are subjective, fixed, secured, directed by interest, and governed by perceptual (gestalt) and processing principles. The asymmetry between the two makes learning a perennial human effort to overcome cognitive limitation in quest of knowledge.

I propose a typology of conceptual learning by two dimensions (intention and awareness) with four types: active conscious learning, passive conscious learning, active unconscious learning, and passive unconscious learning. They encompass Bruner's, Schank's, and Chomsky's version of learning.

A learning continuum represents how a learner moves from imitation to understanding to routinization in dealing with novelty. Concept learning (the acquisition of concepts) and conceptual learning (the acquisition of knowledge through concepts) are two sides of the same coin. Once a learner passes the threshold of learning, he/she is at the learning stage and he/she acquires knowledge by some organizing principles: approximation of key features, growth of mental network, one-dimensional growth pathway, and internal reorganization for meaning, efficiency, and simplicity.

Underlying individual differences in learning are predispositions of persistence, alertness, and positive response patterns. Behind these predispositions are the interaction of at least two background factors in the affective domain: exploratory instinct, and restless potential.

Intelligent Food for Thought V

In view of children's acquisition of concepts, how would they characterize a zebra? Is it a white animal with black stripes or a black animal with white stripes? Why do they think that way? Would a cross between a zebra and a white horse produce more white or black stripes? (Hint: this is more a scientific than a mind problem.)

For solution, see Stephen J. Gould's *Hen's Teeth and Horse's Toes: Further Reflections in Natural History* (1983).

6

Extending Conceptual Thought and Conceptual Learning to New Frontiers: The Development of Creativity

Creativity can be seen as the human enterprise of extending from the known to the unknown, of venturing from existing knowledge and domains of human endeavor to new knowledge and endeavor. It is a cutting edge into new frontiers (Li, 1989). When learning is the acquisition of existing knowledge and skills, creativity is the search for new knowledge and skills. Creativity goes beyond learning. In learning there are the pre-learning stage and learning stage, in which we move from imitation to understanding to routinization. Beyond that point is the post-learning stage, or creation stage, in which we explore for new ideas and possibilities. Creativity can thus be seen as an extension of learning.

THE STUDY OF CREATIVITY

The study of creativity has traditionally been focused almost exclusively on insight. Presumably insight is considered the essence of creativity. Thus Jacques Hadamard (1949) described the phenomenon of insight by four stages: preparation, incubation, illumination, and verification. This was further elaborated by Herbert Simon's (1977) computational explanation of familiarization and selective forgetting. Ohlsson's (1984) theory of insight was to reinterpret creative problem solving as searching through the problem space. One latest theory of scientific insight was offered by Pat Langley and Randolph Jones (1988), who integrated ideas from ten theorists and explained insight as a memory-related search phenomenon. All these theories are narrowly focused on the phenomenon of insight without looking at the whole process of creative thought. On the other hand, Robert Weisberg (1986, 1988) tried to demystify insight and argued that the same creative thought processes underlie psychological laboratory experiments and great people. Robert S. Albert (1990) pointed out that creativity and intelligence are empirically distinguishable, but his study of creatively gifted children did not yield any conclusive results of how eminence can be attained (Li, 1994a). To broaden the scope, Howard Gruber (1981), Gruber and Sara Davis (1988), and Gruber and Doris Wallace (1989) applied the case study method with an evolving-systems approach to the study of creative people, their product and process. This is a broader approach to the study of creative thought. The "multiple intelligences" psychologist Howard Gardner also did some case studies of *Creating Minds* (1993a). Not too surprisingly, his exemplars of creativity fit neatly into his multiple intelligences view: Freud for linguistic and logical creativity (intelligence), Picasso for spatial and bodily creativity (intelligence), Stravinsky for musical creativity (intelligence), and Gandhi for interpersonal intelligence (creativity).

From another approach, Dean Simonton (1990) expands the domain of study to include the "four *ps*" of creativity—person, product, process, and persuasion. Here, Simonton takes a socio-historical view to study genius and creativity. He sees creativity as a form of leadership that entails personal influence over others (1988, p. 386). He treats the complex phenomenon of creativity quantitatively (1976, 1977a, 1977b, 1978, 1984, 1985, 1986a, 1986b, 1987, 1989). By applying mathematics to historical data (probability theory, Poisson and multiple distributions, time-series analysis, nonlinear models, etc.), Simonton comes to the conclusion that creativity is a social phenomenon in that "a creator profoundly alters the thinking habits of other human beings by making a contribution to their quest for enhanced self-organization" (1988, p. 421). His chance-configuration theory (pp. 388-395) is a grand theory of creativity that takes into account chance permutation, configuration formation, and self-organization in the realization of creativity within a millieu.

THE NATURE OF CREATIVITY AND CREATIVE THOUGHT

Creativity as an Extension of Learning

While Herbert Walberg (1988, p. 340) characterizes "creativity and talent as learning," he merely stresses the importance of education but does not provide any theoretical justification. In my view, in-depth learning and in-depth thinking are generally the preconditions of creativity. First, we learn (acquire) existing knowledge. We think through it. We have an in-depth understanding of it. In fact, thinking underlies all conceptual learning. Then we reflect on, evaluate, and criticize it. To go further we reinterpret the whole framework of existing knowledge, sometimes in light of new evidence. Finally we invent new knowledge. This is what we call the creative process. Seen in this light, new knowledge usually cannot possibly exist out of the blue; it can always be traced back with its roots in existing knowledge.

If creativity is the extension of learning, why is the former so much more difficult than the latter? In other words, why is creating knowledge so much more difficult than acquiring knowledge? This may be because we use the same cognitive apparatus (human mind) to acquire knowledge as well as creating knowledge, but the task demand is quite different. In acquiring existing knowledge, the subject matter is well structured and well organized; we can learn it step by step in an orderly manner. We are given a paradigm that defines what problems are, what tools are available, what counts as solution, and where lies the standard of excellence. In other words, there are guidance and milestones in learning. We imitate, we follow through, we keep apprenticing our skills. But once we venture beyond the existing realm of knowledge, everything becomes fuzzy. There is no standard way of reasoning it, no accepted point of entry or departure, no agreed-upon conceptualization. The domain may have a problem, but there is no clear definition. Anything goes, and everything is a possibility. We have to make sense out of this amorphous, unstructured reality. Some researchers have thus characterized problem finding as an important skill for creativity (Csikszentmihalyi & Getzels, 1988). Creating is no easy task.

Creative Thought as an Extension of Conceptual Thought

Creative thought is an extension and special case of conceptual thought. It is the form of thought leading to the creation of new knowledge. Creative thought is an outgrowth of conceptual thought, which is again an outgrowth of rudimentary thought. Thus, human thought follows a growth path from rudimentary thought to conceptual thought, and then from conceptual thought to creative thought.

All existing knowledge is the product of creative thought. If we analyze our cultural artifacts and trace their origins, we would find that they were the invention of some creative persons back in history. In fact culture embodies knowledge, and knowledge originates from creative thought. If we draw a time line in history, we will find outselves always moving in the direction of creating more knowledge and adding it to our stock of cultural heritage. Instead of focusing narrowly on the issue of insight, I will take a broader perspective and try to answer the following more general questions: What is the nature of creative thought? What is its product, process, and mechanism? What are the characteristics of creative thought? How is creative thought possible? How do we create new knowledge?

The Nature of Creative Thought

My starting point is that creative thought is a thought process leading to the creation of new knowledge. This new knowledge can be seen as a product resulting from the interaction between a person's knowledge base and the problem the person tries to solve. If the person's knowledge base is broad, unique, and well matched with the resource requirement of the problem, then the person is likely to provide a creative solution to the problem. Quite often, there is a certain mix between the person's knowledge and the problem demand that renders a problem solvable and its solution creative. Whether a thought is deemed creative is socially defined. Quite often, it is defined in terms of the standard of the professional community of a discipline. Thus, the achievement of Nobel laureates can serve as some index of creative attainment. On the other hand, it is not infrequent that a thought is so creative that it is beyond the recognition of the professional community. For example, Charles Babbage, the father of computing, had a creative vision in 1823 of designing an analytic machine, the modern version of which is a computer. Yet his creative thought was too advanced to be recognized by his peers. Babbage's vision was not realized until 1944, when Howard Aiken built the first computer. Thus creative thought is as inherently possessed by a person as a post hoc given by society, based on social norms, values, and impact the creative product has on society. It follows that a creative thought cannot be understood outside human value, social context, and cultural meaning.

Let me examine how a person's knowledge base interacts with a problem situation, leading to the creation of new knowledge. A person's knowledge base is all the repetories of his/her thinking skills plus his/her knowledge ranging from facts, ideas to beliefs, theories, and systems of thought. His/her knowledge base generally reflects what is prevalent in society, or the existing conventional framework of knowledge. People think and create knowledge; knowledge then becomes a socially shared cultural artifact. Thus a person's knowledge base mostly reflects a part of this shared cultural artifact, though at times represented in an idiocycratic way.

When a person is engaged in problem solving, he/she is making use of quite a number of existing conventional frameworks of knowledge to bear upon a problem. This does not guarantee a solution to every problem because our existing knowledge does not have all the solutions to every problem. Under that situation, a transformation will take place: The person has to search through his/her knowledge base, again, the existing conventional knowledge frameworks represented idiocycratically and internally in him/her. He/she has to reconfigure or reorganize the knowledge in such a way that can match with the demand of the problem. The person may even have to radically expand his/her knowledge base, searching ideas/evidence from fields formerly alien to him/her. Such reconfiguration of knowledge will be subject to existing knowledge constraints. The person may have to break those constraints, leading to a new perspective, a redefinition of the problem-space as well as the adjustment of existing knowledge. In fact, he/she is producing new knowledge. I will illustrate all these with a case.

A CASE STUDY OF CREATIVE THOUGHT: JULIAN JAYNES'S THEORY OF CONSCIOUSNESS

Jaynes's Background and Theory

The Search of Consciousness

One afternoon in the late 1950s, a young and aspiring student living alone in Boston was pondering over the issue of consciousness in epistemology. The student had been studying continuously for about a week and finally lay down in intellectual despair on a couch. In his words,

Suddenly, out of an absolute quiet, there came a firm, distinct loud voice from my upper right which said, "Include the knower in the known!" It lugged me to my feet absurdly exclaiming, "Hello?" looking for whoever was in the room. The voice had an exact location. No one was there! Not even behind the wall where I sheepishly looked. (Jaynes, 1976, p. 86)

Thus started Julian Jaynes's lifelong search for the answer of his hearing voices in hallucination intermingled with his preoccupied problem of consciousness. Twenty years later, Jaynes, then teaching psychology in Princeton, proposed a startling theory in his book *The Origin of Consciousness in the Breakdown of the Bicameral Mind* (1976). The book brought Jaynes to immediate international acclaim, with one book critic complimenting, "As startling . . . as Darwin's dissolution of species, as Einstein's reigning of light."

Jaynes's Thesis of Bicameral Mind

Jaynes's thesis is novel, creative, and intriguing. He pointed out that human consciousness is as much a cultural invention as a change in brain neurophysiological organization. According to Jaynes, ancient people from Mesopotamia to Peru (B.C. 1000-3000), did not "think" as we do and were not conscious. Their brain physiology was probably somewhat different from ours. They had evolved language, which was directed by the Broca's area, Wernicke's area, and supplementary motor area of the left hemisphere. This is quite similar to us: they could speak, listen, and understand a conversation as we do. But Jaynes hypothesised that they have a corresponding speech area on the right hemisphere, connected to the left hemisphere through anterior commissures. This corresponding area on the right hemisphere can "think," "plan," "command," and "speak" to the left hemisphere of ancient people so that they can hear voices and act according to the command of those voices while not conscious of it. Thus ancient people are seen as living in a culture of mass hallucination organized under a hierarchy of theocracies: they were capable of building cities, farming, hunting and livestock rearing, communicating and cooperating with one another, but they were not conscious. Everyone is hearing voices from his/her own god for instructions, especially at novel, anxiety-arousing situations. Their lives were peaceful because their ideas and voices are generally homogeneous. Their minds are split into two parts: one part for themselves, organized by the left hemisphere, and the other part for the voices of the gods by the right hemisphere. They are thus called the bicameral mind.

Jaynes has proposed a theory so novel and strange that it is almost incomprehensible to us. He did try to bridge this gap by a familiar example. Assume you are driving a car with a bicameral man sitting next to you. You are using your hand, foot, eyes to steer and control the car in an automatic processing manner that demands little of your attention and consciousness. At the same time, you are always engaging your consciousness in something else: having a conservation with your passenger, listening to news report, engaging in deep thoughts, and so on. When something unexpected happened, such as an accident ahead, we modern people will automatically switch our consciousness back and plan our action. But the bicameral man will have to wait for his bicameral voice to tell him what to do (Jaynes, 1976, p. 85). Jaynes turned to the study of early agricultural civilizations for evidence to substantiate his claim. His study of Natufian culture (B.C. 9000-10,000) showed that

These Natufians were not conscious. They could not narratize and had no analog selves to 'see' themselves in relation to others. They were what we could call signal-bound, that is, responding each minute to cues in a stimulus-response manner, and controlled by those cues . . . I have suggested that auditory hallucinations may have evolved as a side effect of language and operated to keep individuals persisting at the longer tasks of tribal life . . . But after a time there is no reason not to suppose that such voices could 'think' and solve problems, albeit, of course, unconsciously. (Jaynes, 1976, p. 140)

The Rise of Human Consciousness

The logical development of Jaynes's theory is to account for the breakdown of the bicameral mind and the subsequent rise of human consciousness. This Jaynes did quite creatively, pointing out the inherent instability of bicameral kingdoms due to the invention of written language, the growth of more complex social structures, social and geological catastrophes, and interaction among bicameral cultures with different languages, beliefs, and voices of gods. The cause of the breakdown of the bicameral mind, "between hallucinated voice and automaton action, was that in social chaos the gods could not tell you what to do." (Jaynes, 1976, p. 209). In fact, the bicameral man habituated to obeying voices find it hard to adapt to rapid changes.

Jaynes wrapped up his thesis by pointing to the superiority of consciousness over the bicameral mind. He argued his case convincingly by digging evidence from ancient history of Mesopotamia, Early Greece, and Khabiru, showing the transition from bicameral mind to consciousness.

Analysis of Jaynes's Creative Thought

Jaynes's Existing Knowledge Base and Scholarship

Jaynes's problem is human consciousness: what it is and how it comes about. To answer this question, he searched through philosophy and psychology but did not get a definite answer. It is a problem that "keeps returning, not taking a solution" (p. 2).

Jaynes received his training in psychology but is interested in the problem of consciousness. His early training in psychology is basically under the behaviorist paradigm, which denies the existence of consciousness. Undeterred, Jaynes grabbed the idea of consciousness as learning and began his search for the origin of consciousness by doing experimental work in an attempt to produce signal learning in a mimosa plant. According to Jaynes, "After over a thousand pairings of the light and the tactile stimulus, my patient plant was as green as ever. It was not consciousness" (p. 7). Jaynes's utter failure and his apparent liability of behaviorist/experimental training turned out to be an asset. Throughout the book, Jaynes supported his claim by quoting a lot of cognitive psychological experiments. He even designed sophisticated experiments to demonstrate the relation between right hemisphere and face recognition to justify the claim of relative independence of the right hemisphere (p. 121).

Another deep knowledge base of Jaynes's is in philosophy. His deep understanding of the philosophical implication in the study of consciousness lead him to realize a paradox:

If understanding a thing is arriving at a familiarizing metaphor for it, then we can see that there always will be a difficulty in understanding consciousness. For it should be immediately apparent that there is not and cannot be anything in our immediate experience that is like immediate experience itself. There is therefore a sense in which we shall never be able to understand consciousness in the same way that we can understand things that we are conscious of. (Jaynes, 1976, p. 53)

Seeing this paradox is probably an important turning point for Jaynes to move away from the traditional philosophical search of consciousness and then strive for a novel, hard-to-understand thesis of the origin of consciousness. Thus, Jaynes had two vast knowledge bases: philosophy and psychology, which serve as fertile grounds for his academic growth. What is more, his scholarship is both broad and deep. It is not uncommon to see him refer to texts as old as nineteenth century and early twentieth century in fields such as history, archaeology, religion, and ancient studies. His broad knowledge base fulfils the precondition for the creation of new knowledge.

Crystallizing Experience and Added Academic Resources

Gardner (1988) used the term "crystallizing experience" to characterize "chance (or planned encounter) with some hitherto unfamiliar material or problem has a dramatically motivating effect on the individual" (p. 303). In Jaynes's case, his terrifying, hallucinating experience probably served as a dramatic motivating force, pushing him to the study of psychopathology, such as schizophrenia, hallucination, and split brain research. As we shall see later, such diversity of ideas becomes so instrumental and fundamental in Jaynes's formulation of his theory.

But the above knowledge bases and diversity are not sufficient for the production of a theory on the origin of consciousness. To answer the question of origin, one has to go to history and that is what Jaynes did. He studied ancient history and religion, trying to find evidence from archaeology and related disciplines. Jaynes even ventured into linguistics because he knew there must be some important connections between language and consciousness. In fact, Jaynes formulated his major theory of bicameral mind in 1969; seven years later he also proposed an evolutionary theory of language in Pleistocene (Jaynes, 1976).

The above should have adequately demonstrated that there is nearly nothing we cannot account for Jaynes's theory by his knowledge base, scholarship, crystallizing experience, and added academic resources. They are all part and parcel of the conventional framework of knowledge existing in different fields and generally possessed by a few different individual experts: a philosopher, a psychologist, a neuro-scientist, a linguist, a historian, and so on. What is new is that Jaynes combined all those subbranches of knowledge, configured and reorganized them to the point of proposing a theme to unify them in a meaningful way. His thesis of the bicameral mind is simple but startling, utilizing all the academic resources he could have for explanation and justification. He has to get numerous evidence of support from modern medical research on cases of mental disorder, brain research findings, as well as archaeology and ancient history and the interpretation of texts. Jaynes has literally produced new knowledge and called for the adjustment of existing knowledge frameworks in nearly all the fields he has come across. He forces us to change our thinking on consciousness, hallucination, and the psychohistory of ancient people.

The Links for Reaching Insight

In grand-scale theories such as this, it is not just one insight that pieces everything together. Rather it is an evolving process of discovering insights after insights, finally leading to the formulation of a new theory. In Jaynes's case, I wish to point out a few major links/insights that are essential to the formulation of his theory. First, it must be the realization of the paradox in the study of consciousness that leads Jaynes to search for novel understanding of the problem. Jaynes even admitted that a good theory of consciousness may even be so novel as to be "almost incomprehensible to us" (p. 84). Then, the realization that behaviorism is a dead end as well as hypocrisy leads Jaynes to backup and move to another direction. But the most important insight, of course, is to see the connection/similarity between the description of hallucinating schizophrenics and the mind of ancient people as obedient to the voices of gods. Both are hearing voices and both speak in scanning rhythms or rhyme. Finally, Jaynes wrapped up his theory with a sociological explanation of social and cultural catastrophe.

CHARACTERISTICS OF CREATIVE THOUGHT

The following are a few major characteristics of creative thought. First, creative thought results in new knowledge. New knowledge is often a configuration of existing knowledge. It is just inconceivable that a system of knowledge can exist out of the blue. It must have a developmental process, and its genesis could be found in existing frameworks of conventional knowledge. New knowledge is a creative reconfiguration and reorganization of existing knowledge producing a novel appearance and new understanding or perspective to old problems.

Second, existing knowledge serves as a germinating ground as well as constraining force for new knowledge. A system of new knowledge can provide new interpretation to existing knowledge or reduce existing knowledge to special cases, but it cannot simply disregard existing knowledge without well-reasoned arguments or counterresearch findings. In Jaynes's case, the record in ancient text of self-dialogue between a person and his god is an existing piece of knowledge he cannot deny. Nor can he deny hallucinations. All Jaynes can do is to accept these facts and constraints and develop a theory to encompass them. Another telling example is James Watson and Francis Crick's double-strand helical model of DNA. Initially the two scientists tried to build a model of DNA with three strands because at that time this seemed to be the only viable mechanism connecting the whole system. Once finished for peer commentary, they were embarrassed by their colleagues with expertise in X-ray analysis of DNA who pointed out that it must be incorrect because it is against existing knowledge of DNA evidence.

Thus, Watson and Crick were forced back to be drawing board, but not all the way to the beginning. They retained the helical structure, but changed it in response to new information that became available, in an example of a "local search." Two large changes took place in the structure: The bases were moved between the backbones of the helix, and the number of strands went from three to two. (Weisberg, 1988, p. 162)

Third, it is not always the case that new knowledge has to subject to the constraints of existing knowledge. At times the new knowledge may be so sweeping and encompassing that it provides a new paradigm and leads to the amendment, adjustment, or replacement of existing knowledge.   There are numerous examples in scientific discovery following this path. Einstein's theory of relativity is a far more encompassing theory than Newton's law of motion, amending the latter and reducing it to special cases. In Jaynes's case, he forced us to look at hallucination, ancient history, religion, and linguistics in new lights.

HOW DO WE CREATE NEW KNOWLEDGE?

How is creative thought possible?   How do we create new knowledge? As I pointed out earlier, conventional researchers focus narrowly on the study of insight.   For example, Robert Weisberg pointed out that insight is a common phenomenon tractable in both laboratory experiments and great people, showing the insight has a developmental/evolutionary process subject to the constraints of the problem situation (Weisberg, 1986, 1988).   Sternberg and Davidson (1982, 1983) suggested that insight is explicable through selective encoding, selective combination, and selective comparison.   Still Langley and Jones (1988) argued that insight is cued by external events, to be retrieved through unconscious spreading activation in memory. All these are micro descriptions that can only partially explain the creation of new knowledge. What I have in mind are some general principles that may account for the creation of new knowledge at a grand scale.

The first is to connect existing knowledge with a unifying theme. I have defined new knowledge as reconfiguration of existing knowledge. The important point to note here is that the creator has to use a theme to unify/connect knowledge and evidence from a number of domains. It is like connecting everything by a single thread. With this convergence, a new perspective is formed. How to find this theme is at the heart of insight. Hadamard (1949) called it illumination while Sternberg and Davidson (1982) called it selective encoding. I would characterize this process as selecting and finding the right connection. It is not easy because the creator has to search through his/her repertoire of knowledge, and there is no guarantee of success. However, it appears that a theme is an idea that has preoccupied the creator for a long time, gradually growing and evolving to the point that it unifies and connects many other ideas in his/her repertoire of knowledge. In Jaynes's case, we have seen that his theme of hallucination and bicameral mind is somehow related to his crystallization experience of hallucination. In Darwin's case, his theme of natural selection unifies a lot of phenomena such as inheritance, variation, acquired characteristics, environmental forces,and so on, together with support of the vast collection of facts from his voyage of the *Beagle* (Gruber, 1981). In the creative thought process, what is important is to artfully blend two or more concepts together, blending perspectives and evidences from different domains together, and yet maintaining a coherent and consistent picture.

The second is ramification approach. This is in fact a case of logical deduction, that is, spelling out the full conceptual ramification of an idea that has not been focused by others before. Note that an idea, say, liberty, has an immense ramification and consequences when defined and carried out to the full. In spelling out an idea, the creative person can apply logical reasoning, and scenario analysis as well as empirical data and examples. As in the case of Jaynes, his argument for the decline of the bicameral mind and the rise of consciousness is basically a ramification approach.

Third, any grand system of thought that carries high originality and creativity almost invariably came with a perspective shift. Thus Marx's claim that "All hitherto history is the history of class struggle" (Marx, 1848) is a perspective shift from conventional thinking of history. Generally, a perspective shift includes paradigm shift, problem shift, or problem redefinition. A paradigm shift has been extensively discussed by Thomas Kuhn (1970), and problem shift or redefinition has been termed problem finding and selection by Sternberg (1985). In paradigm shift it may be the growth of anomalies that the existing paradigm cannot account for, or possibly the discovery of new evidence calls for the reinterpretation of the existing paradigm. Problem definition depends very much on the creative person in question, who, with his/her unique or idiocycratic background, may bring in new ideas into a given field.

Fourth, consider the deconstruction approach. I have shown that almost all new ideas have their origins in existing knowledge frameworks. New ideas may elaborate or develop existing ideas further, but it is not uncommon that new ideas bury old ones. For a new idea to take shape, old ideas may have to be destroyed. The creative person may create a new framework, pointing out errors of the old framework, demolishing or reducing it to special cases. In that case, the creative person is proposing a more general and encompassing theory. At times, he/she does not destroy an old framework entirely but merely discovers certain constraints of the old framework and succeeds in breaking it.

Fifth, we can create new knowledge by assigning new meaning to existing empirical framework. Our conventional thinking is deeply rooted in the existing meaning and a realistic framework. Since we understand the world by its meaning to us and ground our experience in a realist/empirical framework, we are very much meaning bound and empirically bound. Our meanings in words do change over time, reflecting changes of our experience in reality. A creative thought may be one of broadening old meanings, or assigning new meanings to old. Take the idea of a game. It originates with children playing games, but it gradually evolves into ideas such as rules, players, optimizing strategies, and so on. John Von Neumann, a brilliant mathematician who made lasting contribution in the early history of computing and programming, took up this idea, assigned new meaning to it and created a new branch of mathematics called game theory. He then applied it in economics to account for economic behavior (Von Neumann & Morgenstern, 1944). Such is a creative undertaking, and it creates new knowledge by assigning new meanings and applying it to new fields and domains. To do so, the creative person must overcome the conventional meaning boundedness and empirical boundedness, exploit the metaphorical power of concepts put in different contexts, detect asymmetrical relations between concepts and contexts, and make use of his/her imagination to create new fields, new domains of knowledge, and subsequently new empirical possibilities.

Finally, there is also methodological consideration. In creating new knowledge, there are considerations such as to reflect on the structure of the theory, its symmetry, aesthetic beauty, and so on. Also criteria such as consistency, coherence, simplicity must also be met. However, methodological consideration serves more as a checking function of creative thought than the creating force of creative thought.

CHAPTER SUMMARY

Creativity is almost an intractable phenomenon. Researchers focus mostly on insight with the latest interpretation as selective forgetting (Simon, 1977) and a memory-related search phenomenon (Langley & Jones, 1983). Howard Gruber (1981) broadened it by the case study method and the evolving-systems approach. Howard Gardner (1993a) also did some case studies based on his theory of multiple intelligences. Dean Simonton (1988) sees creativity as a social phenomenon and proposes a chance-configuration theory to account for chance permutation, configuration formation, and self-organization for creativity.

My characterization is that creativity is the extension of conceptual thought and conceptual learning to new frontiers of knowledge and human endeavors. We venture from the known into the unknown, make sense out of the amorphous reality, and create new knowledge.

Creative thought is the process of transforming existing conventional knowledge into new knowledge. I illustrate the product, process and mechanisms by a case study on Julian Jaynes's theory of consciousness (1976). Here I trace Jaynes's existing knowledge base and scholarship, examine his crystallizing experience, analyze his configuration of existing knowledge, and outline his links for reaching insight.

Existing knowledge is both the germinating ground and the constraining force for new knowledge. New knowledge may be accumulative but sometimes it can be paradigm-setting and replace existing knowledge. A few principles for creating knowledge have been proposed: connecting existing knowledge with a unifying theme, ramification approach, perspective shift, deconstruction approach, new meaning assignment, and so on.

Intelligent Food for Thought VI

While Julian Jaynes studied consciousness, he also toyed with unconsciousness. Want to try unconscious learning?

1. Form a clandestine team of "red lovers" in your workplace. Go around complimenting every girl wearing red. In a week you will be surprised to find red everywhere (in office, corridor, cafeteria restroom, parking lot).
2. Ask someone to say random words to you. Whenever he/she says a plural noun, you smile, repeat it pleasantly, say "good," or do something positive. See how quickly the frequency of his/her plural noun utterances increases.
3. Try this on your professor. The whole class will smile, pay rapt attention, or roar to his/her jokes whenever he/she moves to the right side of the lecture hall. It is possible to train him/her to move out of the door!

Want more examples? See chapter 1 and 2 of Jaynes (1976). Then devise your own experiments.

7

Intelligence and Giftedness

THE NATURE OF HUMAN INTELLIGENCE

Conceptual Thinking and Conceptual Learning as the Essence of Human Intelligence

One unifying theme throughout this book is that conceptual thinking and conceptual learning are the two major unique characteristics of the human species. The capacity to think conceptually and the capacity to learn conceptually are the essence of human intelligence. The case I argue for is in fact an evolving consensus among intelligence researchers since the 1920s. What is lacking is a systematic theoretical treatment which this book attempts to provide. In thinking, I divide it into three levels: rudimentary thought, conceptual thought, and creative thought. While rudimentary thought is present in both lower species and humans, what separates us from other species is our capacity to think through concepts and, subsequently, the creation of new knowledge through creative thought. As for learning, nearly all species (even snails and worms) are capable of some form of behavioral learning, but it is the capacity for conceptual learning that has landed us to a new plateau of learning, through which we achieve understanding and the mastery of knowledge.

Conceptual Thought as an Outcome of Symbolic and Mental Interaction

Conceptual thought is made possible by the creation of concepts, which is the result of interaction between the symbolic world and the mental world. The symbolic world is the world of language symbols while the mental world is the world of mental events and activities. They interact in such a way that thought becomes objective, and language acquires meaning. Language also leads to the creation of concepts for thought to operate on. Language as a human invention has an unprecedented impact on the human species itself. Specifically language allows us to represent reality, to articulate ideas and feelings through concepts. With the advent of concepts, our thought process becomes conceptual thought, which allows us to think effectively and efficiently and also to act intelligently. In the co-evolution between language and thought, we see that rudimentary thought gradually gives way to conceptual thought, which is a more efficient way of thinking. On the one hand, language enhances thought, anchors thought, and gives order to thought. Conversely thought creates language, elevates linguistic functions, and manifests itself in language. In this sense language transforms thought as well as thought transforms language. The culmination of this co-evolution process has made the human species intelligent.

Conceptual Learning and the Human Knowledge Enterprise

One consequence of the co-evolution process is the creation of concepts and conceptual thought. With that the human species enter the phase of conceptual learning, or learning through concepts. This is a much deeper and more powerful way of learning than behavioral learning. Conceptual learning opens up a new domain for the human species, the accumulation and transmission of knowledge. No lower species are said to possess knowledge, though their genetic codes carry information for their growth and survival, which they can neither comprehend nor be conscious of. On the other hand, humans acquire knowledge and are able to understand it and transmit it through concepts, language, and communication. Because of the asymmetry between knowledge characteristics and human cognitive characteristics, learning becomes a perennial human effort to overcome our cognitive limitation in our acquisition of knowledge. My theory of conceptual intelligence is summarized in Figure 7.1.

The Collective Nature of Intelligence

Intelligence theorists have always taken intelligence as an inherent entity existed in individuals. The study of intelligence has always been focused on the cognitive process of an individual (Li, 1993). This "individualistic" approach may be mistaken. According to the theory postulated above, intelligence should be seen as a social collective effort. Intelligence is the logical outcome of language interacting with the

Figure 7.1
Li's Theory of Conceptual Intelligence in Summary

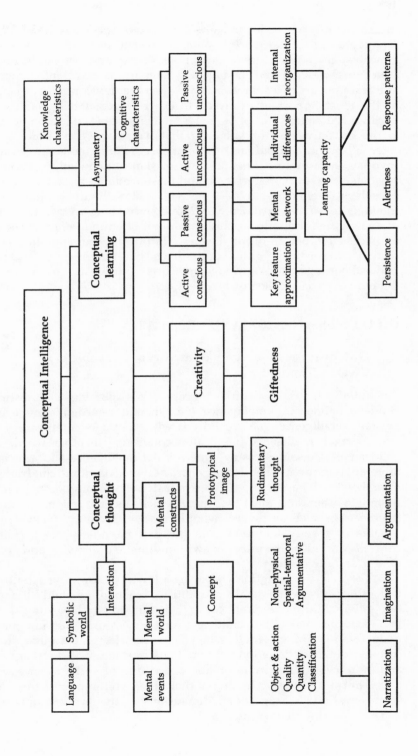

mental world, where language is a collective social product. Without language, our mental world would not be transformed into a world of concepts, and without the development of concepts we would not have conceptual thought and intelligence. Seen in this light, intelligence is a cultural product of a shared heritage with the development of language as the most important catalyst. In other words, intelligence is social because it develops out of language; intelligence is collective because it is the collective use of language that has made conceptual thought internalized in individuals. Intelligence is also cultural because it involves the accumulation and transmission of knowledge and cultural heritage. We learn, understand, and master human knowledge to make ourselves intelligent. While we see vast individual differences in intelligence, so that extraordinary intelligence seems to rest in the minds of a few gifted individuals, this should not obscure the fact of the social and collective nature of intelligence. In other words, intelligence may rest in extraordinary gifted individuals, but they owe it to our rich cultural heritage and knowledge enterprise, particularly to the language the human species collectively invent.

GIFTEDNESS, GENIUS, AND CREATIVITY

Giftedness as Supernormal Intelligence Capable of Creative Thought

Intelligence is a neutral concept. We may make a distinction between subnormal intelligence (i.e., mental retarded/slow learner), normal intelligence (i.e., children with average intelligence), and supernormal intelligence (i.e., gifted children). In other word, gifted children are those possessing supernormal intelligence and are capable of creative thought. Two major characteristics of gifted children stand out: they think better, and they learn faster. For example, they are very fluent in thinking and reasoning, such as induction, deduction, inference, as well as divergent and creative thinking. They are also capable of speedy imitation, and the understanding and learning of concepts and ideas, resulting in swift automatic processing and creation of new and novel ideas.

The above description just gives a broad picture of a gifted child. It does not specify the details of abilities of each gifted child. In fact, no two gifted children are identical in their thinking and learning abilities. For example, one gifted child is a creative thinker but not good at deductive reasoning. Another may learn very fast in the initial stage of certain formats of imitation but not at a later stage. Still another may be and be very efficient in automatic processing of certain concepts and ideas, but not others. The fact is that gifted children exist in different shapes and styles, stages, and dimensions so that we can only give a general description of them.

Everybody Has Gifts: Giftedness Is a Potential and Becoming Concept

Educators of the gifted are always faced with a troubling questions: Doesn't every child have his/her gift? If so, why do you separate the gifted from the nongifted in educating them? My answer based on the above theory is that every child does have his/her gifts—the ability to think and to learn. But there are vast individual differences in the ability to think and to learn too. The individual difference does not start at birth; in fact it starts right after fertilization of the egg. Cells grow exponentially, and there is strong competition among the cells to migrate and to specialize for specific body forms and functions. Before birth the brain has largely been formed, and it can already pick up signals or respond to the external environment. It is not exaggerating to argue that your intelligence starts in your mother's womb during the prenatal stage.

Then a child is born with different sex, weight, brain size, height, race, and so on. He/she is also born with different predisposition and faculties, behavioral tendencies, temperament, expectations, preferences, response strategies, energy level, and so forth. Malleable to some extent in early childhood, this gradually propels the child into a developmental pathway of his/her own, forming a unique configuration of attitudes, character traits, cognitive capabilities and affective sensitivity. All along there is the complex interaction between the genetic endowment and the environment (Storfer, 1990). Some speculated about the uneven growth spurts during brain development (Epstein, 1978; McQueen, 1984). Thus giftedness is not a fixed genetic given, but is a process of always becoming (Clark, 1988). A child without much apparent talent and interest in learning may, by undergoing some programs or crystallizing experience, become a motivated and efficient learner. Educators should acknowledge this and help all children enhance their potentials.

My theory has posited the pivotal role of language in thought. By extension of this theory, it seems that linguistic and conceptual fluency is an indicator of giftedness. For example, if a child has a vocabulary richer than his/her peers, is able to use linguistic forms (questions, answers, narration, discussion) more advanced than his/her age, or can describe things in detail and argue cogently, it is likely he/she may be gifted. On the conceptual side, if a child has a rich association network in his/her memory, if he/she is able to generalize experience efficiently and creatively, if he/she is able to see more similarities and differences in comparison, if he/she possesses a richer conceptual framework, these are all indicators of giftedness. Linguistic and conceptual fluency, however, does not show up until a child has acquired language, at least two or three years old, so that we may have to find other indicators of early giftedness, such as "perceptual efficiency" proposed by John

Borkowski and Virginia Peck (1986). In addition, the capacity to learn, or learning potential, especially on the conceptual level, is another major indicator of intellectual giftedness.

Distinction Between Child Giftedness and Adult Giftedness

Throughout the literature on giftedness, the term has been used to conveniently denote both gifted children and gifted adults. But the two are so qualitatively different that a clear distinction is badly needed. By extension of my theory, gifted children have a less stringent criterion than gifted adults. A gifted child may simply think better and learn faster. He/she may display creative thought such as solving a problem in a novel way, finding his/her way home from a strange place by unconventional cues, or come up with an original idea on, say, how to play a game and so on. Their creativity, however, is unmatched with real creative products produced by gifted adults such as great thinkers, scientists, writers, and leaders. Thus a child is considered gifted so long as he/she displays supernormal intelligence, that is, thinks better and learns faster, but an adult has to testify his/her giftedness by a creative product or performance. What is more, a gifted adult is *not* a simple continuation of a gifted child. Many gifted children fall short of the stringent criterion of producing creative works when they become adults (Tannenbaum, 1983). On the other hand, gifted adults do not necessary have their gifts shown or recognized as children. Then for the handful of gifted children who finally make it to qualify themselves as gifted adults, there are a lot of complicated extra-intellectual factors that have brought to their outstanding accomplishment and eminence (Gruber & Wallace, 1989) to the extent that Feldman called it coincidence (Feldman, 1991) and Tannenbaum (1983) called it the chance factor.

As argued in the above theory, a rich knowledge base is the precondition for creative thought and the creation of new knowledge. This I have demonstrated in the case study of Julian Jaynes. What is important here is to note that in this age of knowledge specialization and explosion, it is not enough to be acquainted with only one field; expertise in a variety of fields seems necessary for the production of new knowledge, as in Jaynes's case. Moreover, the gifted adult must have a genuine interest in the problem, must be willing to carry and labor through the problem for a long time, sometimes decades, and to possess a clear mind undrowned in the sea of data of different disciplines.

Can We Create Giftedness?

The answer is both yes and no. Yes, since giftedness is a potential concept and is always in the process of becoming; educators of the gifted can always enhance the potentials of their students to reach for more creativity. Moreover, I have shown that conceptual thinking is the essence on humans and all persons with normal intelligence are capable of conceptual thinking. From the basis of conceptual thinking, it can lead to creative thinking, which is the highest form of thinking. Creative thinking is in principle attainable by any normal person, and the process as I demonstrated it is not at all mysterious. Education can enhance creativity and giftedness (Li, 1989, 1994b). In fact creative thinking later becomes cultural artifacts, and we are all capable of learning them. Morever, metalearning—learning how to learn and monitoring ones learning—can enhance knowledge acquisition, a precondition for the development of intellectual giftedness (Li, 1995b).

On the other hand, very few people have the personality needed for the final attainment of creative thinking, such as risk taking, and tolerance of ambiguity (Sternberg, 1988a), purpose, ego strength, motivation (Gruber & Wallace, 1989) and so on. Even if they do, the creation of extraordinary products was shaped by unique circumstances, events, friends, peers, family, mentors, cultural tradition, existence of domain, domain-talent fit (Feldman, 1988), which are all beyond the capability of educators. In this respect, the impact of the family is especially important, which I have demonstrated in an Asian context (Li, 1992, 1995a). In conclusion, educators can enhance the potentials for giftedness but it is beyond their ability to produce gifted adults who can finally produce creative thinking and new knowledge. Surprisingly, statesmen can create giftedness and genius if they make more wars and sufferings, as Simonton's analysis of historical data shows (1984, 1988).

POSITIONING MY THEORY IN THE CONTEMPORARY SCENE

The theory in this book stands in sharp contrast with most contemporary theories of intelligence. Generally speaking, it has a broader scope and a sharper focus. Instead of theorizing intelligence in an abstract way, the theory starts from the contemporary consensus that thinking and learning are the two major components of intelligence and tries to explain thinking and learning in a systematic manner. In the process, it has answered the following basic questions: How is thinking possible? How does the human species grow into thinking? What are the nature and scope thinking? How does the advent of language transform thinking? What are the relations between language and thought? How are concepts formed, and how do they facilitate thinking? What are the nature and processes of conceptual thought and creative thought? How is the human species different from other species in learning? How is conceptual learning possible? How does conceptual learning take place? What are the nature, scope, content, and principles of conceptual learning, and how does it contribute to intelligence?

The Information-Processing Paradigm

The information-processing tradition is best represented by Sternberg's triarchic theory of intelligence (Sternberg, 1984, 1985). For Sternberg, intelligence is a cognitive phenomenon and process to be explained. This he explained by three subtheories: the contextual sub-theory, the experiential subtheory and the componential subtheory. He did not explicitly theorize about thinking, but implicitly studied reasoning by applying componential analysis to it. In other words, Sternberg is narrowly focused on the processing aspect of reasoning only, and his scope is limited to inductive reasoning and deductive reasoning. Sternberg did offer some localized theories for reasoning, such as the transitive chain theory of deductive reasoning (Guyote & Sternberg, 1981) and the componential theory of information processing in inductive reasoning (Sternberg, 1977), but they do not have the character of a general theory covering all types of reasoning and thinking.

My approach is different from Sternberg's. Instead of taking intelligence as a cognitive phenomenon and process to be explained, I take it as having two major components, thinking and learning, and examine them one by one. My study of thinking is a broad concern that answers many basic questions stated above. In so doing I have to examine the nature of language, the nature of concepts, the growth of conceptual thought and creative thought, and so on. I am also concerned about the conceptual thought process and postulate three modes of thought: narratization, imagination, and argumentation. In other words, I have a different starting point and approach from the information-processing paradigm.

The Factor-Analytic Paradigm and Learning Paradigm

The factor-analytic paradigm treats intelligence as a performance concept, or performance scores in intelligence tests. Its main concern is on factoring and measuring intelligent behaviors, which are supposed to manifest in intelligence test scores. As stated earlier, this paradigm is more concerned about whether there exists single or multiple abilities (intelligence) and how to measure them. It has eschewed more general and foundational issues such as how intelligence comes into being, what relation exists between intelligence, thinking, and learning, and so on. On the whole, the factor-analytic paradigm has no foundation theory to offer, at least about thinking and learning.

As regards to the existence of single or multiple intelligence (abilities), Horn (1989) posited the existence of seven important human abilities (see chapter 2). I have pointed out that five of them are basic cognitive abilities while the remaining two abilities, crystallized intelligence and fluid intelligence, are higher-level intellectual abilities. In fact, Horn's fluid intelligence is very similar to a category for reasoning. In contrast with Horn's, my concept of thinking is broader in scope, covering rudimentary thought, conceptual thought, and creative thought. Within conceptual thought I postulate three modes of thought: narratization, imagination and argumentation. As regards crystallized intelligence, it is related to domain-specific knowledge and learning. Here Ackerman 1989 provides a model for skill acquisition while I offer a theory of conceptual learning.

The learning paradigm is concerned about the role of learning in intelligence, but most treatments are inadequate, as they lack the status or structure of a theory. They have seldom touched the issues of knowledge characteristics and acquisition principles. In addition, many theorists stress only one aspect of learning while I attempt to offer a broader typology. By making a distinction between behavioral learning and conceptual learning, I hope to point to a new direction in our search for acquisition principles.

The Cognitive-Developmental Paradigm

My theory can be viewed as an integration of the learning paradigm and the cognitive-development paradigm, from which I gain many insights. The founding father of the cognitive-developmental paradigm is Jean Piaget. Another major figure is Howard Gardner. In fact Piaget's theory has inspired a whole generation of researchers— the Neo-Piagetians and Gardner, among others—in their study of intelligence. While I enjoy Gardner's eloquence and welcome the Neo-Piagetian effort, I will discuss only Piaget here.

It is embarrassing to compare my theory of intelligence with Piaget's. As I said earlier, my concern in intelligence, thinking and learning, is in fact a domain shared and studied extensively by Piaget. Piaget offers a very powerful and sophisticated theory of intelligence, focused on thinking and learning. It is a system of thought with a whole set of concepts, terms, notions, explanatory schemes, forming a theoretical construct and giving a descriptive account of intelligence in its development and stages. It is hard to deny Piaget's substantive contribution to theories of intelligence.

Piaget offers a rich taxonomy and theory to capture the many aspects of growth of the human intellect from childhood to adolescents, with thinking and learning as a unifying theme. Undeniably Piaget offers a very broad and general theory of intelligence. When it comes to thinking, Piaget has his own concepts and terminologies: logico-mathematical knowledge, reflective abstraction, differentiation and integration, relativization of concepts, quantification of relations. In representing formal thought (adolescent thinking), Piaget offers a logical model of 16 logical binary operations and the INRC group.

I hope, however, that my theory supplements Piaget's. I have a different starting point and come up with an entirely different picture of the problem. I did not approach the problem of thinking from a child-growth perspective. Instead I start from the nature of language and mental events and show the interaction between the symbolic world and mental world in the creation of concepts. I outline the co-evolution between language and thought, the development of conceptual thought, creative thought, and so on. In spelling out my theory, I also develop many concepts, arguments, and constructs. As for learning, Piaget is concerned with development, learning in a general sense, while I am concerned with learning in a conceptual sense, or learning in the specific sense of knowledge transmission. Our theories are of course wide apart.

Do Piaget's theory and mine ever meet? If both of us have the same concern, how can we differ so greatly? Who is correct? I tend to think of it with an analogy: we are both going to the top of a mountain but we take different routes. Both routes can lead to the top of the mountain, but they differ in steps and direction. In fact our perspectives are different: Piaget takes the perspective of a developmental psychologist, but I am an educationalist, integrating linguistics, philosophy, and psychology in my perspective for the purpose of education. Finally we do meet at the top of the mountain: Piaget's formal thought is the same as my conceptual thought and creative thought. Here again we speak different languages. If in any small way can my ideas go beyond Piaget, it is because I have the opportunity to read and benefit from his.

SYNTHESIS IN THE NINETIES

Synthesis is a perennial human effort in the human knowledge enterprise and this also happens in human intelligence theories. In the 1990s we see, for example, Miles Storfer integrating *Intelligence and Giftedness* (1990). Storfer argued cogently that "[t]he quality of children's educational environments during infancy and toddlerhood can make a dramatic and lasting difference in their measured intelligence" (p. xiv). Below I will review Mike Anderson's and David Perkins's integrating effort, and suggest some synthesis with mine.

Anderson's Minimal Cognitive Architecture

Mike Anderson is a new wave in intelligence research with an ambitious attempt to integrate the factor-analytic paradigm and the cognitive-developmental paradigm.   Educated in Edinburgh and Oxford and later joining the British Medical Research Council doing research on cognitive development, Mike found himself in an unfavorable research environment.   After Cyril Burt's scandal of masquerading data on intelligence research, British psychologists generally look upon intelligence with scepticism and suspicion. Undeterred and with the support of fellow researchers, Mike spent four years building his minimal cognitive architecture of intelligence, an exhilarating synthesizing effort that represents among the best work in contemporary intelligence theories. While Anderson alludes to major figures in intelligence research such as Sternberg, Gardner, Guilford, and Vernon, his main thrust comes from theorists of two entirely opposing camps: Piaget and Jensen. From Piaget and Neo-Piagetians such as Juan Pascual-Leone, Robbie Case and G. S. Halford, Anderson finds support for qualitative change in cognitive development. From Jensen, he takes the IQ/RT correlation studies to show the existence of Spearman's g of and gets the inspiration that "intelligence must be a processing parameter underlying knowledge, knowledge use and knowledge acquisition" (p. 44).

Facts, Postulates, and Architecture

Anderson starts with five significant facts which, he argues, must be accounted for by any theory of intelligence:

(1)   Cognitive abilities increase with development (p. 6).
(2)   Individual differences are remarkably stable in development (p. 7).
(3)   Cognitive abilities co-vary (p. 8).
(4)   There are also specific cognitive abilities (p. 9).
(5)   There are cognitive mechanisms that are universal for human beings and which show no individual differences (p. 10).

These all sound common sense, but Anderson shows us they are conflicting facts. For example, individual differences shown in measured IQ as in (2) conflict with universal cognitive mechanisms showing no individual differences in (5). Nor is stability in IQ (2) compatible with increase in cognitive abilities in (1). Moreover, are not cognitive abilities and intelligence two sides of the same coin? To make matters even more confusing, Anderson proposes two startling hypotheses:

H1: Intelligence does not develop (p.1).
H2: Intelligence constrains development (p. 3).

Anderson tries to convince readers that this is "not merely an exercise in semantics" (p. 1). He did so by drawing many diagrams of his minimal cognitive architecture (p. 74, 97, 107, 110) and creating a metaphor of a law firm, Anderson and Anderson, with secretary, partners and specialists (p. 101-6). Finally I was convinced, not by his rhetoric but by his scholarship. In his minimal cognitive architecture, Anderson postulates the existence of a few components:

- One basic processing mechanism;
- Two specific processors;
- A few modules.

The Anderson Black Boxes

I reorganize Anderson's architecture in two black boxes for easy understanding (Figure 7.2). Calling them black boxes are entirely legitimate, even for Anderson. In his words, "the theory does not, as yet, embody a computational model. That is to say, the theory could not be used at the moment to explain precisely how someone solves even the simplest of problems" (p. 213).

Figure 7.2
The Anderson Black Boxes of Intelligence and Cognitive Development

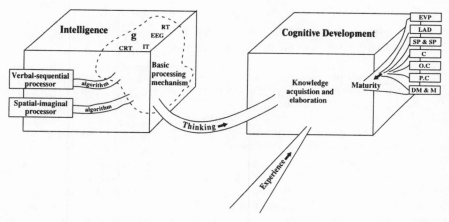

Key :

g	=	Psychometric g
IT	=	Inspection time
RT	=	Reaction time
EEG	=	Electroencephalogram
CRT	=	Complex reaction time
EVP	=	Ecological visual perception
DM & M	=	Decoupling mechanism & metarepresentation
LAD	=	Language acquisition device
SP & SP	=	Speech perception & syntactic parsing
C	=	Causality
OC	=	Object concept
PC	=	Perceptual categories

Basically Anderson makes a distinction between intelligence and cognitive development, the former as envidenced in measured IQ and the latter as detailed in Piagetian terms. Although Piaget is at war with IQ—he worked in Binet Laboratory in 1920 and later turned against the IQ test gang (see my chapter 1), Anderson tries to combine the two by thinking, a term he uses to denote "the process which most knowledge is acquired" (p. 104).

According to Anderson, the intelligence black box contains a basic processing mechanism which varies in speed among individuals. The performance of basic processing mechanism can be approximated in knowledge-free measures such as reaction time (RT), choice reaction time (CRT), inspection time (IT) or average evoked potentials (AEP). "There has been growing evidence . . . [that they] are significantly related to high-level differences in cognition measured by psychometric tests of intelligence" (p. 57). Though Anderson concedes that "these data are by no means as unequivocal" (p. 57), he nevertheless takes this as evidence that "there are low-level cognitive processes that underlie intelligent thinking" (p. 58). Thus Anderson "posits that a major component of intelligence is the basic processing mechanism and that it is responsible for the phenomenon of psychometric g, because it varies in its speed among individuals in the population" (p. 58).

Connecting Intelligence with Cognitive Development

Since the basic processing mechanism is basically genetic and stable, this explains his significant fact (2) and supports his H1: Intelligence does not develop. In addition, Anderson postulates that inside the intelligence black box are two specific processors, the verbal-propositional processor and the spatial-imaginal processor. They generate problem-solving algorithms for the basic processing mechanism to implement, a process Anderson calls "thinking" (p. 99), and the result is "knowledge acquisition." By this architecture, Anderson explains significant fact (4) and connects intelligence with cognitive development. Since the speed of the basic processing mechanism constrains the performance of the two specific processors, it also explains significant fact (3).

But the intelligence black box has a hard time explaining many complex human abilities discoverd by cognitive scientists, such as the acquisition of language, the capacity of extracting three-dimensional structure, the language of thought (Fodor, 1975), and so on. So Anderson postulates modules—specialized computationally complex mechanisms. Modules are input systems that exist because of evolutionary advantage, and they must satisfy three conditions: "(1) the information they provide increases the organism's chances of survival; (2) the information base for those mechanisms is likely to be invariant for members of the species; (3) the information cannot be provided by more general-purpose knowledge-acquisition mechanisms in an ecologically useful time frame" (p. 62-63). Among the more important modules are capabilities related to ecological visual perception, language acquisition, speech perception and syntactic parsing, causality, object concept, perceptual categories, decoupling mechanism (Leslie, 1987) and meta-representation (see Figure 7.2). By postulating the existence of modules, Anderson explains significant fact (5). Since modules mature in stages, Anderson explains significant fact (1).

Now we reach the cognitve development black box. Here cognitive development is manifest in knowledge acquisition and elaboration, which can be attained, independently as well as simultaneously, from three routes: thinking, experience, and module maturity (indicated by arrows in figure 7.2). Since intelligence can influence cognitive development via thinking and knowledge acquisition, this is the same as saying H2: Intelligence constrains development. So Anderson finally reaches an apparently paradoxical conclusion: *Intelligence does not develop but cognitive abilities grow.* Anderson's architecture is a bold conjecture of the complicated inner-working mechanisms of human intelligence. For one thing, I applaud his courage to taking a strong stance which is subject to scientific refutation.

Perkins's Mindware

Written a few years after Anderson's *Intelligence and Development* (1992), David Perkins's *Outsmarting IQ—The Emerging Science of Learnable Intelligence* (1995) tries to integrate not only Anderson's work but also many recent research findings on thinking, such as Deanna Kuhn's (1991) *The Skills of Argument,* Jonathan Baron and his associates' (1993) *Decision-making Bias,* and Ellen Langer's (1989) *Mindfulness.* One unifying theme across these researches is that adults do not think intelligently: they are biased, mindless, one-sided in their arguments, and think illogically. Perkins laments at adults' poor reasoning and prescribes reflective thinking, the major component of his learnable intelligence. (See chapter 2 of this book for review.)

While Perkins pointed out that "Anderson's map stands separate from the main concern of [my] book, reflective intelligence" (1995, p. 306), I find it interesting to contrast them. Anderson postulates two black boxes (intelligence and cognitive development) while Perkins proposes three intelligences (neurological, experiential and reflective). Upon closer look, Perkins's neurological intelligence is as old as Spearman's *g*, which is Anderson's version of basic processing mecha-nism. And Perkins's experiential intelligence stressing the importance of content-specific knowledge is surprisingly similar to Anderson's knowledge acquisition and elaboration in the cognitive development black box. This in fact reflects research consensus of the 1990s. The difference between the two lies rather in that Perkins postulates reflective intelligence (the mindware), while Anderson proposes two specific processors and a few modules. Are they merely different labels of the same thing or are they conceptually different structures?

My view is that they are different. By Anderson's account, modules are complex input and processing systems that are universal among the human species. They are prewired and cannot be learned. As for Perkins, his reflective intelligence (the mindware), can be improved through learning. Thus, Anderson's is a descriptive account of intelligence while Perkins's is a prescriptive account similar to Baron's rational thinking (1985), and choice-theoretic prescription of intelligence. On the other hand, Anderson has not been very clear about whether his specific processors are prewired or learned, though he insists that the latent power of these processors is often constrained and under-manifested by the speed of basic processing mechanism. Since specific processors generate problem-solving algorithms for basic processing mechanism to execute, they may well be the likely candidate of Perkins's mindware. However, Perkins is talking about the software function of the mind (1995, p. 13), and Anderson is alluding to a hardware architecture. Even if we can reconcile the two, they are surely not a difference in semantics.

Further Synthesis

While Anderson, Perkins, and I hold different theoretical orientations, a comparison may throw light on the nature of problems we each try to address (Table 7.1).

Both Anderson and Perkins try to find the neurological basis of intelligence, thus Anderson's basic processing mechanism and Perkins's neurological intelligence. I have barely touched this issue, apart from postulating a learning capacity with some underlying predispositions. While Anderson hypothesizes two separate processors—the verbal-propositional processor and the spatial-imaginal processor, I suggest that language (symbolic world) and mental events (mental world) interact in the creation of concepts and thus conceptual intelligence. Then Anderson's modules overlap with my notion of cognitive residues. As for the developmental process, Anderson and Perkins both acknowledge the important role of knowledge and experience in intelligence, while I propose conceptual learning and detail the asymmetry between knowledge and cognition. When Perkins postulates reflective intelligence (the mindware), I theorize on conceptual thinking. Finally I extend my theory to explain creativity and giftedness while Anderson finds support of his theory from research on mentally-retarded subjects.

Table 7.1
Approaches to Intelligence in Comparison: Anderson, Perkins, and Li

	Anderson (1992)	Perkins (1995)	Li (1996)
Theory	Minimal Cognitive Architecture	Learnable Intelligence	Conceptual Intelligence
Architecture	Basic processing mechanism	Neurological intelligence	
	Verbal processor and spatial processor		Symbolic-mental interaction and concept
	Modules		Cognitive residues
Developmental Process	Knowledge acquisition and elaboration	Experiential Intelligence	Conceptual learning
		Reflective Intelligence and mindware	Conceptual thinking
Scope of Explanation	Mental retardation		Giftedness
			Creativity

In management we like to contrast the top-down with the bottom-up approach. In comparing Anderson's approach with mine, it makes sense to say that his is an "inside-out" approach while I am working on an "outside-in approach." That is, I try to conceptualize the intelligence phenomenon and theorize from its ontology (i.e., thinking and learning) to its mechanisms. From the other side, Anderson theorizes from the intelligence mechanisms (black boxes) to the intelligence phenomenon.

Further synthesis may work in the direction of bridging the gap between the phenomenon and the mechanisms. On the phenomenal side, it is the issue of specifying the rules and organizing principles of conceptual thought, the nature and characteristics of learning capacity, the stages of conceptual development, and the growth paths of thinking and learning. On the mechanism side, it is the problem of detailing the problem-solving algorithms of specific processors, the rules of knowledge acquisition and elaboration, and the maturity of modules. If the two approaches can slowly move toward each other, we may be nearer to opening the Anderson black boxes.

CHAPTER SUMMARY

The capacity to think and to learn conceptually are the essence of human intelligence. Conceptual thought is made possible by the creation of concepts, which is the result of interaction between the symbolic world of language and the mental world of rudimentary thought. In the co-evolution between language and thought, language enhances, anchors and gives order to thought, while thought creates language, elevates linguistic functions and manifests itself in language.

Conceptual learning is a consequence of conceptual thought; it is a much deeper and more powerful way of learning than behavioral learning. Conceptual learning opens up a new universe for the human species—the building of the knowledge enterprise through knowledge accumulation and transmission.

Intelligence has its social and collective nature. It is a cultural product, a shared heritage of the human knowledge enterprise. Intelligence can be better understood in social and cultural context.

Based on the theory of conceptual intelligence, gifted children are defined as those possessing supernormal intelligence and are capable of creative thought: they think better, learn faster, and are capable of speedy imitation, efficient understanding, swift automatic processing, and the creation of new and novel ideas. Linguistic and conceptual fluency are indicators of giftedness.

Everybody has gifts: giftedness is a potential and becoming concept. Education can enhance creativity and giftedness because creative thinking, an outgrowth of conceptual thought, can be taught and learned.

It is necessary to make a distinction between child giftedness and adult giftedness. A gifted adult is not a simple continuation of a gifted child. Many gifted children do not produce creative works when they become adults and many gifted adults do not have their gifts recognized as children. A lot of complicated extra-intellectual factors affect adult giftedness and accomplishment.

My theory starts from the contemporary consensus of thinking and learning as the major components of intelligence. I try to explain the human intelligence phenomenon by the notion of conceptual thinking and conceptual learning. My approach is very different from the information-processing paradigm and the factor-analytic paradigm. It is an integration of the learning paradigm and the cognitive-developmental paradigm from which I draw research findings heavily for support. Finally I am indebted to Piaget for his ideas and insights, which I try hard to go beyond.

The 1990s saw some integrating effort, notably Mike Anderson's minimal cognitive architecture and David Perkins's learnable intelligence.   The former is a bold conjecture of the inner working mechanisms of human intelligence while the latter gives a prescriptive account of how to outsmart IQ. Further synthesis may try to bridge the gap between theories on the phenomenon of intelligence and theories on its mechanisms.

References

Ackerman, P. L. (1989). Individual differences and skill acquisition. In P. L. Ackerman, R. S. Sternberg & R. Glaser (Eds.), *Learning and individual differences* (pp. 164-217). New York: W. H. Freeman.

_____. (1994). Intelligence, attention, and learning: Maximal and typical performance. In D. K. Detterman (Ed.), *Current Topics in Human Intelligence; Volume 4: Theories of Intelligence* (pp. 1-27). Norwood: Ablex.

Ackerman, P. L., & Goff, M. (1995). Intelligence, personality, and interests: Historical review and a model for adult intellect. Submitted to *Psychological Bulletin* (under review).

Albert, R. S. (1990). Identity, experiences, career choice among the exceptionally gifted and eminent. In M. A. Runco & R. S. Albert (Eds.), *Theories of creativity*. Newbury Park, CA: Sage.

Anderson, J. R. (1983). *The architecture of cognition*. Cambridge: Harvard University Press.

_____. (1990). *Cognitive psychology and its implications* (3rd ed.). New York: W. H. Freeman.

Anderson, M. (1992). *Intelligence and development: A cognitive theory*. Cambridge: Blackwell.

Arlin, P. (1975). Cognitive development in adulthood: A fifth stage? *Developmental Psychology, 11*, 602-606.

Ayer, A. J. (1936). *Language, truth and logic*. New York: Pelican Books (reprint 1971).

Baron, J. (1985). *Rationality and intelligence*. Cambridge: Cambridge University Press.

_____. (1986). Capacities, dispositions, and rational thinking. In R. J. Sternberg & D. S. Detterman (Eds.), *What is intelligence? Contemporary viewpoints and its nature and definition* (pp. 29-33). Norwood, NJ: Ablex.

Baron, J., Granato, L., Spranca, M., & Teubal, E. (1993). Decision-making biases in children and early adolescents: exploratory studies. *Merrill-Palmer Quarterly, 39*(1), 22-46.

Barsalou, L. W. (1983). Ad hoc categories. *Memory and Cognition,* 11, 211-227.

Bigge, M. L. (1982). *Learning theories for teachers* (4th ed.). New York: Harper & Row.

Biggs, J. B., & Telfer, R. (1987). *The process of learning* (2nd ed.). Australia: Prentice-Hall.

Bloom, L. (1973). *One word at a time: The use of single word utterances before syntax.* The Hague: Mouton.

_____. (Ed.). (1978). *Readings in language development.* New York: Wiley.

_____. (1991). *Language development from two to three.* Cambridge: Cambridge University Press.

_____. (1993). *The transition from infancy to language: Acquiring the power of expression.* Cambridge: Cambridge University Press.

Boring, E. G. (1923). Intelligence as the tests test it. *New Republic, 34,* 35-36.

Borkowski, J. G., & Peck, V. A. (1986). Causes and consequences of metamemory in gifted children. In R. J. Sternberg & J. E. Davidson (Eds.), *Conceptions of giftedness* (pp. 182-200). Cambridge: Cambridge University Press.

Bower, G. H., Black, J. B., & Turner, T. J. (1979). Scripts in memory for text. *Cognitive Psychology, 11,* 177-220.

Brentano, F. S. (1874). *Psychologie vom empirischem Standpunkt.* Vol. 3. Vom. London: Routledge & Kegan Paul (1981).

Broca, P. (1861). Sur le volume et la forme du cerveau suivant les individus et suivant les races. *Bulletin Societe d'Anthropologie Paris 2,* 139-207, 301-321, 441-446.

Brown, A. L., & Campione, J. C. (1984a). Learning ability and transfer propensity as sources of individual differences in intelligence. In P. H. Brooks, C. McCauley, & R. Sperber (Eds.), *Learning and cognition in the mentally retarded* (pp. 265-294). Hillsdale, NJ: Erlbaum.

_____. (1984b). Three faces of transfer: Implications for early competence, individual differences, and instruction. In M. Lamb, A. Brown, & B. Rogoff (Eds.), *Advances in developmental psychology* (Vol. 3, pp. 143-192). Hillsdale, NJ: Erlbaum.

_____. (1985). *Dynamic assessment: One approach and some initial data.* Cambridge: Bolt, Beranek & Newman.

_____. (1986). Academic intelligence and learning potential. In R. J. Sternberg & D. S. Detterman (Eds.), *What is intelligence? Contemporary viewpoints and its nature and definition* (pp. 39-43). Norwood, NJ: Ablex.

Brown, H. D. (1987). *Principles of language learning and teaching* (2nd ed.). Englewood Cliffs, NJ: Prentice-Hall.

Bruner, J. S. (1960). *The process of education.* Cambridge: Harvard University Press.

_____. (1966). *Toward a theory of instruction.* Cambridge: Harvard University Press.

_____. (1983). *Child's talk: Learning how to use language.* New York: Norton.

_____. (1984). Narrative and paradigmatic modes of thought. Invited address to American Psychological Association. Toronto, August 25. *Yearbook of National Society for the Study of Education,* 1984-85. (pp. 97-115). Chicago: University of Chicago Press.

Bruner, J. S., & Anglin, J. M. (1973). *Beyond the information given: Studies in the psychology of knowing.* New York: Norton.

Bruner, J. S., Goodnow, J. J., & Austin, G. A. (1956). *A study of thinking*. New York: Wiley.

Bruner, J. S., Olver, R. R., & Greenfield, P. M. (1966). *Studies in cognitive growth*. New York: Wiley.

Buhler, K. (1934). *Sprachtheorie: die Darstellungsfunktion der Sprache*. Jena: Gustav Fischer.

Burks, B. S., Jensen, D. W., & Terman, L. M. (1930). *The promise of youth: Follow-up studies of a thousand gifted children*. *Genetic studies of genius* (Vol. 3). Stanford, CA: Stanford University Press.

Butterfield, E. C. (1986). Intelligent action, learning and cognitive development might all be explained in the same theory. In R. J. Sternberg & D. S. Detterman (Eds.), *What is intelligence? Contemporary viewpoints and its nature and definition* (pp. 45-49). Norwood, NJ: Ablex.

Butterfield, E. C., & Feretti, R. P. (1989). Intelligence as a correlate of children's problem-solving. *Journal of Mental Retardation, 93* (4), 423-433.

Campione, J. C. (1989). Assisted assessment: A taxonomy of approaches and an outline of strengths and weaknesses. *Journal of Learning Disabilities, 22* (3), 55-65.

Carey, S. (1985). *Conceptual change in childhood*. Cambridge: MIT Press.

Carroll, J. B. (1976). Psychometric tests as cognitive tasks: A new "structure of intellect." In L. B. Resnick (Ed.), *The nature of intelligence*. Hillsdale, NJ: Erlbaum.

_____. (1980). *Individual difference relations in psychometric and experimental cognitive tasks* (NR 150-406 ONR Final Report). Chapel Hill: L.L. Thurstone Psychometric Laboratory, University of North Carolina.

Case, R. (1978). Intellectual development from birth to adulthood: A neo-Piagetian interpretation. In R. S. Siegler (Ed.), *Children's thinking: What develops?* (pp. 37-71). Hillsdale, NJ: Erlbaum.

Cattell, R. B. (1971). *Abilities: Their structure, growth and action*. Boston: Houghton Mifflin.

Chapman, L. J., & Chapman, J. P. (1959). Atmosphere effect re-examined. *Journal of Experimental Psychology, 58*, 220-226.

Chomsky, N. (1959). A review of B. F. Skinner's verbal behavior. *Language, 35*, 26-58.

_____. (1965). *Aspects of the theory of syntax*. Cambridge: MIT Press.

_____. (1970). *The acquistion of syntax in children from 5 to 10*. Cambridge: MIT Press.

_____. (1980). Human language and other semiotic systems. In T. A. Seboek and D. J. Umiker-Sebeok (Eds.), *Speaking of apes* (pp. 429-440). New York: Plenum Press.

Churchland, P. M. (1988). *Matter and consciousness: A contemporary introduction to the philosophy of mind* (rev. ed.). Cambridge: MIT Press.

Clark, B. (1988). *Growing up gifted* (3rd ed.). Columbus, OH: Merrill.

Clark, H. H. (1969). Linguistic processes in deductive reasoning. *Psychological Review, 76*, 387-404.

_____. (1972). Difficulties people have answering the question "where is it?" *Journal of Verbal Learning and Verbal Behavior, 11*, 265-277.

Commons, M. L., Richards, F. A., & Kuhn, D. (1982). Systematic and metasystematic reasoning: A case for levels of reasoning beyond Piaget's stage of formal operations. *Child Development, 53*, 1058-1069.

Csikszentmihalyi, M., & Getzels, J. W. (1988). Creativity and problem finding in art. In F. H. Farley & R. W. Neperud (Eds.), *The foundations of aesthetics, art, and art education.* Westport, CT: Praeger.

de Bono, E. (1986). *Six thinking hats.* New York: Viking.

_____. (1987). *CoRT thinking program: Workcards and teacher's notes.* Chicago: Science Research Associates.

_____. (1992). *Teach your child how to think.* New York: Viking.

Dennett, D. (1978). *Brainstorms.* Cambridge: MIT Press.

Dewey, J. (1933). *How we think: A restatement of the relation of reflective thinking to the educative process.* Boston: D.C. Health.

Dickstein, L. S. (1978). The effect of figure on syllogistic reasoning. *Memory & Cognition, 6,* 76-83.

Dryden, G., & Vos, J. (1995). *The learning revolution: A life-long learning program for the world's finest computer—your amazing brain.* Torrance, CA: Jalmar Press.

Eccles, J. C. (1991). *Evolution of the brain: Creation of the self.* London: Routledge.

Egan, K. (1988). *Primary understanding: Education in early childhood.* New York: Routledge.

_____. (1990). *Romantic understanding: The development of rationality and imagination. Ages 8-15.* New York: Routledge.

Epstein, H. (1978). Growth spurts during brain development: Implications for educational policy and practice. In J. Chall & A. Mirsky (Eds.), *Education and the brain, the 77th yearbook of the National Society for the Study of Education* (Pt. 2, pp. 343-370). Chicago: University of Chicago Press.

Erickson, J. R. (1974). A set analysis theory of behavior in formal syllogistic reasoning tasks. In R. Solso (Ed.), *Loyola symposium on cognition* (Vol. 2). Hillsdale, NJ: Erlbaum.

_____. (1978). Research on syllogistic reasoning. In R. Revlin & R. E. Mayer (Eds.), *Human reasoning.* Washington, DC: Winston.

Eysenck, H. J. (1979). *The structure and measurement of intelligence.* New York: Springer.

_____. (Ed.). (1982). *A model for intelligence.* New York: Springer.

_____. (1986a). Is intelligence? In R. J. Sternberg, & D. K. Detterman (Eds.), *What is intelligence?* (pp. 69-72). Norwood, NJ: Ablex.

_____. (1986b). The theory of intelligence and the psychophysiology of cognition. In R. J. Sternberg (Ed.), *Advances in the psychology of human intelligence* (Vol. 3). Hillsdale, NJ: Erlbaum.

_____. (1993). The biological basis of intelligence. In P. A. Vernon (Ed.), *Biological approaches to the study of human intelligence* (pp. 1-32). Norwood, NJ: Ablex.

Feldman, D. H. (1988). Creativity: Dreams, insights, and transformations. In R. J. Sternberg (Ed.), *The nature of creativity* (pp. 272-297). Cambridge: Cambridge University Press.

_____. (1991). *Nature's gambit: Child prodigies and the development of human potential.* New York: Teachers College, Columbia University.

Feyeraband, P. K. (1963). Mental events and the brain. *Journal of Philosophy, 60* (11), 295-296.

Flanagan, O. (1991). *The science of the mind* (2nd ed.). Cambridge: MIT Press.

Flavell, J. H. (1977). *Cognitive development*. Englewood Cliffs, NJ: Prentice-Hall.

Fodor, J. (1968). *Psychological explanation*. New York: Random House.

_____. (1975). *The language of thought*. New York: Thomas Y. Crowell.

_____. (1980). On the impossibility of acquiring "more powerful" structures. In M. Piattelli-Palmarini (Ed.), *Language and learning: The debate between Jean Piaget and Noam Chomsky* (pp. 142-162). London: Routledge & Kegan Paul.

_____. (1983). *The modularity of mind*. Cambridge: MIT Press.

Fung, Y. L. (1948). *A short history of Chinese philosophy*. New York: Macmillan

Gagne, R. M. (1970). *The conditions of learning* (2nd ed.). New York: Holt, Rinehart and Winston.

_____. (1989). Some reflections of learning and individual differences. In P. L. Ackerman, R. J. Sternberg, & R. Glaser (Eds.), *Learning and individual differences: Advances in theory and research* (pp.1-11). New York: W. H. Freeman.

Gallagher, J. M., & Reid, D. K. (1981). *The learning theory of Piaget and Inhelder*. Monterey, CA: Brooks/Cole Publishing Co.

Galton, F. (1869). *Hereditary genius*. New York: D. Appleton.

Gardner, H. (1983). *Frames of mind: The theory of multiple intelligences*. New York: Basic Books.

_____. (1985). *The mind's new science: A history of the cognitive revolution*. New York: Basic Books.

_____. (1988). Creative lives and creative works: A synthetic scientific approach. In R. J. Sternberg (Ed.), *The nature of creativity* (pp. 298-324). Cambridge: Cambridge University Press.

_____. (1989). *To open minds: Chinese clues to the dilemma of contemporary education*. New York: Basic Books.

_____. (1991). *The unschooled mind: How children think and how schools should teach*. New York: Basic Books.

_____. (1993a). *Creating minds: An anatomy of creativity seen through the lives of Freud, Einstein, Picasso, Stravinsky, Eliot, Graham and Gandhi*. New York: Basic Books.

_____. (1993b). *Multiple intelligences: The theory in practice*. New York: Basic Books.

Gelman, S. A., & Markman, E. M. (1986). Categories and induction in young children. *Cognition, 23*, 183-208.

_____. (1987). Young children's inductions from natural kinds: The role of categories and appearances. *Child Development, 58*, 1532-1541.

Geschwind, N. (1965). Disconnection syndromes in animal and man. Part 1. *Brain 88*, 237-294.

Ginsburg, H. P., & Opper, S. (1988). *Piaget's theory of intellectual development* (3rd ed.). Englewood Cliffs, NJ: Prentice-Hall.

Glaser, R. (1976). The processes of intelligence and education. In L. B. Resnick (Ed.), *The nature of intelligence*. Hillsdale, NJ: Erlbaum.

_____. (1986). Intelligence as acquired proficiency. In R. J. Sternberg & D. S. Detterman (Eds.), *What is intelligence? Contemporary viewpoints and its nature and definition* (pp. 77-83). Norwood, NJ: Ablex.

Glaser, R., & Rabinowitz , M. (1985). Cognitive structure and process in highly competent performance. In F. D. Horowitz & M. O'Brien (Eds.), *The gifted*

and talented: Developmental perspectives (pp. 75-98).   Washington, DC:
American Psychological Association.

Goddard, H. H. (1914). *Feeble-mindedness: Its causes and consequences.* New
York: Macmillan.

Goodall, J. (1971). *In the shadow of man.* Boston, MA: Houghton Mifflin.

Gould, S. J. (1981). *The mismeasure of man.* New York: Norton.

_____. (1983). *Hen's teeth and horse's toes: Further reflections in natural history.*
New York: Norton.

Greene, M. (1978). *Landscape of learning.* New York: Teachers College Press.

Griffiths, A. P. (Ed.). (1967). *Knowledge and belief.* London: Oxford University
Press.

Grinder, R. E. (1967). *A history of genetic psychology: The first science of human
development.* New York: Wiley.

_____. (1985). The gifted in our midst: By their divine deeds, neuroses, and
mental test scores we have known them. In F. D. Horowitz & M. O'Brien
(Eds.), *The gifted and talented, developmental perspectives* (pp. 5-35).
Washington, DC: American Psychological Association.

Gruber, H. E. (1981). *Darwin on man: A psychological study of scientific creativity*
(2nd ed.). Chicago, IL: University of Chicago Press.

Gruber, H. E., & Davis, S. N. (1988). Inching our way up Mount Olympus: The
evolving systems approach to creative thinking. In R. J. Sternberg (Ed.),
The nature of creativity (pp. 243-270). Cambridge: Cambridge University
Press.

Gruber, H. E., & Wallace, D. B. (Eds.). (1989). *Creative people at work: Twelve
cognitive case studies.* New York: Oxford University Press.

Guilford, J. P. (1967). *The nature of human intelligence.* New York: McGraw-Hill.

Guthrie, E. R. (1942). Conditioning: A theory of learning in terms of stimulus,
response, and association. In N. B. Henry (Ed.), *The forty-first year book of
the National Society of Education: II. The psychology of learning* (pp. 17-60).
Chicago: University of Chicago Press.

Guyote, M. J., & Sternberg, R. J. (1981). A transitive-chain theory of syllogistic
reasoning. *Cognitive Psychology, 13,* 461-525.

Hadamard, J. (1949). *The psychology of invention in the mathematical field.*
Princeton, NJ: Princeton University Press.

Hamlyn, D. W. (1978). *Experience and the growth of understanding.* London:
Routledge & Kegan Paul.

Haygood, R. C., & Bourne, L. E. (1965). Attribute and rule learning aspects of
conceptual behavior. *Psychological Review, 72,* 175-195.

Hebb, D. O. (1949). *The organization of behavior.* New York: Wiley.

Herrnstein, R., & Murray, C. (1994). *The Bell curve: Intelligence and class structure
in American life.* New York: Free Press.

Hill, W. F. (1985). *Learning: A survey of psychological interpretations* (4th ed.).
New York: Harper & Row.

Hirst, P. H. (1974). *Knowledge and the curriculum: A collection of philosophical
papers.* London: Routledge & Kegan Paul.

Holzman, M. (1984). Evidence for a reciprocal model of language development.
Journal of Psycholinguistic Research, 13, 119-146.

Horn, J. L. (1965). *Fluid and crystallized intelligence.* Unpublished doctoral
dissertation, University of Illinois, Urbana-Champaign.

_____. (1985). Remodeling old models of intelligence: Gf-Gc theory. In B. B. Wolman (Ed.), *Handbook of intelligence* (pp. 462-503). New York: Wiley.

_____. (1989).   Models of intelligence.   In R. L. Linn (Ed.), *Intelligence: Measurement, theory and public policy* (pp. 29-73). Urbana: University of Illinois Press.

Horn, J. L., & Cattell, R. B. (1966). Refinement and test of the theory of fluid and crystallized intelligence. *Journal of Educational Psychology, 57*, 253-270.

Hospers, J. (1967). *An introduction to philosophical analysis* (rev. ed.). Englewood Cliffs, NJ: Prentice-Hall.

Houston, J. P. (1986). *Fundamentals of learning and memory* (3rd ed.). New York: Harcourt Brace Jovanovich.

Hull, C. L. (1943). *Principles of behavior.* New York: Appleton.

_____. (1952). *A behavior system.* New Haven, CT: Yale University Press.

Humphreys, L. G. (1979). The construct of general intelligence. *Intelligence, 3,* 105-120.

_____. (1986). Describing the elephant. In R. J. Sternberg & D. S. Detterman (Eds.), *What is intelligence? Contemporary viewpoints and its nature and definition* (pp. 97-100). Norwood, NJ: Ablex.

Hunt, E. B. (1978). Mechanics of verbal ability. *Psychological Review, 85,* 109-130.

_____. (1980). Intelligence as an informatin processing concept. *British Journal of Psychology, 71,* 449-74.

Huttenlocher, J., & Higgins, E. T. (1971).   Adjectives, comparatives, and syllogisms. *Psychological Review, 78,* 487-504.

Jackendoff, R. (1987). *Consciousness and the computational mind.* Cambridge: MIT Press.

Jackson, F. (1982). Epiphenomenal qualia. *Philosophical Quarterly, 32* (127).

James, W. (1890). *The principles of psychology. 3 vols.* Cambridge: Harvard University Press (reprint 1976).

Jaynes, J. (1976). *The origin of consciousness in the breakdown of the bicameral mind.* Boston: Houghton Mifflin.

Jensen, A. R. (1969). How much can we boost IQ and scholastic achievement? *Harvard Educational Review, 39,* 1-123.

_____. (1980). *Bias in mental testing.* New York: Free Press.

_____. (1982).   Reaction time and psychometric *g.* In H. J. Eysenck (Ed.), *A model for intelligence* (pp. 93-132). New York: Springer-Verlag.

_____. (1984). Test validity: *g* versus the specificity doctrine. *Journal of Social and Biological Sciences, 7,* 93-118.

_____. (1986). Intelligence: "Definition," measurement, and future research. In R. J. Sternberg & D. K. Detterman (Eds.), *What is intelligence?* (pp. 109-112). Norwood, NJ: Ablex.

Johnson-Laird, P. N., & Steedman, M. (1978). The psychology of syllogisms. *Cognitive Psychology, 10,* 64-99.

Johnson-Laird, P. N., & Wason, P. C. (1977). *Thinking: Readings in cognitive science.* Cambridge: Cambridge University Press.

Kamin, L. (1974). *The science and politics of IQ.* Hillsdale, NJ: Erlbaum.

Kamin, L., & Eysenck H. J. (1981). *The intelligence controversy.* New York: Wiley.

Keil, F. C. (1989). *Concepts, kinds, and cognitive development.* Cambridge: MIT Press.

Kellogg, R. T. (1983). Age differences in hypothesis testing and frequency processing in concept learning. *Bulletin of the Psychonomic Society, 21,* 101-104.

Klein, S. B. (1991). *Learning: Principles and applications* (2nd ed.). New York: McGraw-Hill.

Kohler, W. (1927). *The mentality of apes.* New York: Harcourt Brace Jovanovich.

Kossan, N. E. (1981). Developmental differences in concept acquisition strategies. *Child Development, 52,* 290-298.

Kripke, S. (1972). Naming and necessity. In D. Davidson and G. Harman (Eds.). *Semantics of natural language.* Dordrecht, Holland: Reidel.

Kuhn, D. (1991). *The skills of argument.* Cambridge: Cambridge University Press.

Kuhn, T. S. (1970). *The structure of scientific revolution* (2nd ed.). Chicago: University of Chicago Press.

_____. (1977). *The essential tension: Selected studies in scientific tradition and change.* Chicago: University of Chicago Press.

Langer, E. J. (1989). *Mindfulness.* Menlo Park, CA: Addison-Wesley.

Langley, P., & Jones, R. (1988). A computational model of scientific insight. In R. J. Sternberg (Ed.), *The nature of creativity* (pp. 177-201). Cambridge: Cambridge University Press.

Lenneberg, E. H. (1967). *The biological foundations of language.* New York: Wiley.

Leslie, A. M. (1987). Pretense and representation: the origins of 'theory of mind'. *Psychological review, 94,* 412-26.

Lewis, D. (1966). An argument for the identity theory. *Journal of Philosophy, 63* (1).

Li, R. (1989). *Education and creativity.* Hong Kong: Gifted Education Council. (In Chinese).

_____. (1992). *Education and research of the gifted in Taiwan, Mainland China and Hong Kong: A comparative study.* Hong Kong: Gifted Education Council.

_____. (1993). *Recent advances in theories of intelligence.* Paper presented at the National Conference on the Research on and Education of Gifted Children, October, Beijing. (In Chinese).

_____. (1994a). *From giftedness to eminence: A review of Albert studies.* Hong Kong: IES Book Review.

_____. (1994b). *Hong Kong gifted programs on creativity: Program implementation and evaluation.* Paper presented at The 3rd Asia-Pacific Conference on Giftedness, August 1-4, Seoul, Korea.

_____. (1995a). *A study of parent-child relations among gifted Chinese children.* Unpublished doctoral dissertation, Teachers College, Columbia University.

_____. (1995b). *How to teach critical thinking and creativity to Chinese students.* Workshop presentation at the 11th World Conference on Gifted and Talented Children, July 31-August 4, Hong Kong.

Lieberman, P. (1975). *On the origins of language.* New York: Macmillan.

Locurto, C. M. (1991). *Sense and nonsense about IQ: The case for uniqueness.* Westport, CT: Praeger.

Markman, E. M. (1989). *Categorization and naming in children: Problems of induction.* Cambridge: MIT Press.

Marshack, A. (1985). *Hierarchical evolution of the human capacity: The paleolithic evidence. 54th James Arthur lecture on the evolution of the human brain, 1984.* New York: American Museum of Natural History.

Marshalek, B., Lohman, D. F., & Snow, R. E. (1983). The complexity continuum in the radex and hierarchical models of intelligence. *Intelligence, 7,* 107-127.

Marzano, R. J. (1989). *Dimensions of thinking: A framework for curriculum and instruction.* U.S.A.: Association for Supervision and Curriculum Development.

Marx, K. (1848). *The communist manifesto.* Harmondoworth, UK: Penguin Books (reprint 1967).

Matthews, G. B. (1977). Consciousness and life. *Philosophy,* 52(199), 13-26.

McArthur, T. (1983). *A foundation course for language teachers.* Cambridge: Cambridge University Press.

McNeill, D. (1966). Developmental psycholinguistics. In F. Smith & G. A. Miller (Eds.), *The genesis of language: A psychological approach.* Cambridge: MIT Press.

McQueen, R. (1984). Spurts and plateaus in brain growth: A critique of the claims of Herman Epstein. *Educational Leadership, 41* (5), 66-69.

Mithaug, D. E. (1993). *Self-regulation theory: How optimal adjustment maximizes gain.* Westport, CT: Praeger.

Murphy, G. L., & Medin, D. (1985). The role of theories in conceptual coherence. *Psychological Review, 92,* 289-316.

Neimark, E. (1975). Intellectual development during adolescence. In F. Horowitz (ed.), *Review of child development research* Vol. IV. Chicago: University of Chicago Press.

Nickerson, R. S., Perkins, D. N., & Smith, E. (1985). *The teaching of thinking.* Hillsdale, NJ: Erlbaum.

Norman, E. R. (1985). Differences in intelligence and automatic memory process. *Intelligence, 1* (9), 3, 265-274.

Novak, J. D., & Gowin D. B. (1984). *Learning how to learn.* Cambridge: Cambridge University Press.

Ohlsson, S. (1984). Restructuring revisited: Summary and critique of the gestalt theory of problem solving. *Scandinavian Journal of Psychology, 25,* 65-78.

Passow, A. H. (1986). Reflections on three decades of education of the gifted. *Reoper Review, 4,* May, 223-226.

Pei, M. (1966). *Glossary of linguistic terminology.* New York: Anchor Books.

Peters, R. S. (1966). *Ethics and education.* London: Allen & Unwin.

Perkins, D. N. (1992). *Smart schools: From training memories to educating minds.* New York: Free Press.

_____. (1995). *Outsmarting IQ: The emerging science of learnable intelligence.* New York: Free Press.

Perkins, D. N., & Simmons, R. (1988). Patterns of misunderstanding: An integrative model of misconceptions in science, mathematics, and programming. *Review of Educational Research, 58(3),* 303-326.

Phillips, D. C., & Soltis, J. F. (1985). *Perspectives on learning.* New York: Teachers College Press.

Piaget, J. (1926). *The language and thought of the child*, (M. Gabain Trans.) London: Routledge & Kegan Paul.

———. (1950). *The psychology of intelligence* (M. Percy & D. E. Berlyne, Trans.). London: Routledge & Kegan Paul.

———.(1951). *Play, dreams and imitation in childhood* (C. Gattegno & F. M. Hodgson, Trans.). New York: Norton.

———. (1952). *The origins of intelligence in children.* (M. Cook, Trans.). New York: International Universities Press.

———. (1971). *Genetic epistemology* (E. Duckworth, Trans.). New York: Columbia University Press.

———. (1974). *Adaptation vitale et psychologie de L'intelligence: Selection organique et phenocopie.* Paris: Hermann.

———. (1978). What is psychology? *American Psychologist, 33,* 648-52.

———. (1980). The psychogenesis of knowledge and its epistemological significance. In M. Piattelli-Palmarini (Ed.), *Language and learning: The debate between Jean Piaget and Noam Chomsky* (pp. 23-34). London: Routledge & Kegan Paul.

Piaget, J., & Inhelder, B. (1958). *The growth of logical thinking from childhood to adolescence.* A. Parsons and S. Seagrin., Trans. New York: Basic Books.

Popper, K. R. (1963). *Conjectures and refutations.* London: Routledge & Kegan Paul.

———. (1972). *Objective knowledge: An evolutionary approach.* Oxford: Oxford University Press.

Pressley, M. & associates. (1990). *Cognitive strategy instruction that really improves children's academic performance.* Cambridge: Brookline Books.

Putnam, H. (1975). The meaning of meaning. In H. Putnam, (Ed.), *Mind, language and reality.* Vol. 2. Cambridge: Cambridge University Press.

Quine, W. V. O. (1977). Natural kinds. In S. P. Schwartz, (Ed.), *Naming, necessity, and natural kinds.* Ithaca, NY: Cornell University Press.

Resnick, L. B. (Ed.) (1976). *The nature of intelligence.* Hillsdale, NJ: Erlbaum.

Rimoldi, H. J. (1948). Study of some factors related to intelligence. *Psychometrika, 13,* 27-46.

Rips, L. J., & Marcus, S. L. (1977). Supposition and the analysis of conditional sentences. In M. A. Just & P. A. Carpenter (Eds.), *Cognitive processes in comprehension.* Hillsdale, NJ: Erlbaum.

Rorty, R. (1979). *Philosophy and the mirror of nature.* Princeton, NJ: Princeton University Press.

Rosch, E. (1973). On the internal structure of perceptual and semantic categories. In T. E. Moore (Ed.), *Cognitive development and the acquisition of language.* New York: Academic Press.

———. (1978). Principles of categorization. In E. Rosch & B. Lloyd (Eds.), *Cognition and categorization* (pp. 28-48). Hillsdale, NJ: Erlbaum.

Rosch, E., Mervis, C. B., Gray, W. D., Johnson, D. M., & Boyes-Braem, P. (1976). Basic objects in natural categories. *Cognitive Psychology, 8,* 382-439.

Ross, G. (1980). Categorization in 1- to 2- year-olds. *Developmental Psychology, 16,* 391-396.

Rousseau, J. J. (1762). *Emile.* W. Boyd (Ed. and Trans., 1956). New York: Teachers College Press.

Rumbaugh, D. M. (1980). Language behavior of apes. In T. A. Sebeok and D. J. Umiker-Sebeok (Eds.), *Speaking of apes* (pp. 231-259) New York: Plenum Press.

Rumelhart, D. E., & Abrahamson, A. A. (1973). A model for analogical reasoning. *Cognitive Psychology, 5*, 1-28.

Rumelhart, D. E., & Norman, D. A. (1975). The problem of reference. In D. A. Norman & D. E. Rumelhart (Eds.), *Explorations in cognition.* San Francisco: Freeman.

Russell, B. (1912). *Problems of philosophy.* London: Oxford University Press.

Ryle, G. (1949). *The concept of mind.* London: Hutchinson.

Sattler, J. M. (1988). *Assessment of children* (3rd ed.). San Francisco: Jerome M. Sattler, Publisher.

Schank, R. C. (1982). *Dynamic memory: A theory of learning in computers and people.* Cambridge: Cambridge University Press.

_____. (1986). Explaining intelligence. In R. J. Sternberg, & D. K. Detterman (Eds.), *What is intelligence?* (pp. 121-131). Norwood, NJ: Ablex.

Schank, R. C., & Abelson, R. (1977). *Scripts, plans, goals and understanding.* Hillsdale, NJ: Erlbaum.

Schucard, D. W., & Horn, J. L. (1972). Cortical evoked potentials and measurement of human abilities. *Journal of Comparative and Physiological Psychology, 78*, 59-68.

Schultz, A. (1932). *The phenomenology of the social world.* Vienna: Julius Springner. (G. Walsh & F. Lehnert, Trans.) (reprint 1967, 1980). London: Heinemann.

Schwartz, S. P. (1980). Natural kinds and nominal kinds. *Mind, 89*, 182-195.

Senge, P. (1990). *The fifth discipline: The art and practice of the learning organization.* New York: Doubleday.

Shaffer, J. (1963). Mental events and the brain. *Journal of Philosophy, 60* (6), 160-166.

Shepherd, R. N., & Metzler, J. (1971). Mental rotation of three-dimensional objects. *Science, 171*, 701-703.

Shore, B. M., & Dover, A. C. (1987). Metacognition, intelligence and giftedness. *Gifted Child Quarterly, 31, (1)* 37-39.

Shweder, R. A. (1977). Culture and thought. In B. B. Wolman (Ed.), *International encyclopedia of neurology, psychiatry, psychoanalysis, and psychology* (p. 446). New York: Van Nostrand Reinhold.

Siegl, L. S. (1978). The relationship of language and thought in the preoperational child: A reconsideration of non-verbal alternatives to Piagetian tasks. In L. S. Siegel & C. J. Brainerd, (Eds.), *Alternatives to Piaget: Critical essays on the theory.* New York: Academic Press.

Siegler, R. S., & Richards, D. D. (1982). The development of intelligence. In R. J. Sternberg (Ed.)., *Handbook of human intelligence* (pp. 897-971). Cambridge: Cambridge University Press.

Simon, H. A. (1977). *Boston studies in the philosophy of science: Vol. 54. Models of discovery.* Boston: Reidel.

Simonton, D. K. (1976). Philosophical eminence, beliefs, and zeitgeist: An individual generational analysis. *Journal of Personality and Social Psychology, 34*, 630-640.

_____. (1977a). Creative productivity, age, and stress: A biographical time series analysis of 10 classical composers. *Journal of Personality and Social Psychology, 35,* 791-804.

_____. (1977b). Eminence, creativity, and geographic marginality: A recursive structural equation model. *Journal of Personality and Social Psychology, 35,* 805-816.

_____. (1978). Independent discovery in science and technology: A closer look at the Poisson distribution. *Social Studies of Science, 8,* 521-532.

_____. (1984). *Genius, creativity, and leadership.* Cambridge: Harvard University Press.

_____. (1985). Intelligence and personal influence in groups: Four nonlinear models. *Psychological Review, 92,* 532-547.

_____. (1986a). Multiples, Poisson distributions, and chance: An analysis of the Brannigan-Wanner model. *Scientometrics, 9,* 127-137.

_____. (1986b). Stochastic models of multiple discovery. *Czechoslovak Journal of Physics, 36,* 138-141.

_____. (1987). *Why presidents succeed.* New Haven, CT: Yale University Press.

_____. (1988). Creativity, leadership, and chance. In R. J. Sternberg (Ed.), *The nature of creativity* (pp. 386-428). Cambridge: Cambridge University Press.

_____. (1989). *Scientific genius.* Cambridge: Cambridge University Press.

_____. (1990). History, chemistry, psychology and genius: An intellectual autobiography of historiometry. In M. A. Runco & R. S. Albert (Eds.), *Theories of creativity.* Newbury Park, CA: Sage.

Skemp, R. R. (1979). *Intelligence, learning and action : A foundation for theory and practices in education.* New York: Wiley.

Skinner, B. F. (1957). *Verbal behavior.* New York: Appleton-Century-Crofts.

Slobin, D. I. (1971). *Psycholinguistics.* Glenview, IL: Scott, Foresman.

_____. (Ed.). (1986). *The crosslinguistic study of language acquisition.* Hillsdale, NJ: Erlbaum.

Smart, J. J. (1962). Sensations and brain processes. In V. C. Chappell (Ed.), *The philosophy of mind* (pp. 16-172). Englewood Cliffs, NJ: Prentice-Hall.

Smith, S. M., Brown, H. O., Toman, J. E. P., & Goodman, L. S. (1947). The lack of cerebral effects of d-Tubercurarine. *Anesthesiology, 8,*1-14.

Smoke, K. L. (1933). Negative instances in concept learning. *Journal of Experimental Psychology, 16,* 583-588.

Snow, R. E. (1978). Theory and method for research on aptitude processes. *Intelligence, 2,* 255-278.

_____. (1980). Intelligence for the year 2001. *Intelligence, 4,* 185-199.

_____. (1981). Toward a theory of aptitude for learning intelligence: Fluid and crystallized abilities and their correlates. In M. P. Friedman, J. P. Das, & N. O' Connor (Eds.), *Intelligence and learning* (pp. 345-362). New York: Plenum.

_____. (1986). On Intelligence. In R. J. Sternberg & D. S. Detterman (Eds.), *What is intelligence? Contemporary viewpoints and its nature and definition* (pp. 133-139). Norwood, NJ: Ablex.

Snow, R. E., Kyllonen, P. C., & Marshalek, B. (1984). The topography of ability and learning correlations. In R. J. Sternberg (Ed.), *Advances in the psychology of human intelligence* (Vol. 2, pp. 47-103). Hillsdale, NJ: Erlbaum.

Snow, R. E., & Lohman, D. F. (1984). Toward a theory of cognitive aptitude for learning from instruction. *Journal of Educational Psychology, 76,* 347-376.

Snyderman, M., & Rothman, S. (1988). *The IQ controversy: The media and public policy.* New Brunswick, NJ: Transaction Books.

Solso, R. L. (1988). *Cognitive psychology* (2nd ed). Boston: Allyn & Bacon.

Spearman, C. (1904). "General intelligence," objectively determined and measured. *American Journal of Psychology, 15,* 201-293.

_____. (1927). *The abilities of man: Their nature and measurement.* New York: Macmillan.

Staudenmayer, H. (1975). Understanding conditional reasoning with meaningful propositions. In R. J. Falmagne (Ed.), *Reasoning: Representation and process in children and adults.* Hillsdale, NJ: Erlbaum.

Stern, C. (1928). *Die Kindersprache.* Leipzig: Barth.

Sternberg, R. J. (1977). *Intelligence, information processing, and analogical reasoning: The componential analysis of human abilities.* Hillsdale, NJ: Erlbaum.

_____. (1980). Representation and process in linear syllogistic reasoning. *Journal of Experimental Psychology, 109,* 119-159.

_____. (1982). Natural, unnatural, and supernatural concepts. *Cognitive Psychology, 14,* 451-488.

_____. (1984). Toward a triarchic theory of human intelligence. *Behavioral and Brain Sciences, 7*(2), 269-316.

_____. (1985). *Beyond IQ: A triarchic theory of human intelligence.* Cambridge: Cambridge University Press.

_____. (1986a). A framework for understanding conceptions of intelligence. In R. J. Sternberg & D. K. Detterman (Eds.). *What is intelligence?* (pp. 3-15). Norwood, NJ: Ablex.

_____. (1986b). Intelligence is mental self-government. In R. J. Sternberg & D. K. Detterman (Eds.), *What is intelligence?* (pp. 141-148). Norwood, NJ: Ablex.

_____. (1988a). A three-facet model of creativity. In R. J. Sternberg (Ed.), *The nature of creativity* (pp. 125-147). Cambridge: Cambridge University Press.

_____. (1988b). *The triarchic mind—A new theory of human intelligence.* New York: Penguin Books.

_____. (1990a). *Wisdom: Its nature, origins and development.* Cambridge: Cambridge University Press.

_____. (1990b). *Metaphors of mind: Conceptions of the nature of intelligence.* Cambridge: Cambridge University Press.

Sternberg, R. J., & Davidson, J. E. (1982). The mind of the puzzler. *Psychology Today, 16,* June, 37-44.

_____. (1983). Insight in the gifted. *Educational Psychology, 18,* 51-57.

_____. (1985). Cognitive development in the gifted and talented. In F. D. Horowitz & M. O'Brien (Eds.), *The gifted and talented: Developmental perspectives* (pp. 37-74). Washington, DC: American Psychological Association.

Sternberg, R. J., & Detterman, D. S. (Eds.). (1986). *What is intelligence? Contemporary viewpoints and its nature and definition.* Norwood, NJ: Ablex.

Sternberg, R. J., & Downing, C. (1982). The development of higher-order reasoning in adolescence. *Child Development, 53,* 209-221.

Sternberg, R. J., & Gardner, M. K. (1982). A componential interpretation of the general factor in human intelligence. In H. J. Eysenck (Ed.), *A model for intelligence*. Berlin: Springer-Verlag.

_____. (1983). Unities in inductive reasoning. *Journal of Experimental Psychology, 112,* 80-116.

Sternberg, R. J., & Powell, J. S. (1982). Theories of intelligence. In R. J. Sternberg (Ed.), *Handbook of human intelligence* (pp. 975-1005). Cambridge: Cambridge University Press.

_____. (1983). The development of intelligence. In P. H. Mussen (Ed.), *Handbook of child psychology* (4th ed., pp. 341-418). Vol. 3, *Cognitive Development* (J. H. Flavell & E. H. Markman, 3rd vol. eds.). New York: Wiley.

Stevens, C. F. (1988). The neuron. In R. R. Llinas (Ed.), *The biology of the brain, from neurons to networks* (pp. 1-19). New York: W. H. Freeman.

Storfer, M. D. (1990). *Intelligence and giftedness*. San Francisco: Jossey-Bass Publishers.

Tannenbaum, A. J. (1983). *Gifted children: Psychological and educational perspectives*. New York: Macmillan.

Taplin, J. E. (1971). Reasoning with conditional sentences. *Journal of Verbal Learning and Verbal Behavior, 10,* 218-225.

Tennyson, R. D. (1989). Cognition science and instructional technology: Improvements in higher order thinking strategies. *Proceedings of selected research papers at the Annual Meeting of the Association for Educational Communication and Technology,* February 1-5.

Terman, L. M. (1925). *Mental and physical traits of a thousand gifted children. Genetic studies of genius* (Vol. 1). Stanford, CA: Stanford University Press.

Terman, L. M., & Oden, M. H. (1947). *The gifted child grows up: Twenty-five years' follow-up of a superior group. Genetic studies of genius* (Vol. 4). Stanford, CA: Stanford University Press.

_____. (1959). *The gifted group at mid-life: Thirty-five years' follow-up of the superior child. Genetic studies of genius* (Vol. 5). Stanford, CA: Stanford University Press.

Thomson, G. A. (1919). On the cause of hierarchical order among correlation coefficients. *Proceedings of the Royal Society, A, 95,* 400-408.

Thorndike, E. L. (1898). Animal intelligence: An experimental study of the associative processes in animals. *Psychological Review Monograph Supplement, 2,* 1-109.

_____. (1913). *Educational psychology*. (Vol. 1). New York: Teachers College Press.

_____. (1924). Mental discipline in high school studies. *Journal of Educational Psychology 15,* no. 2, February, 95.

Thorndike,E. L., & Woodworth, R. S. (1901). The influence of improvement in one mental function upon the efficiency of other functions. *Psychological Review 8,* 247-261; 384-395; 553-564.

Thurstone, L. L. (1935). *Vectors of the mind*. Chicago: University of Chicago Press.

_____. (1938). *Primary mental abilities*. Chicago: University of Chicago Press.

_____. (1947). *Multiple factor analysis*. Chicago: University of Chicago Press.

Tobias, P. V. (1983). Recent advances in the evolution of the hominids with special reference to brain and speech. In C. Chagas (Ed.), *Recent advances in the evolution of primates* (pp. 85-140). Vatican City: Pontificiae Academiae Scientiarum Scripta Varia.

———. (1987). The brain of homo habilis: A new level of organization in cerebral evolution. *Journal of Human Evolution, 16,* 741-761.

Tolman, E. C. (1959). Principles of purposive behavior. In S. Koch (Ed.), *Psychology: A study of a science* (Vol. 2, pp. 92-157). New York: McGraw-Hill.

Vernon, P. E. (1971). *The structure of human abilities.* London: Methuen.

Vernon, P. A. (Ed.) (1989). *Speed of information processing and intelligence.* Norwood, NJ: Ablex.

Von Neumann, J., & Morgenstern, O. (1944). *The theory of games and economic behavior.* Princeton, NJ: Princeton University Press.

Vygotsky, L. (1934). *Thought and language.* A. Kozulin (Ed. and Trans.). Cambridge: MIT Press (reprint 1986).

Walberg, H. J. (1988). Creativity and talent as learning. In R. J. Sternberg (Ed.), *The nature of creativity* (pp. 340-385). Cambridge: Cambridge University Press.

Walker, S. (1985). *Animal thought.* London: Routledge & Kegan Paul.

Wanner, E., & Gleitman, L. R. (1982). *Language acquisition: The state of the art.* Cambridge: Cambridge University Press.

Wason, P. C., & Johnson-Laird, P. N. (1972). *Psychology of reasoning: Structure and content.* Cambridge: Harvard University Press.

Wechsler, D. (1991). *Manual of Wechsler intelligence scale for children* (3rd ed.). New York: Psychological Corporation.

Weisberg, R. W. (1986). *Creativity: Genius and other myths.* New York: W. H. Freeman.

———. (1988). Problem solving and creativity. In R. J. Sternberg (Ed.), *The nature of creativity* (pp. 148-176). Cambridge: Cambridge University Press.

Wellman, H. M. (1990). *The child's theory of mind.* Cambridge: MIT Press.

Werner, H. (1948). *Comparative psychology of mental development* (2nd ed). New York: International Universities Press.

Werner, H., & Kaplan, B. (1963). *Symbol formation: An organismic-developmental approach to language and the expression of thought.* New York: Wiley.

Wesman, A. (1944). A study of transfer of training from high school subjects to intelligence. *Teachers College Record,* October, 391-393.

Whorf, B. L. (1956). *Language, thought, and reality.* Cambridge: MIT Press.

Woodrow, H. (1938). The relation between abilities and improvement with practice. *Journal of Educational Psychology, 29,* 215-230.

Woodworth, R. S., & Sells, S. B. (1935). An atmospheric effect in formal syllogistic reasoning. *Journal of Experimental Psychology, 18,* 451-460.

Zeaman, D., & House, B. J. (1967). The relation of IQ and learning. In R. M. Gagne (Ed.), *Learning and individual differences.* Columbus, OH: Merrill.

Zigler, E. (1984). *Conceptions of social competence.* Paper presented at the Mediax Conference, April, Washington, DC.

———. (1986). Intelligence: A developmental approach. In R. J. Sternberg & D. S. Detterman (Eds.), *What is intelligence?* (pp. 149-152). Norwood, NJ: Ablex.

Zigler, E., & Butterfield, E. C. (1968). Motivational aspects of changes in IQ test
    performances of culturally deprived nursery school children. *Child
    Development, 39,* 1-14.
Zigler, E. F., & Finn-Stevenson, M. (1987). *Children: Development and social
    issues.* Lexington, MA: D. C. Health.

Author Index

Subject Index

About the Author

REX LI is Chairman of the Gifted Education Council, an international organization based in Hong Kong. He is Research Director of the Asian Center for the Study of Giftedness, Board Chairman of the Mathematical Olympiad School, and Director of the Supermind Institute of Hong Kong. He has published extensively in Chinese and English on gifted education.

ISBN 0-275-95326-2

EAN

9 780275 953263

HARDCOVER BAR CODE